From an Erie Railroad timetable dated 1875

MIDNIGHT SPECIALS

MIDNIGHT SPECIALS

An Anthology for Train Buffs
and Suspense Aficionados

Edited by Bill Pronzini

The Bobbs-Merrill Company, Inc.
INDIANAPOLIS / NEW YORK

Illustration on page 186 by Paul Orban from *Astounding Science Fiction*, December 1950. Copyright by Street and Smith, 1950.

Published by the Bobbs-Merrill Company, Inc.
Indianapolis   New York

Designed by Ingrid Beckman
Manufactured in the United States of America

First printing

Library of Congress Cataloging in Publication Data
Main entry under title

Midnight specials.

    Bibliography: p.
    CONTENTS: 1870-1925: Dickens, C. The signal-man.
Lutz, J. The shooting of Curly Dan. Twain, M.
The invalid's story. Wharton, E. A journey.
Hoch, E. D. The problem of the locked caboose.
Noyes, A. Midnight express. [etc.]
    1. Railroads—Trains—Fiction. 2. Detective and
mystery stories. I. Pronzini, Bill.
PZ1.M586   [PN6071.R3]   808.83'872   76-46227
ISBN 0-672-52308-6

ACKNOWLEDGMENTS

THE SHOOTING OF CURLY DAN, by John Lutz. Copyright © 1973 by John Lutz. First published in *Ellery Queen's Mystery Magazine*. Reprinted by permission of the author.

A JOURNEY, by Edith Wharton. From *The Collected Short Stories of Edith Wharton* and reprinted by permission of Charles Scribner's Sons.

THE PROBLEM OF THE LOCKED CABOOSE, by Edward D. Hoch. Copyright © 1976 by Edward D. Hoch. First published in *Ellery Queen's Mystery Magazine*. Reprinted by permission of the author.

MIDNIGHT EXPRESS, by Alfred Noyes. Reprinted by permission of Hugh Noyes (Lisle Combe, St. Lawrence, Isle of Wight, England), executor for the estate of Alfred Noyes.

FAITH, HOPE AND CHARITY, by Irvin S. Cobb. Copyright © 1934 by Irvin S. Cobb, renewed 1962 by Laura Baker Cobb. From *Faith, Hope and Charity*, by Irvin S. Cobb. Reprinted by permission of The Bobbs-Merrill Company, Inc.

DEAD MAN, by James M. Cain. Copyright © 1936 by James M. Cain. First published in *The American Mercury*. Reprinted by permission of the author and the author's agents, Harold Ober Associates, Inc.

CONTENTS

1951-TODAY — AND TOMORROW . . .

INTRODUCTION

THOMAS WOLFE, that immensely talented contemporary of Hemingway and Steinbeck, once wrote: "The rails go westward in the dark. Brother, have you seen starlight on the rails? Have you heard the thunder of the fast express?"

The answer for most of us, of course, is yes: even if we have never personally ridden a train, we have at some time or other heard the thunder of the fast express, and smelled smoke and cinders and hot diesel oil, and seen the bright Cyclopian eye of a locomotive's headlight, and listened to the mournful cry of a whistle or an air horn echoing in the night. And the more romantically inclined of us have perhaps had secret desires to ride in an empty boxcar on an outbound freight, or to stand beside the engineer in the cab of a highballing special, or to occupy a compartment on the Orient Express bound for Istanbul.

If, like me, you are one of those people—if to you a train is not just a mode of transportation (and a nearly outdated one in the eyes of many) but a symbol of adventure, intrigue, suspense—I think you'll particularly enjoy your journey on the "midnight specials" in this anthology. For you'll travel on a variety of passenger, freight, and subway trains in this country, in Europe, and in other places strange and wonderful; you'll venture from the early days of railroading through the present and into tomorrow; you'll meet signalmen, gandy dancers, hoboes, highballing engineers, foreign correspondents, detectives, thieves, spies, and murderers, as well as people just like yourself.

The stories told about and by these fellow travelers and train personnel, you'll find, are as diverse in type and suspense as the writers whose tales they are. There are detective stories by such practitioners of the art as Georges Simenon, Ellery Queen, and Edward D. Hoch; ghost and supernatural stories by Charles Dickens, Alfred Noyes, and August Derleth; psychological studies by Edith Wharton and Charles Beaumont; sociological examinations by James M. Cain and Howard Schoenfeld; pure action and adventure by Cornell Woolrich and Harold Lamb; fantasy and science-fiction excursions by Robert Bloch and Barry N. Malzberg; murder and crime stories by John Lutz, Irvin S. Cobb, and William P. McGivern; and an item by no less a personage than Mark Twain which defies categorization.

In short, I hope there is something for you and for everyone, above and beyond the lure of trains. And while you may not like all of the things you see and all of the people you meet in the hours to come, I'm pretty sure you'll be entertained by them.

When you've finished your journey, perhaps you will be motivated to take others in the future; to that end, I've included a lengthy bibliography of train-oriented suspense stories, novels, nonfiction (works which are as factually suspenseful as most tales of the imagination), plays, and films.

Before we proceed with the first of the "midnight specials," I would like to offer my thanks to those individuals who helped in the compilation of the bibliography and assisted with other internal matters: my wife, Bruni; Barbara Norville, editor at Bobbs-Merrill; Bill Blackbeard, of the San Francisco Academy of Art; Connie diRienzo, of *Ellery Queen's Mystery Magazine;* and fellow writers and anthologists Edward D. Hoch, Frederic Dannay, Cedric Clute, Francis M. Nevins, Barry Malzberg, and Jack Leavitt.

BILL PRONZINI

San Francisco, California
September 1976

1870–1925

The Signal-Man

By Charles Dickens

*T*HE *author of such literary masterpieces as* Oliver Twist, David Copperfield, A Christmas Carol, *and* Dombey and Son *(which contains a marvelously grim train sequence) hardly needs an introduction. There is, however, another authorial side to Charles Dickens which bears mentioning here: his "popular fictions" written for a variety of British weekly periodicals in the mid-1800s, of which "The Signal-Man" is a prime example.*

Dickens wrote these stories to supplement his income and thus help to finance a wide range of extra-literary interests—charitable organizations, social reform, travels in Europe and America, and the managing of a theatrical company. Most modern readers are regrettably unaware of his popular fictions, and yet they are an important part of the Dickens canon, for they reflect his storytelling mastery, his insight into and complex use of symbolism, and his fascination with the psychological and the macabre.

In this tale of a train signalman who occupies a lonely shack at

3

the mouth of a long tunnel, Dickens creates a dark, brooding atmosphere akin to that which pervades some of his more prominent works. The result is a chilling examination of things beyond human knowledge and human understanding.

"Halloa! Below there!"

When he heard a voice thus calling to him, he was standing at the door of his box, with a flag in his hand, furled round its short pole. One would have thought, considering the nature of the ground, that he could not have doubted from what quarter the voice came; but instead of looking up to where I stood on the top of the steep cutting nearly over his head, he turned himself about, and looked down the Line. There was something remarkable in his manner of doing so, though I could not have said for my life what. But I know it was remarkable enough to attract my notice, even though his figure was foreshortened and shadowed, down in the deep trench, and mine was high above him, so steeped in the glow of an angry sunset, that I had shaded my eyes with my hand before I saw him at all.

"Halloa! Below!"

From looking down the Line, he turned himself about again, and, raising his eyes, saw my figure high above him.

"Is there any path by which I can come down and speak to you?"

He looked up at me without replying, and I looked down at him without pressing him too soon with a repetition of my idle question. Just then there came a vague vibration in the earth and air, quickly changing into a violent pulsation, and an oncoming rush that caused me to start back, as though it had force to draw me down. When such vapour as rose to my height from this rapid train had passed me, and was skimming away over the landscape, I looked down again, and saw him refurling the flag he had shown while the train went by.

I repeated my inquiry. After a pause, during which he seemed to regard me with fixed attention, he motioned with his rolled-up flag towards a point on my level, some two or three hundred yards distant. I called down to him, "All right!" and made for that point. There, by dint of looking closely about me, I found a rough zigzag descending path notched out, which I followed.

The cutting was extremely deep and unusually precipitous. It was made through a clammy stone, that became oozier and wetter as I went down. For these reasons, I found the way long enough to give me time to recall a singular air of reluctance or compulsion with which he had pointed out the path.

When I came down low enough upon the zigzag descent to see him again, I saw that he was standing between the rails on the way by which the train had lately passed, in an attitude as if he were waiting for me to appear. He had his left hand at his chin, and that left elbow rested on his right hand, crossed over his breast. His attitude was one of such expectation and watchfulness that I stopped a moment, wondering at it.

I resumed my downward way, and stepping out upon the level of the railroad, and drawing nearer to him, saw that he was a dark, sallow man, with a dark beard and rather heavy eyebrows. His post was in as solitary and dismal a place as ever I saw. On either side a dripping-wet wall of jagged stone, excluding all view but a strip of sky; the perspective one way only a crooked prolongation of this great dungeon; the shorter perspective in the other direction terminating in a gloomy red light, and the gloomier entrance to a black tunnel, in whose massive architecture there was a barbarous, depressing, and forbidding air. So little sunlight ever found its way to this spot that it had an earthy, deadly smell; and so much cold wind rushed through it that it struck chill to me, as if I had left the natural world.

Before he stirred, I was near enough to him to have touched him. Not even then removing his eyes from mine, he stepped back one step, and lifted his hand.

This was a lonesome post to occupy (I said), and it had riveted my attention when I looked down from up yonder. A visitor was a rarity, I should suppose; not an unwelcome rarity, I hoped? In me he merely saw a man who had been shut up within narrow limits all his life, and who, being at last set free, had a newly-

awakened interest in these great works. To such purpose I spoke
to him; but I am far from sure of the terms I used, for, besides
that I am not happy in opening any conversation, there was
something in the man that daunted me.

He directed a most curious look towards the red light near the
tunnel's mouth, and looked all about it, as if something were
missing from it, and then looked at me.

That light was part of his charge, was it not?

He answered in a low voice, "Don't you know it is?"

The monstrous thought came into my mind, as I perused the
fixed eyes and the saturnine face, that this was a spirit, not a man.
I have speculated since whether there may have been infection in
his mind.

In my turn I stepped back. But in making the action, I detected
in his eyes some latent fear of me. This put the monstrous thought
to flight.

"You look at me," I said, forcing a smile, "as if you had a
dread of me."

"I was doubtful," he returned, "whether I had seen you
before."

"Where?"

He pointed to the red light he had looked at.

"There?" I said.

Intently watchful of me, he replied (but without sound), "Yes."

"My good fellow, what should I do there? However, be that as
it may, I never was there, you may swear."

"I think I may," he rejoined. "Yes; I am sure I may."

His manner cleared, like my own. He replied to my remarks
with readiness, and in well-chosen words. Had he much to do
there? Yes—that was to say, he had enough responsibility to
bear; but exactness and watchfulness were what was required of
him, and of actual work—manual labour—he had next to none.
To change that signal, to trim those lights, and to turn this iron
handle now and then, was all he had to do under that head.
Regarding those many long and lonely hours of which I seemed
to make so much, he could only say that the routine of his life
had shaped itself into that form, and he had grown used to it.

He had taught himself a language down here—if only to know it by sight, and to have formed his own crude ideas of its pronunciation, could be called learning it. He had also worked at fractions and decimals, and tried a little algebra; but he was, and had been as a boy, a poor hand at figures. Was it necessary for him when on duty always to remain in that channel of damp air, and could he never rise into the sunshine from between those high stone walls? Why, that depended upon times and circumstances. Under some conditions there would be less upon the Line than under others; and the same held good as to certain hours of the day and night. In bright weather, he did choose occasions for getting a little above these lower shadows; but, being at all times liable to be called by his electric bell, and at such times listening for it with redoubled anxiety, the relief was less than I would suppose.

He took me into his box, where there was a fire, a desk for an official book in which he had to make certain entries, a telegraphic instrument with its dial, face, and needles, and the little bell of which he had spoken. On my trusting that he would excuse the remark that he had been well educated, and (I hoped I might say without offence) perhaps educated above that station, he observed that instances of slight incongruity in such wise would rarely be found wanting among large bodies of men; that he had heard it was so in workhouses, in the police force, even in that last desperate resource the army; and that he knew it was so, more or less, in any great railway staff. He had been, when young (if I could believe it, sitting in that hut—he scarcely could), a student of natural philosophy, and had attended lectures; but he had run wild, misused his opportunities, gone down, and never risen again. He had no complaint to offer about that. He had made his bed, and he lay upon it. It was far too late to make another.

All that I have here condensed he said in a quiet manner, with his grave dark regards divided between me and the fire. He threw in the word "Sir" from time to time, and especially when he referred to his youth—as though to request me to understand that he claimed to be nothing but what I found him. He was several times interrupted by the little bell, and had to read off messages, and send replies. Once he had to stand without the door, and display a flag as a train passed, and make some verbal communication to the driver. In the discharge of his duties, I observed him to be remarkably exact and vigilant, breaking off his discourse at a syllable, and remaining silent until what he had to do was done.

In a word, I should have set this man down as one of the safest of men to be employed in that capacity, but for the circumstance that while he was speaking to me he twice broke off with a fallen colour, turned his face towards the little bell when it did NOT ring, opened the door of the hut (which was kept shut to exclude the unhealthy damp), and looked out towards the red light near the mouth of the tunnel. On both of those occasions, he came back to the fire with the inexplicable air upon him which I had re-marked, without being able to define, when we were so far asunder.

Said I, when I rose to leave him, "You almost make me think that I have met with a contented man."

(I am afraid I must acknowledge that I said it to lead him on.)

"I believe I used to be so," he rejoined, in the low voice in which he had first spoken; "but I am troubled, sir, I am troubled."

He would have recalled the words if he could. He had said them, however, and I took them up quickly.

"With what? What is your trouble?"

"It is very difficult to impart, sir. It is very, very difficult to speak of. If ever you make me another visit, I will try to tell you."

"But I expressly intend to make you another visit. Say, when shall it be?"

"I go off early in the morning, and I shall be on again at ten to-morrow night, sir."

"I will come at eleven."

He thanked me, and went out at the door with me. "I'll show my white light, sir," he said, in his peculiar low voice, "till you have found the way up. When you have found it, don't call out! And when you are at the top, don't call out!"

His manner seemed to make the place strike colder to me, but I said no more than, "Very well."

"And when you come down to-morrow night, don't call out! Let me ask you a parting question. What made you cry, 'Halloa! Below there!' to-night?"

"Heaven knows," said I. "I cried something to that effect—"

"Not to that effect, sir. Those were the very words. I know them well."

"Admit those were the very words. I said them, no doubt, because I saw you below."

"For no other reason?"

"What other reason could I possibly have?"

"You had no feeling that they were conveyed to you in any supernatural way?"

"No."

He wished me good-night, and held up his light. I walked by the side of the down Line of rails (with a very disagreeable sensation of a train coming behind me) until I found the path. It was easier to mount than to descend, and I got back to my inn without any adventure.

Punctual to my appointment, I placed my foot on the first notch of the zigzag next night, as the distant clocks were striking eleven. He was waiting for me at the bottom, with his white light on. "I have not called out," I said, when we came close together; "may I speak now?" "By all means, sir." "Good-night, then, and here's my hand." "Good-night, sir, and here's mine." With that we walked side by side to his box, entered it, closed the door, and sat down by the fire.

"I have made up my mind, sir," he began, bending forward as soon as we were seated, and speaking in a tone but a little above a whisper, "that you shall not have to ask me twice what troubles me. I took you for some one else yesterday evening. That troubles me."

"That mistake?"

"No. That Some one else."

"Who is it?"

"I don't know."

"Like me?"

"I don't know. I never saw the face. The left arm is across the face, and the right arm is waved—violently waved. This way."

I followed his action with my eyes, and it was the action of an arm gesticulating, with the utmost passion and vehemence, "For God's sake, clear the way!"

"One moonlight night," said the man, "I was sitting here, when I heard a voice cry, 'Halloa! Below there!' I started up, looked from that door, and saw this Some one else standing by the red light near the tunnel, waving as I just now showed you. The voice seemed hoarse with shouting, and it cried, 'Look out! Look out!' And then again, 'Halloa! Below there! Look out!' I caught up my lamp, turned it on red, and ran towards the figure, calling, 'What's wrong? What has happened? Where?' It stood just outside the blackness of the tunnel. I advanced so close upon it that I wondered at its keeping the sleeve across its eyes. I ran right up at it, and had my hand stretched out to pull the sleeve away, when it was gone."

"Into the tunnel?" said I.

"No. I ran on into the tunnel, five hundred yards. I stopped, and held my lamp above my head, and saw the figures of the measured distance, and saw the wet stains stealing down the walls and trickling through the arch. I ran out again faster than I had run in (for I had a mortal abhorrence of the place upon me), and I looked all round the red light with my own red light, and I went up the iron ladder to the gallery atop of it, and I came down again, and ran back here. I telegraphed both ways, 'An alarm has been given. Is anything wrong?' The answer came back, both ways, 'All well.'"

Resisting the slow touch of a frozen finger tracing out my spine, I showed him how that this figure must be a deception of his sense of sight; and how that figures, originating in disease of the delicate nerves that minister to the functions of the eye, were known to have often troubled patients, some of whom had become conscious of the nature of their affliction, and had even proved it by experiments upon themselves. "As to an imaginary cry," said I, "do but listen for a moment to the wind in this unnatural valley while we speak so low, and to the wild harp it makes of the telegraph wires."

That was all very well, he returned, after we had sat listening for a while, and he ought to know something of the wind and the wires—he who so often passed long winter nights there, alone and watching. But he would beg to remark that he had not finished.

I asked his pardon, and he slowly added these words, touching my arm,—

"Within six hours after the Appearance, the memorable accident on this Line happened, and within ten hours the dead and wounded were brought along through the tunnel over the spot where the figure had stood."

A disagreeable shudder crept over me, but I did my best against it. It was not to be denied, I rejoined, that this was a remarkable coincidence, calculated deeply to impress his mind. But it was unquestionable that remarkable coincidences did continually occur, and they must be taken into account in dealing with such a subject. Though to be sure I must admit, I added (for I thought I saw that he was going to bring the objection to bear upon me), men of common sense did not allow much for coincidences in making the ordinary calculations of life.

He again begged to remark that he had not finished.

I again begged his pardon for being betrayed into interruptions.

"This," he said, again laying his hand upon my arm, and glancing over his shoulder with hollow eyes, "was just a year ago. Six or seven months passed, and I had recovered from the surprise and shock, when one morning, as the day was breaking, I, standing at the door, looked towards the red light, and saw the spectre again." He stopped, with a fixed look at me.

"Did it cry out?"

"No. It was silent."

"Did it wave its arm?"

"No. It leaned against the shaft of the light, with both hands before the face. Like this."

Once more I followed his action with my eyes. It was an action of mourning. I have seen such an attitude in stone figures on tombs.

"Did you go up to it?"

"I came in and saw down, partly to collect my thoughts, partly because it had turned me faint. When I went to the door again, daylight was above me, and the ghost was gone."

"But nothing followed? Nothing came of this?"

He touched me on the arm with his forefinger twice or thrice, giving a ghastly nod each time:—

"That very day, as a train came out of the tunnel, I noticed, at a carriage window on my side, what looked like a confusion of hands and heads, and something waved. I saw it just in time to signal the driver, Stop! He shut off, and put his brake on; but the train drifted past here a hundred and fifty yards or more. I ran after it, and, as I went along, heard terrible screams and cries. A beautiful young lady had died instantaneously in one of the compartments, and was brought in here, and laid down on this floor between us."

Involuntarily I pushed my chair back, as I looked from the boards at which he pointed to himself.

"True, sir. True. Precisely as it happened, so I tell it you."

I could think of nothing to say, to any purpose, and my mouth was very dry. The wind and the wires took up the story with a long lamenting wail.

He resumed. "Now, sir, mark this, and judge how my mind is troubled. The spectre came back a week ago. Ever since, it has been there, now and again, by fits and starts."

"At the light?"

"At the Danger-light."

"What does it seem to do?"

He repeated, if possible with increased passion and vehemence, that former gesticulation of, "For God's sake, clear the way!"

Then he went on: "I have no peace or rest for it. It calls to me, for many minutes together, in an agonized manner, 'Below there! Look out! Look out!' It stands waving to me. It rings my little bell—"

I caught at that. "Did it ring your bell yesterday evening when I was here, and you went to the door?"

"Twice."

"Why, see," said I, "how your imagination misleads you. My eyes were on the bell, and my ears were open to the bell, and if I am a living man, it did NOT ring at those times. No, nor at any other time, except when it was rung in the natural course of physical things by the station communicating with you."

He shook his head. "I have never made a mistake as to that yet, sir. I have never confused the spectre's ring with the man's. The ghost's ring is a strange vibration in the bell that it derives from nothing else, and I have not asserted that the bell stirs to the eye. I don't wonder that you failed to hear it. But *I* heard it."

"And did the spectre seem to be there when you looked out?"

"It was there."

"Both times?"

He repeated firmly, "Both times."

"Will you come to the door with me and look for it now?"

He bit his under lip, as though he were somewhat unwilling, but arose. I opened the door, and stood on the step, while he stood in the doorway. There was the Danger-light. There was the dismal mouth of the tunnel. There were the high, wet stone walls of the cutting. There were the stars above them.

"Do you see it?" I asked him, taking particular note of his face. His eyes were prominent and strained, but not very much more so, perhaps, than my own had been when I had directed them earnestly towards the same spot.

"No," he answered. "It is not there."

"Agreed," said I.

We went in again, shut the door, and resumed our seats. I was thinking how best to improve this advantage, if it might be called one, when he took up the conversation in such a matter-of-course way, so assuming that there could be no serious question of fact between us, that I felt myself placed in the weakest of positions.

"By this time you will fully understand, sir," he said, "that what troubles me so dreadfully is the question, What does the spectre mean?"

I was not sure, I told him, that I did fully understand.

"What is its warning against?" he said, ruminating, with his eyes on the fire, and only by times turning them on me. "What is the danger? Where is the danger? There is danger overhanging somewhere on the Line. Some dreadful calamity will happen. It is not to be doubted this third time, after what has gone before. But surely this is a cruel haunting of *me*. What can *I* do?''

He pulled out his handkerchief, and wiped the drops from his heated forehead.

''If I telegraph Danger, on either side of me, or on both, I can give no reason for it,'' he went on, wiping the palms of his hands. ''I should get into trouble, and do no good. They would think I was mad. This is the way it would work:—Message: 'Danger! Take care!' Answer: 'What Danger? Where?' Message: 'Don't know. But, for God's sake, take care!' They would displace me. What else could they do?''

His pain of mind was most pitiable to see. It was the mental torture of a conscientious man, oppressed beyond endurance by an unintelligible responsibility involving life.

''When it first stood under the Danger-light,'' he went on, putting his dark hair back from his head, and drawing his hands outward across his temples in an extremity of feverish distress, ''why not tell me where that accident was to happen—if it must happen? Why not tell me how it could be averted—if it could have been averted? When on its second coming it hid its face, why not tell me, instead, 'She is going to die. Let them keep her at home'? If it came, on those two occasions, only to show me that its warnings were true, and so to prepare me for the third, why not warn me plainly now? And I, Lord help me! A mere poor signal-man on this solitary station! Why not go to somebody with credit to be believed, and power to act?''

When I saw him in this state, I saw that for the poor man's sake, as well as for the public safety, what I had to do for the time was to compose his mind. Therefore, setting aside all question of reality or unreality between us, I represented to him that whoever thoroughly discharged his duty must do well, and that at least it was his comfort that he understood his duty, though he did not understand these confounding Appearances. In this effort I succeeded far better than in the attempt to reason him out of his conviction. He became calm; the occupations incidental to his post as the night advanced began to make larger demands on his attention; and I left him at two in the morning. I had offered to stay through the night, but he would not hear of it.

That I more than once looked back at the red light as I ascended the pathway, that I did not like the red light, and that I should have slept but poorly if my bed had been under it, I see no reason to conceal. Nor did I like the two sequences of the accident and the dead girl. I see no reason to conceal that either.

But what ran most in my thoughts was the consideration how ought I to act, having become the recipient of this disclosure? I had proved the man to be intelligent, vigilant, painstaking, and exact; but how long might he remain so, in his state of mind? Though in a subordinate position, still he held a most important trust; and would I (for instance) like to stake my own life on the chances of his continuing to execute it with precision?

Unable to overcome a feeling that there would be something treacherous in my communicating what he had told me to his superiors in the Company, without first being plain with himself and proposing a middle course to him, I ultimately resolved to offer to accompany him (otherwise keeping his secret for the present) to the wisest medical practitioner we could hear of in those parts, and to take his opinion. A change in his time of duty would come round next night, he had apprised me, and he would be off an hour or two after sunrise, and on again soon after sunset. I had appointed to return accordingly.

Next evening was a lovely evening, and I walked out early to enjoy it. The sun was not yet quite down when I traversed the field-path near the top of the deep cutting. I would extend my walk for an hour, I said to myself, half an hour on and half an hour back, and it would then be time to go to my signal-man's box.

Before pursuing my stroll, I stepped to the brink, and mechanically looked down from the point from which I had first seen him. I cannot describe the thrill that seized upon me when, close at the mouth of the tunnel, I saw the appearance of a man, with his left sleeve across his eyes, passionately waving his right arm.

The nameless horror that oppressed me passed in a moment, for in a moment I saw that this appearance of a man was a man indeed, and that there was a little group of other men, standing at a short distance, to whom he seemed to be rehearsing the gesture he made. The Danger-light was not yet lighted. Against its shaft, a little low hut, entirely new to me, had been made of some wooden supports and tarpaulin. It looked no bigger than a bed.

With an irresistible sense that something was wrong—with a flashing self-reproachful fear that fatal mischief had come of my leaving the man there, and causing no one to be sent to overlook or correct what he did—I descended the notched path with all the speed I could make.

"What is the matter?" I asked the men.

"Signal-man killed this morning, sir."

"Not the man belonging to that box?"

"Yes, sir."

"Not the man I know?"

"You will recognize him, sir, if you knew him," said the man who spoke for the others, solemnly uncovering his own head, and raising an end of the tarpaulin, "for his face is quite composed."

"Oh, how did this happen—how did this happen?" I asked, turning from one to another as the hut closed in again.

"He was cut down by an engine, sir. No man in England knew his work better. But somehow he was not clear of the outer rail. It was just at broad day. He had struck the light, and had the lamp in his hand. As the engine came out of the tunnel, his back was towards her, and she cut him down. That man drove her, and was showing how it happened. Show the gentleman, Tom."

The man who wore a rough dark dress stepped back to his former place at the mouth of the tunnel.

"Coming round the curve in the tunnel, sir," he said, "I saw him at the end, like as if I saw him down a perspective-glass. There was not time to check speed, and I knew him to be very careful. As he didn't seem to take heed of the whistle, I shut it off when we were running down upon him, and called to him as loud as I could call."

"What did you say?"

"I said, 'Below there! Look out! For God's sake, clear the way!' "

I started.

"Ah! it was a dreadful time, sir. I never left off calling to him. I put this arm before my eyes not to see, and I waved this arm to the last; but it was no use."

Without prolonging the narrative to dwell on any one of its curious circumstances more than on any other, I may, in closing it, point out the coincidence that the warning of the Engine-Driver included, not only the words which the unfortunate Signal-Man had repeated to me as haunting him, but also the words which I myself—not he—had attached, and that only in my own mind, to the gesticulation he had imitated.

The Shooting of Curly Dan

By John Lutz

*T*HERE *is something almost legendary about the men who built and watched over the tracks of the great iron horse in the latter half of the nineteenth century—the section gangs, the rail-splitters, the gandy dancers, the steel-driving men. They seem larger than life, like "John Henry" in perhaps the most stirring of all railroad folksongs; giants, heroic figures from an age that, unlike our own, paid homage and accorded respect to individuals of strength, endurance, and high spirit. And yet in truth, of course, they were fallible mortals given to the same failings and weaknesses as everyone else: greed, jealousy, lust, and murder.*

John Lutz, a young contemporary writer whose credits include more than one hundred published short stories and two excellent suspense novels, The Truth of the Matter *(1971) and* Buyer

Beware (1976), accomplishes the difficult feat of combining legend and fact in "The Shooting of Curly Dan"—a memorable story which, in the words of Ellery Queen, "reads like American folklore."

Ollie Robinson was my great-great-grandfather, and he didn't know himself how old he was or where he was born. He was a smart man, but he didn't have much education, and he kept to himself most of the time because of how the other kids would make fun of him. When I was younger I used to laugh at him myself; then all of a sudden one day I got to thinking, I was 13, and he was—what? 113? But I had found out that when he told a story, it was worth listening to, because he was a man who'd done things and been places and met people.

One night when Mom and Dad weren't home he told me the story of Curly Dan's murder that happened when Grandpa Ollie—that's what I called him—was a gandy dancer for the Alton and Southern Railroad. That railroad is gone now, and so are gandy dancers, I expect. Grandpa Ollie didn't tell me how long ago it happened, but it had to be a long, long time. It didn't matter to him, though, because for Grandpa Ollie, sitting there half crippled in his cane chair, chin stuck out and skin loose and wrinkled like an old dollar bill, the past was sometimes right there all around him.

I was sitting near his chair, listening to the even in-and-out rhythm of his breathing and thinking he was asleep. Way off somebody was beating on something metal with a hammer, and maybe that's what kept him from dozing off like he usually did. But he wasn't asleep, and he began talking to me in a voice clearer than his usual voice—younger-sounding, like he was really back there living what he was telling me, living it all over again. . . .

All the railroads had crews of gandy dancers in them days [Grandpa Ollie began], eight or ten strong men to a crew and a caller. I was a gandy dancer for three years with the A & S, but I guess you don't know what a gandy dancer be. When trains go over and over a set of rails, them rails gets crooked and outa line with each other, and somebody's got to set 'em straight again. They got a machine does it now, but then it was done like most things, with sweat and muscle.

There was nine men on each Alton and Southern line crew, 'long with a line chief usually. The company engine would drop us off way out where the rails didn't have no care for a long time and we'd walk along carryin' our pry bars while the line chief kept his eye on the rails that needed work done on 'em. There was a flat cart with water and tools that we pushed along with us, 'cause we done other work besides just truin' the rails. Sometimes we'd have to take a hammer and drive loose spikes, or shovel earth under a section of roadbedding that had give way.

The day Curly Dan was killed we didn't have a line boss, like we didn't sometimes the day before payday, 'cause the foreman, he be workin' on the payroll and paperwork, and he figured ol' Ivy Joe was good enough to be caller and boss both. The line boss and his crew was over on a section of track the other side of a rise, close enough so we could hear the ringin' of their steel and sometimes their voices.

Ivy Joe—that wasn't his true name, but his initials was I. V., so that's what we called him. Now we'd walk along the track, carryin' our pry bars, till Joe spotted a place needed work. Our pry bars was about five feet long and tempered steel, kinda curved and flattened on one end. When we wanted to line track we'd stand in a row 'longside it and put the flattened ends of the bars under the rail. Then, like the big boss always told us, everything depended on rhythm. Nine men had to move like one. That's where Ivy Joe's callin' came in, and he was the best caller the A & S ever had.

When we all had our pry bars 'neath the rail, ready to use 'em like long levers, that's when Ivy Joe started callin' and we'd all tap the rail in rhythm. Then at the last of his chant he'd raise his voice sudden and we'd all put our backs in it together and there'd be a loud ring of steel and we'd move that rail. Over and over we'd do it till the rails was true, then we'd walk on downtrack to the next bad spot.

It were a hot day when the murder happened, and we hadn't had a water break since middle mornin' and the sun was near high. Steel was ringin' and Ivy Joe was callin' the rhythm:

Tell me line boss eyes be blind
How he gonna tell if the rails in line?

And we'd all pull back together and strike steel in rhythm to inch the rail over. We stopped for a water break after that bad section were trued, and I can tell you ain't none of us didn't need it.

Then we worked on ahead, leavin' the water and tool cart sittin' behind as usual till we found another bad place. We was workin' hard on a bend in the rails for some time 'fore Ivy Joe noticed Curly Dan wasn't with us.

"Where that Curly Dan?" he says, standin' with his big fists on his hips. "You know, Slim?"

Slim Deacon was the one helped Curly Dan read letters from Albany. His lean body kinda bent and he shook his head.

"Chaney?"

Chaney was a big man, always grinnin', and he grinned wider and shrugged his heavy shoulders.

"Ollie," Ivy Joe says to me, "you run on back to the tool cart an' see if that lazy Curly Dan be layin' out on us."

I took out runnin', listenin' to the ringin' rhythm of the line crew across the rise while my feet hit the ties.

When I rounded the bend and ran a ways, there be Curly Dan, layin' on his side, kinda curled up around the water jug that was still sittin' on the ground. His blue shirt back were covered with blood where he'd been shot, the bullet goin' clear through, and when I got closer I could see he'd been shot in the back of the head, too, like someone wanted to make sure he be dead.

Everything seemed unnatural quiet and still there. Even the water just below the top of the jug were as calm and still as Curly Dan hisself.

I run back halfway round the bend, yellin' and wavin', and the rest of the crew followed me back to Curly Dan's body. For a while we all stood and stared, lookin' from one to the other.

"How come we didn't hear no shot?" Arky said. He was a short wide man from Arkansas that always had a blade of grass in his teeth.

Ivy Joe looked round him towards the rise and a grove of trees. " 'Cause the killer timed his shot with the rhythm," he says. "Brogan's crew be workin' over the rise when we was here, and when they hit steel hard is when the killer pulled the trigger from the trees over there."

Then Ivy Joe walks over to the grove of trees and a while later comes back holdin' a pistol. "It be a small gun," he said, "and I found where the brush was flattened down where the killer was hidin'." Then he looked real close at the body, standin' there holdin' the pistol and thinkin'. "Load Curly Dan onto the tool cart," he said, and we did that and put up the tools and water jug that was still layin' there from our last work break. Kelly, a bowlegged man with a big mustache, and a man name of Tall Al slid Curly Dan well to the back so's he wouldn't get blood on any of the tools.

"What we gonna do now?" Chaney asked, standin' with his arms crossed.

"We gonna work," Ivy Joe told him. "We gonna work on." And we went on down the tracks.

"Who'd have any reason to shoot Curly Dan?" Ben Zebo said while we was walkin' back to where we'd left off workin'.

Nobody answered 'cause everybody know'd who. There was three men on the crew coulda done it for reason. Chaney was sweet on Curly's little gal, Molly Ann Parker, who'd been all his till Curly Dan took her over. And a man named Handy Billy Grover, he was awful sweet on her too, and he and Curly Dan'd had a fight about her just a few days ago. If any of 'em had any sense they'd just waited, 'cause Molly Ann woulda come round to 'em again. Then there was Arky, who Curly Dan owed fifty dollars to, and who'd been in a argument with him last week over Curly Dan not payin' up.

Ivy Joe know'd all these things, but he didn't say any of 'em as we kept on walkin' 'long the tracks, listenin' to Brogan's crew ringin' steel on the return line over the rise. Kelly with the big mustache was laggin' behind us, pushin' the cart along the tracks real slow and keepin' his distance from Curly Dan.

We got to where we was linin' track, took our places again 'long the outside rail, and slid our pry bars under the steel. Ivy Joe started to clink his bar in rhythm and sing like always.

> *Work be hard but I ain't gonna moan*
> *Work my han's till I see de bone!*

Steel rung and we moved that rail 'bout an inch. It were a song Ivy Joe'd sung lots before and we was all in rhythm, pullin' hard and together.

'Long the bend we was workin' was the worst section of track on the Alton and Southern but for the Gibsey Hill, and we could look ahead in the sun and see rail shimmerin' outa line for a long ways. We worked on and sweat was runnin' down us all.

> *Somebody hide an' shoot Curly Dan*
> *Shame to kill dat young good man!*

All the while Ivy Joe sang we was tappin' rhythm on the steel, all together and bendin' our backs to it at the last when he'd raise his fine voice. Movin' rail, we was, and then walkin' on to more rail. The sun be high and hot as I ever felt it, and we was all walkin'-weary soon, throats dry and eyes burnin' with sweat. I seen Arky in front of me, staggerin' some as we walk on down the line.

"When we gonna stop for water?" Chaney yelled, but Ivy Joe, he didn't hear and kept right on workin'.

> *Somebody on de railroad crew*
> *Know how to shoot when the rhythm do!*

And the steel clang together like one clang, all through the song, then loud like to make your head hurt.

We work on for must've been hours like that, in kind of a daze like you'd get when Ivy Joe was callin' rhythm. We was all tired and achin', and I remember how my back felt like it was blazin' and it pained me to lean. Still we kept the rhythm, 'cause the job, it be all rhythm.

There be sorrow for Molly Ann
Somebody done gone an' shoot her man!

I pulled up and back on my pry bar, feelin' a pain down my stomach, and the rail hardly move and I heard a little clink just a eyewink after the other men had pulled hard together.

"Water," Handy Billy called out, and we all called out for water. Billy's clothes was stickin' to him and his face be all swollen where he kept wipin' his sleeve to keep the sweat outa his eyes.

Someone here he done hang back
Kill Curly Dan when we move downtrack!

Much pain as there be, we still tried to keep up the rhythm. My mouth was dry as sand and the pain almost kept me from straightenin' as the steel rang, and again I heard that clang of a pry bar outa time.

One man kill fo' a woman's all
Now a rope gonna stop his fall!

"I got to have water!" Handy Billy yelled again with his voice all cracked when the steel ring, and I could hardly hear if there was a late ring that time.

The heat be risin' from the ground, and I know'd any time I was gonna fall flat on my face, but we worked on, gaspin' for breath and tryin' to ignore the achin'. Then again there was a late ring of steel, this time later than before, and there was a thuddin' sound too, and we turned and seen the last man in the crew layin' out on the ties with his chest heavin'.

Ivy Joe walked on back and looked down at him. "You the one killed Curly Dan, Chaney," he said like he know'd for sure.

Chaney just looked up at him and kinda croaked.

Then Ivy Joe let us all have water, but not Chaney. Ivy Joe standed over him with the ladle full after everybody else drunk. He let a few drops fall down on Chaney's forehead.

"You killed him," Ivy Joe said again.

"I done it," Chaney said in a raw voice. "I done it to get Molly Ann, an' I used her gun. Danny, he had it comin' to him!" He raised up a hand what was all bloody and blistered like everybody else. "Now gimme some water!"

Ivy Joe let him drink then, and I didn't think Chaney was ever gonna stop drinkin'.

"How'd you know it were him?" Handy Bill asked, wonderin' on his luck at bein' Molly Ann's one and only again. "It didn't have to be a railroad man to time his shot with the rhythm."

"It be a railroad man," Ivy Joe said. "That's why he left the gun, so's we wouldn't find it on him. I know'd it was prob'ly one of three men at first: Arky, Chaney, or you, Handy Billy. I figured it wasn't Arky that shot a man who owed him money, 'cause it's day before payday. Least he'd do is wait a day or two."

Ivy Joe looked back towards where we come from. "Instead of linin' up for water, the killer hid in them trees during water break, seein' Curly Dan was last in line for a drink, then picked him off when the rest of us was walkin' away uptrack. Then he caught up with us 'fore we missed him and was there to help us move track."

"But it coulda been somebody else," Billy said. "It coulda been somebody from the crew over the rise."

"I know'd it were someone from our crew," Ivy Joe said, " 'cause of the way Curly Dan was layin' curled round the water jug where he'd been drinkin'. He musta been shot first in the back, then fell, 'cause the bullet come out the front and there were no hole in the jug, or the jug wouldn't be full like we found it.

"Now from that distance a shot in the head is a funny way to make sure you done finished a man off, but that's where Curly Dan was shot again while he was layin' there on the ground. Why in the head? Like I said, so's not to break the water jug and lose our water. So then I know'd the killer was on our crew and was the only one hadn't had a water break since early mornin'. In this heat, first man to drop from thirst would likely be Curly Dan's killer. And when it were Chaney that dropped first I know'd."

Ivy Joe sent a man on ahead, and we stayed where we was till a whistle blowed and smoke raised up and the big company engine come on down those straight true rails to take Chaney back to the company yards. To take him back where by and by the hangman be waitin' for him.

Then we started workin' again.

The Invalid's Story

By Mark Twain

IT would be presumptuous of me to attempt to say anything
about Mark Twain that has not already been said by people far
more learned than I am. So I will only repeat the irrefutable
fact that Samuel Langhorne Clemens was both the premier
American humorist and one of the most insightful chroniclers of
life and times in the United States for the period 1860-1900. What
more need be said?

As to "The Invalid's Story," however, a certain amount of
commentary is necessary, since a good argument can be made that
it does not belong in an anthology of suspense stories. It deals
with no crime of any sort, and while it surely conforms to Webster's
definition of suspense as a "pleasant excitement as to a decision
or outcome," it contains none of the elements with which the
modern concept of suspense fiction is associated (i.e., danger,
adventure, mystery, the supernatural).

Why, then, did I select it? Well, when my wife reminded me

*of the story, I reread it for the first time in several years and
promptly told her that although it had a good train background,
it really wasn't suitable for the book. But then, as sometimes
happens with a story, I could not get it out of my mind. I still
couldn't weeks later, with the obvious result. The only other
reason I can offer is that it is so wonderfully bizarre, so blackly
humorous, so patently an exercise in* reductio ad absurdum *that
only Mark Twain could have written it and gotten away with
publishing it. Which is, in itself, I think, sufficient justification
for presenting it here.*

*In any case, I leave it up to the reader to decide on the
wisdom of my decision. I would be willing to wager, though, that
most of you will be on my side after finishing it.*

I seem sixty and married, but these effects are due to my
condition and sufferings, for I am a bachelor, and only forty-one.
It will be hard for you to believe that I, who am now but a shadow,
was a hale, hearty man two short years ago—a man of iron, a very
athlete!—yet such is the simple truth. But stranger still than this
fact is the way in which I lost my health. I lost it through helping to
take care of a box of guns on a two-hundred-mile railway journey
one winter's night. It is the actual truth, and I will tell you about
it.

I belong in Cleveland, Ohio. One winter's night, two years
ago, I reached home just after dark, in a driving snow-storm,
and the first thing I heard when I entered the house was that
my dearest boyhood friend and schoolmate, John B. Hackett,
had died the day before, and that his last utterance had been a
desire that I would take his remains home to his poor old father
and mother in Wisconsin. I was greatly shocked and grieved,
but there was no time to waste in emotions; I must start at
once. I took the card, marked "Deacon Levi Hackett, Bethlehem,

Wisconsin," and hurried off through the whistling storm to the railway-station. Arrived there I found the long white-pine box which had been described to me; I fastened the card to it with some tacks, saw it put safely aboard the express-car, and then ran into the eating-room to provide myself with a sandwich and some cigars. When I returned, presently, there was my coffin-box *back again*, apparently, and a young fellow examining around it, with a card in his hands, and some tacks and a hammer! I was astonished and puzzled. He began to nail on his card, and I rushed out to the express-car, in a good deal of a state of mind, to ask for an explanation. But no—that was my box, all right, in the express-car; it hadn't been disturbed. (The fact is that without my suspecting it a prodigious mistake had been made. I was carrying off a box of *guns* which that young fellow had come to the station to ship to a rifle company in Peoria, Illinois, and *he* had got my corpse!) Just then the conductor sang out, "All aboard," and I jumped into the express-car and got a comfortable seat on a bale of buckets. The expressman was there, hard at work—a plain man of fifty, with a simple, honest, good-natured face, and a breezy, practical heartiness in his general style. As the train moved off a stranger skipped into the car and set a package of peculiarly mature and capable Limburger cheese on one end of my coffin-box—I mean my box of guns. That is to say, I know *now* that it was Limburger cheese, but at that time I never had heard of the article in my life, and of course was wholly ignorant of its character. Well, we sped through the wild night, the bitter storm raged on, a cheerless misery stole over me, my heart went down, down, down! The old expressman made a brisk remark or two about the tempest and the arctic weather, slammed his sliding doors to, and bolted them, closed his window down tight, and then went bustling around, here and there and yonder, setting things to rights, and all the time contentedly humming "Sweet By and By," in a low tone, and flatting a good deal. Presently I began to detect a most evil and searching odor stealing about on the frozen air. This depressed my spirits still more, because of course I attributed it to my poor departed friend. There was something infinitely saddening about his calling himself to my remembrance in this dumb, pathetic way, so it was hard to keep the tears back. Moreover, it distressed me on account of the old expressman, who, I was afraid, might notice it. However, he went humming tranquilly on, and gave no sign; and for this I was grateful. Grateful, yes, but still uneasy; and soon I began to feel more and more uneasy every minute, for every minute that went by that odor thickened up the more, and got to be more and more gamy and hard to stand. Presently, having got things arranged to his satisfaction, the expressman got some wood and made up a tremendous fire in his stove. This distressed me more than I could tell, for I could not but feel that it was a mistake. I was sure that the effect would be deleterious upon my poor departed friend. Thompson—the expressman's name was Thompson, as I found out in the course of the night—now went poking around his car, stopping up whatever stray cracks he could find, remarking that it didn't make any difference what kind of a night it was outside, he calculated to make *us* comfortable, anyway. I said nothing, but I believed he was not choosing the right way. Meantime he was humming to himself just as before; and meantime, too, the stove was getting hotter and hotter, and the place closer and closer. I felt myself growing pale and qualmish, but grieved in silence and said nothing. Soon I noticed that the "Sweet By and By" was gradually fading out; next it ceased altogether, and there was an ominous stillness. After a few moments Thompson said—

"Pfew! I reckon it ain't no cinnamon 't I've loaded up thish-yer stove with!"

He gasped once or twice, then moved toward the cof—gun-box, stood over that Limburger cheese part of a moment, then came back and sat down near me, looking a good deal impressed. After a contemplative pause, he said, indicating the box with a gesture—

"Friend of yourn?"

"Yes," I said with a sigh.

"He's pretty ripe, *ain't* he!"

Nothing further was said for perhaps a couple of minutes, each being busy with his own thoughts; then Thompson said, in a low, awed voice—

"Sometimes it's uncertain whether they're really gone or not—
seem gone, you know—body warm, joints limber—and so,
although you *think* they're gone, you don't really know. I've
had cases in my car. It's perfectly awful, becuz *you* don't know
what minute they'll rise up and look at you!" Then, after a pause,
and slightly lifting his elbow toward the box,—"But *he* ain't in
no trance! No, sir, I'd go bail for *him!*"

We sat some time, in meditative silence, listening to the wind
and the roar of the train; then Thompson said, with a good deal
of feeling:

"Well-a-well, we've all got to go, they ain't no getting around
it. Man that is born of woman is of few days and far between,
as Scriptur' says. Yes, you look at it any way you want to, it's
awful solemn and cur'us: they ain't *nobody* can get around it;
all's got to go—just *everybody*, as you may say. One day
you're hearty and strong"—here he scrambled to his feet and broke
a pane and stretched his nose out at it a moment or two, then
sat down again while I struggled up and thrust my nose out at
the same place, and this we kept on doing every now and then—
"and next day he's cut down like the grass, and the places
which knowed him then knows him no more forever, as Scriptur'
says. Yes'ndeedy, it's awful solemn and cur'us; but we've all
got to go, one time or another; they ain't no getting around it."

There was another long pause; then—

"What did he die of?"

I said I didn't know.

"How long has he ben dead?"

It seemed judicious to enlarge the facts to fit the probabilities;
so I said:

"Two or three days."

But it did no good; for Thompson received it with an injured
look which plainly said, "Two or three *years*, you mean." Then
he went right along, placidly ignoring my statement, and gave his
views at considerable length upon the unwisdom of putting off
burials too long. Then he lounged off toward the box, stood a
moment, then came back on a sharp trot and visited the broken
pane, observing:

" 'Twould 'a' ben a dum sight better, all around, if they'd started him along last summer."

Thompson sat down and buried his face in his red silk handkerchief, and began to slowly sway and rock his body like one who is doing his best to endure the almost unendurable. By this time the fragrance—if you may call it fragrance—was just about suffocating, as near as you can come at it. Thompson's face was turning gray; I knew mine hadn't any color left in it. By and by Thompson rested his forehead in his left hand, with his elbow on his knee, and sort of waved his red handkerchief toward the box with his other hand, and said:

"I've carried a many a one of 'em—some of 'em considerable overdue, too—but, lordy, he just lays over 'em all!—and does it *easy*. Cap, they was heliotrope to *him!*"

This recognition of my poor friend gratified me, in spite of the sad circumstances, because it had so much the sound of a compliment.

Pretty soon it was plain that something had got to be done. I suggested cigars. Thompson thought it was a good idea. He said:

"Likely it'll modify him some."

We puffed gingerly along for a while, and tried hard to imagine that things were improved. But it wasn't any use. Before very long, and without any consultation, both cigars were quietly dropped from our nerveless fingers at the same moment. Thompson said, with a sigh:

"No, Cap, it don't modify him worth a cent. Fact is, it makes him worse, becuz it appears to stir up his ambition. What do you reckon we better do, now?"

I was not able to suggest anything; indeed, I had to be swallowing and swallowing all the time, and did not like to trust myself to speak. Thompson fell to maundering, in a desultory and low-spirited way, about the miserable experiences of this night; and he got to referring to my poor friend by various titles—sometimes military ones, sometimes civil ones; and I noticed that as fast as my poor friend's effectiveness grew, Thompson promoted him accordingly—gave him a bigger title. Finally he said:

"I've got an idea. Suppos'n' we buckle down to it and give the

Colonel a bit of a shove toward t'other end of the car?—about ten foot, say. He wouldn't have so much influence, then, don't you reckon?"

I said it was a good scheme. So we took in a good fresh breath at the broken pane, calculating to hold it till we got through; then we went there and bent over that deadly cheese and took a grip on the box. Thompson nodded "All ready," and then we threw ourselves forward with all our might; but Thompson slipped, and slumped down with his nose on the cheese, and his breath got loose. He gagged and gasped, and floundered up and made a break for the door, pawing the air and saying hoarsely, "Don't hinder me!—gimme the road! I'm a-dying; gimme the road!" Out on the cold platform I sat down and held his head awhile, and he revived. Presently he said:

"Do you reckon we started the Gen'rul any?"

I said no; we hadn't budged him.

"Well, then, *that* idea's up the flume. We got to think of something else. He's suited wher' he is, I reckon; and if that's the way he feels about it, and has made up his mind that he don't wish to be disturbed, you bet he's a-going to have his own way in the business. Yes, better leave him right wher' he is, long as he wants it so; becuz he holds all the trumps, don't you know, and so it stands to reason that the man that lays out to alter his plans for him is going to get left."

But we couldn't stay out there in that mad storm; we should have frozen to death. So we went in again and shut the door, and began to suffer once more and take turns at the break in the window. By and by, as we were starting away from a station where we had stopped a moment Thompson pranced in cheerily, and exclaimed:

"We're all right, now! I reckon we've got the Commodore this time. I judge I've got the stuff here that'll take the tuck out of him."

It was carbolic acid. He had a carboy of it. He sprinkled it all around everywhere; in fact he drenched everything with it, rifle-box, cheese and all. Then we sat down, feeling pretty hopeful. But it wasn't for long. You see the two perfumes began to mix, and then—well, pretty soon we made a break for the door;

and out there Thompson swabbed his face with his bandanna
and said in a kind of disheartened way:

"It ain't no use. We can't buck agin *him*. He just utilizes
everything we put up to modify him with, and gives it his own
flavor and plays it back on us. Why, Cap, don't you know, it's
as much as a hundred times worse in there now than it was
when he first got a-going. I never *did* see one of 'em warm up
to his work so, and take such a dumnation interest in it. No,
sir, I never did, as long as I've ben on the road; and I've carried
a many a one of 'em, as I was telling you."

We went in again after we were frozen pretty stiff; but my,
we couldn't *stay* in, now. So we just waltzed back and forth,
freezing, and thawing, and stifling, by turns. In about an hour we
stopped at another station; and as we left it Thompson came in
with a bag, and said—

"Cap, I'm a-going to chance him once more—just this once;
and if we don't fetch him this time, the thing for us to do, is to
just throw up the sponge and withdraw from the canvas. That's
the way *I* put it up."

He had brought a lot of chicken feathers, and dried apples,
and leaf tobacco, and rags, and old shoes, and sulphur, and
asafetida, and one thing or another; and he piled them on a
breadth of sheet iron in the middle of the floor, and set fire
to them.

When they got well started, I couldn't see, myself, how even
the corpse could stand it. All that went before was just simply
poetry to that smell—but mind you, the original smell stood up out
of it just as sublime as ever—fact is, these other smells just
seemed to give it a better hold; and my, how rich it was! I
didn't make these reflections there—there wasn't time—made them
on the platform. And breaking for the platform, Thompson got
suffocated and fell; and before I got him dragged out, which I
did by the collar, I was mighty near gone myself. When we
revived, Thompson said dejectedly:

"We got to stay out here, Cap. We got to do it. They ain't
no other way. The Governor wants to travel alone, and he's fixed
so he can outvote us."

And presently he added:

"And don't you know, we're *pisoned*. It's *our* last trip, you can make up your mind to it. Typhoid fever is what's going to come of this. I feel it a-coming right now. Yes, sir, we're elected, just as sure as you're born."

We were taken from the platform an hour later, frozen and insensible, at the next station, and I went straight off into a virulent fever, and never knew anything again for three weeks. I found out, then, that I had spent that awful night with a harmless box of rifles and a lot of innocent cheese; but the news was too late to save *me*; imagination had done its work, and my health was permanently shattered; neither Bermuda nor any other land can ever bring it back to me. This is my last trip; I am on my way home to die.

A Journey

By Edith Wharton

*E*DITH *WHARTON, one of the foremost figures in American belles-lettres in the early part of this century, was an author who understood the human condition and wrote of it with considerable sensitivity and intensity. Among her many social and historical novels is the tragic love story* Ethan Frome, *highly acclaimed by critics when it was first published in 1911 and still required reading today in a number of college literature courses. She also published short fiction (her ghost stories rank with the finest of Saki, Lord Dunsany, and Sheridan LeFanu), poems, and travel books in a prolific career that ended with her death in 1937, at the age of seventy-five.*

As evidenced in "A Journey," her themes and her quiet style are all the more powerful for their deceptive simplicity.

Not many writers past or present could transform an account of the train journey of a woman and her seriously ill husband into a moving and shattering study of pain and the kind of terror that comes from internal as well as external forces.

As she lay in her berth, staring at the shadows overhead, the rush of the wheels was in her brain, driving her deeper and deeper into circles of wakeful lucidity. The sleeping-car had sunk into its night-silence. Through the wet window-pane she watched the sudden lights, the long stretches of hurrying blackness. Now and then she turned her head and looked through the opening in the hangings at her husband's curtains across the aisle. . . .

She wondered restlessly if he wanted anything and if she could hear him if he called. His voice had grown very weak within the last months and it irritated him when she did not hear. This irritability, this increasing childish petulance seemed to give expression to their imperceptible estrangement. Like two faces looking at one another through a sheet of glass they were close together, almost touching, but they could not hear or feel each other: the conductivity between them was broken. She, at least, had this sense of separation, and she fancied sometimes that she saw it reflected in the look with which he supplemented his failing words. Doubtless the fault was hers. She was too impenetrably healthy to be touched by the irrelevancies of disease. Her self-reproachful tenderness was tinged with the sense of his irrationality: she had a vague feeling that there was a purpose in his helpless tyrannies. The suddenness of the change had found her so unprepared. A year ago their pulses had beat to one robust measure; both had the same prodigal confidence in an exhaustless future. Now their energies no longer kept step: hers still bounded ahead of life, pre-empting unclaimed regions of hope and activity, while his lagged behind, vainly struggling to overtake her.

When they married, she had such arrears of living to make up:

her days had been as bare as the whitewashed school-room where
she forced innutritious facts upon reluctant children. His coming
had broken in on the slumber of circumstance, widening the
present till it became the encloser of remotest chances. But
imperceptibly the horizon narrowed. Life had a grudge against
her: she was never to be allowed to spread her wings.

At first the doctors had said that six weeks of mild air would
set him right; but when he came back this assurance was
explained as having of course included a winter in a dry climate.
They gave up their pretty house, storing the wedding presents
and new furniture, and went to Colorado. She had hated it there
from the first. Nobody knew her or cared about her; there was no
one to wonder at the good match she had made, or to envy her
the new dresses and the visiting-cards which were still a surprise
to her. And he kept growing worse. She felt herself beset with
difficulties too evasive to be fought by so direct a temperament.
She still loved him, of course; but he was gradually, undefinably
ceasing to be himself. The man she had married had been
strong, active, gently masterful: the male whose pleasure it is to
clear a way through the material obstructions of life; but now
it was she who was the protector, he who must be shielded from
importunities and given his drops or his beef-juice though the
skies were falling. The routine of the sick-room bewildered her;
this punctual administering of medicine seemed as idle as some
uncomprehended religious mummery.

There were moments, indeed, when warm gushes of pity swept
away her instinctive resentment of his condition, when she still
found his old self in his eyes as they groped for each other through
the dense medium of his weakness. But these moments had grown
rare. Sometimes he frightened her: his sunken expressionless face
seemed that of a stranger; his voice was weak and hoarse; his
thin-lipped smile a mere muscular contraction. Her hand avoided
his damp soft skin, which had lost the familiar roughness of
health: she caught herself furtively watching him as she might
have watched a strange animal. It frightened her to feel that
this was the man she loved; there were hours when to tell him
what she suffered seemed the one escape from her fears. But in

general she judged herself more leniently, reflecting that she had perhaps been too long alone with him, and that she would feel differently when they were at home again, surrounded by her robust and buoyant family. How she had rejoiced when the doctors at last gave their consent to his going home! She knew, of course, what the decision meant: they both knew. It meant that he was to die; but they dressed the truth in hopeful euphuisms, and at times, in the joy of preparation, she really forgot the purpose of their journey, and slipped into an eager allusion to next year's plans.

At last the day of leaving came. She had a dreadful fear that they would never get away; that somehow at the last moment he would fail her; that the doctors held one of their accustomed treacheries in reserve; but nothing happened. They drove to the station, he was installed in a seat with a rug over his knees and a cushion at his back, and she hung out of the window waving unregretful farewells to the acquaintances she had really never liked till then.

The first twenty-four hours had passed off well. He revived a little and it amused him to look out of the window and to observe the humors of the car. The second day he began to grow weary and to chafe under the dispassionate stare of the freckled child with the lump of chewing-gum. She had to explain to the child's mother that her husband was too ill to be disturbed: a statement received by that lady with a resentment visibly supported by the maternal sentiment of the whole car. . . .

That night he slept badly and the next morning his temperature frightened her: she was sure he was growing worse. The day passed slowly, punctuated by the small irritations of travel. Watching his tired face, she traced in its contractions every rattle and jolt of the train, till her own body vibrated with sympathetic fatigue. She felt the others observing him too, and hovered restlessly between him and the line of interrogative eyes. The freckled child hung about him like a fly: offers of candy and picture-books failed to dislodge her: she twisted one leg around the other and watched him imperturbably. The porter, as he passed, lingered with vague proffers of help, probably inspired by philanthropic passengers swelling with the sense that "something ought to be done"; and one nervous man in a skull-cap was audibly concerned as to the possible effect on his wife's health.

The hours dragged on in a dreary inoccupation. Toward dusk she sat down beside him and he laid his hand on hers. The touch startled her. He seemed to be calling her from far off. She looked at him helplessly and his smile went through her like a physical pang.

"Are you very tired?" she asked.

"No, not very."

"We'll be there soon now."

"Yes, very soon."

"This time tomorrow—"

He nodded and they sat silent. When she had put him to bed and crawled into her own berth she tried to cheer herself with the thought that in less than twenty-four hours they would be in New York. Her people would all be at the station to meet her—she pictured their round unanxious faces pressing through the crowd. She only hoped that they would not tell him too loudly that he was looking splendidly and would be all right in no time: the subtler sympathies developed by long contact with suffering were making her aware of a certain coarseness of texture in the family sensibilities.

Suddenly she thought she heard him call. She parted the curtains and listened. No, it was only a man snoring at the other end of the car. His snores had a greasy sound, as though they passed through tallow. She lay down and tried to sleep. . . . Had she not heard him move? She started up trembling. . . . The silence frightened her more than any sound. He might not be able to make her hear—he might be calling her now. . . . What made her think of such things? It was merely the familiar tendency of an over-tired mind to fasten itself on the most intolerable chance within the range of its forebodings. . . . Putting her head out, she listened; but she could not distinguish his breathing from that of the other pairs of lungs about her. She longed to get up and look at him, but she knew the impulse was a mere vent for her restlessness, and the fear of disturbing him restrained her. . . . The regular movement of his curtain reassured her, she knew not why; she remembered that he had wished her a cheerful goodnight; and the sheer inability to endure her fears a moment longer made her put them from her with an effort of her whole sound tired body. She turned on her side and slept.

She sat up stiffly, staring out at the dawn. The train was rushing through a region of bare hillocks huddled against a lifeless sky. It looked like the first day of creation. The air of the car was close, and she pushed up her window to let in the keen wind. Then she looked at her watch: it was seven o'clock, and soon the people about her would be stirring. She slipped into her clothes, smoothed her disheveled hair and crept to the dressing-room. When she had washed her face and adjusted her dress she felt more hopeful. It was always a struggle for her not to be cheerful in the morning. Her cheeks burned deliciously under the coarse towel, and the wet hair about her temples broke into strong upward tendrils. Every inch of her was full of life and elasticity. And in ten hours they would be at home!

She stepped to her husband's berth: it was time for him to take his early glass of milk. The window-shade was down, and in the dusk of the curtained enclosure she could just see that he lay sideways, with his face away from her. She leaned over him and drew up the shade. As she did so she touched one of his hands. It felt cold. . . .

She bent closer, laying her hand on his arm and calling him by name. He did not move. She spoke again more loudly; she grasped his shoulder and gently shook it. He lay motionless. She caught hold of his hand again: it slipped from her limply, like a dead thing. A dead thing? . . . Her breath caught. She must see his face. She leaned forward, and hurriedly, shrinkingly, with a sickening reluctance of the flesh, laid her hands on his shoulders and turned him over. His head fell back; his face looked small and smooth; he gazed at her with steady eyes.

She remained motionless for a long time, holding him thus; and they looked at each other. Suddenly she shrank back: the longing to scream, to call out, to fly from him, had almost overpowered her. But a strong hand arrested her. Good God! If it were known that he was dead they would be put off the train at the next station—

In a terrifying flash of remembrance there arose before her a scene she had once witnessed in traveling, when a husband and wife, whose child had died in the train, had been thrust out at some chance station. She saw them standing on the platform with the child's body between them; she had never forgotten the dazed look with which they followed the receding train. And this was what would happen to her. Within the next hour she might find herself on the platform of some strange station, alone with her husband's body. . . . Anything but that! It was too horrible— She quivered like a creature at bay.

As she cowered there, she felt the train moving more slowly. It was coming then—they were approaching a station! She saw again the husband and wife standing on the lonely platform; and with a violent gesture she drew down the shade to hide her husband's face.

Feeling dizzy, she sank down on the edge of the berth, keeping away from his outstretched body, and pulling the curtains close, so that he and she were shut into a kind of sepulchral twilight. She tried to think. At all costs she must conceal the fact that he was dead. But how? Her mind refused to act: she could not plan, combine. She could think of no way but to sit there, clutching the curtains, all day long. . . .

She heard the porter making up her bed; people were beginning to move about the car; the dressing-room door was being opened and shut. She tried to rouse herself. At length with a supreme effort she rose to her feet, stepping into the aisle of the car and drawing the curtains tight behind her. She noticed that they still parted slightly with the motion of the car, and finding a pin in her dress she fastened them together. Now she was safe. She looked around and saw the porter. She fancied he was watching her.

"Ain't he awake yet?" he inquired.

"No," she faltered.

"I got his milk all ready when he wants it. You know you told me to have it for him by seven."

She nodded silently and crept into her seat.

At half-past eight the train reached Buffalo. By this time the other passengers were dressed and the berths had been folded back for the day. The porter, moving to and fro under his burden of sheets and pillows, glanced at her as he passed. At length he said: "Ain't he going to get up? You know we're ordered to make up the berths as early as we can."

She turned cold with fear. They were just entering the station.

"Oh, not yet," she stammered. "Not till he's had his milk. Won't you get it, please?"

"All right. Soon as we start again."

When the train moved on he reappeared with the milk. She took it from him and sat vaguely looking at it: her brain moved slowly from one idea to another, as though they were stepping-stones set far apart across a whirling flood. At length she became aware that the porter still hovered expectantly.

"Will I give it to him?" he suggested.

"Oh, no," she cried, rising. "He—he's asleep yet, I think—"

She waited till the porter had passed on; then she unpinned

the curtains and slipped behind them. In the semi-obscurity her husband's face stared up at her like a marble mask with agate eyes. The eyes were dreadful. She put out her hand and drew down the lids. Then she remembered the glass of milk in her other hand: what was she to do with it? She thought of raising the window and throwing it out; but to do so she would have to lean across his body and bring her face close to his. She decided to drink the milk.

She returned to the seat with the empty glass and after a while the porter came back to get it.

"When'll I fold up his bed?" he asked.

"Oh, not now—not yet; he's ill—he's very ill. Can't you let him stay as he is? The doctor wants him to lie down as much as possible."

He scratched his head. "Well, if he's *really* sick—"

He took the empty glass and walked away, explaining to the passengers that the party behind the curtains was too sick to get up just yet.

She found herself the center of sympathetic eyes. A motherly woman with an intimate smile sat down beside her.

"I'm really sorry to hear your husband's sick. I've had a remarkable amount of sickness in my family and maybe I could assist you. Can I take a look at him?"

"Oh, no—no, please! He mustn't be disturbed."

The lady accepted the rebuff indulgently.

"Well, it's just as you say, of course, but you don't look to me as if you'd had much experience in sickness and I'd have been glad to assist you. What do you generally do when your husband's taken this way?"

"I—I let him sleep."

"Too much sleep ain't any too healthful either. Don't you give him any medicine?"

"Y-yes."

"Don't you wake him to take it?"

"Yes."

"When does he take the next dose?"

"Not for—two hours—"

The lady looked disappointed. "Well, if I was you I'd try giving it oftener. That's what I do with my folks."

After that many faces seemed to press upon her. The passengers were on their way to the dining-car, and she was conscious that as they passed down the aisle they glanced curiously at the closed curtains. One lantern-jawed man with prominent eyes stood still and tried to shoot his projecting glance through the division between the folds. The freckled child, returning from breakfast, waylaid the passers with a buttery clutch, saying in a loud whisper, "He's sick"; and once the conductor came by, asking for tickets. She shrank into her corner and looked out of the window at the flying trees and houses, meaningless hieroglyphs on an endlessly unrolled papyrus.

Now and then the train stopped, and the newcomers on entering the car stared in turn at the closed curtains. More and more people seemed to pass—their faces began to blend fantastically with the images surging in her brain. . . .

Later in the day a fat man detached himself from the mist of faces. He had a creased stomach and soft pale lips. As he pressed himself into the seat facing her she noticed that he was dressed in black broadcloth, with a soiled white tie.

"Husband's pretty bad this morning, is he?"

"Yes."

"Dear, dear! Now that's terribly distressing, ain't it?" An apostolic smile revealed his gold-filled teeth. "Of course you know there's no sech thing as sickness. Ain't that a lovely thought? Death itself is but a deloosion of our grosser senses. On'y lay yourself open to the influx of the sperrit, submit yourself passively to the action of the divine force, and disease and dissolution will cease to exist for you. If you could indooce your husband to read this little pamphlet—"

The faces about her again grew indistinct. She had a vague recollection of hearing the motherly lady and the parent of the freckled child ardently disputing the relative advantages of trying several medicines at once, or of taking each in turn; the motherly lady maintaining that the competitive system saved time; the other objecting that you couldn't tell which remedy had effected the cure; their voices went on and on, like bell-buoys droning through a fog. . . . The porter came up now and then with questions that she did not understand, but that somehow she must have answered since he went away again without repeating them; every two hours the motherly lady reminded her that her husband ought to have his drops; people left the car and others replaced them. . . .

Her head was spinning and she tried to steady herself by clutching at her thoughts as they swept by, but they slipped away from her like bushes on the side of a sheer precipice down which she seemed to be falling. Suddenly her mind grew clear again and she found herself vividly picturing what would happen when the train reached New York. She shuddered as it occurred to her that he would be quite cold and that someone might perceive he had been dead since morning.

She thought hurriedly: "If they see I am not surprised they will suspect something. They will ask questions; and if I tell them the truth they won't believe me—no one would believe me! It will be terrible"—and she kept repeating to herself: "I must pretend I don't know. I must pretend I don't know. When they open the curtains I must go up to him quite naturally—and then I must scream." . . . She had an idea that the scream would be very hard to do.

Gradually new thoughts crowded upon her, vivid and urgent: she tried to separate and restrain them, but they beset her clamorously, like her school-children at the end of a hot day, when she was too tired to silence them. Her head grew confused, and she felt a sick fear of forgetting her part, of betraying herself by some unguarded word or look.

"I must pretend I don't know," she went on murmuring. The words had lost their significance, but she repeated them mechanically, as though they had been a magic formula, until she heard herself saying: "I can't remember, I can't remember!"

Her voice sounded very loud, and she looked about her in terror; but no one seemed to notice that she had spoken.

As she glanced down the car her eye caught the curtains of her husband's berth, and she began to examine the monotonous arabesques woven through their heavy folds. The pattern was intricate and difficult to trace; she gazed fixedly at the curtains, and as she did so the thick stuff grew transparent and through it she saw her husband's face—his dead face. She struggled to avert her look, but her eyes refused to move and her head seemed to be held in a vice. At last, with an effort that left her weak and shaking, she turned away; but it was of no use; close in front of her, small and smooth, was her husband's face. It seemed to be suspended in the air between her and the false braids of the woman who sat in front of her. With an uncontrollable gesture she stretched out her hand to push the face away, and suddenly she felt the touch of his smooth skin. She repressed a cry and half started from her seat. The woman with the false braids looked around, and feeling that she must justify her movement in some way she rose and lifted her traveling-bag from the opposite seat. She unlocked the bag and looked into it; but the first object her hand met was a small flask of her husband's, thrust there at the last moment, in the haste of departure. She locked the bag and closed her eyes . . . his face was there again, hanging between her eye-balls and lids like a waxen mask against a red curtain. . . .

She roused herself with a shiver. Had she fainted or slept? Hours seemed to have elapsed; but it was still broad day, and the people about her were sitting in the same attitudes as before.

A sudden sense of hunger made her aware that she had eaten nothing since morning. The thought of food filled her with disgust, but she dreaded a return of faintness, and remembering that she had some biscuits in her bag she took one out and ate it. The dry crumbs choked her, and she hastily swallowed a little brandy from her husband's flask. The burning sensation in her throat acted as a counter-irritant, momentarily relieving the dull ache of her nerves. Then she felt a gently stealing warmth, as though a soft air fanned her, and the swarming fears relaxed their clutch, receding through the stillness that enclosed her, a stillness soothing as the spacious quietude of a summer day. She slept.

Through her sleep she felt the impetuous rush of the train.

It seemed to be life itself that was sweeping her on with headlong inexorable force—sweeping her into darkness and terror, and the awe of unknown day. Now all at once everything was still—not a sound, not a pulsation. . . . She was dead in her turn, and lay beside him with smooth upstaring face. How quiet it was!— and yet she heard feet coming, the feet of men who were to carry them away. . . . She could feel too—she felt a sudden prolonged vibration, a series of hard shocks, and then another plunge into darkness: the darkness of death this time—a black whirlwind on which they were both spinning like leaves, in wild uncoiling spirals, with millions and millions of the dead. . . .

She sprang up in terror. Her sleep must have lasted a long time, for the winter day had paled and the lights had been lit. The car was in confusion, and as she regained her self-possession she saw that the passengers were gathering up their wraps and bags. The woman with the false braids had brought from the dressing-room a sickly ivy-plant in a bottle, and the Christian Scientist was reversing his cuffs. The porter passed down the aisle with his impartial brush. An impersonal figure with a gold-banded cap asked for her husband's ticket. A voice shouted "Baig-gage express!" and she heard the clicking of metal as the passengers handed over their checks.

Presently her window was blocked by an expanse of sooty wall, and the train passed into the Harlem tunnel. The journey was over; in a few minutes she would see her family pushing their joyous way through the throng at the station. Her heart dilated. The worst terror was past. . . .

"We'd better get him up now, hadn't we?" asked the porter, touching her arm.

He had her husband's hat in his hand and was meditatively revolving it under his brush.

She looked at the hat and tried to speak; but suddenly the car grew dark. She flung up her arms, struggling to catch at something, and fell face downward, striking her head against the dead man's berth.

The Problem of the Locked Caboose

By Edward D. Hoch

*T*HE *classic locked-room mystery, wherein a murder or other crime appears to take place under impossible circumstances, has long been a favorite of detective-story writers. Seldom, though, has this type of story been adapted to the environment of a fast-moving train—and, until the publication early last year of this novelette, never (at least to my knowledge) to that most ubiquitous of railroad cars, the caboose.*

Perhaps it is only fitting that Edward D. Hoch should have created the first "locked caboose" mystery, for he is unquestionably the heir apparent to such worthy practitioners of formal crime fiction as John Dickson Carr and Agatha Christie. He specializes in short stories—and an amazing and apparently inexhaustible flow of "impossible crime" plots; he has published upwards of six hundred tales since he began writing professionally in the early 1950s, and his knowledge of the criminous short has won him the editorship of the prestigious annual, Best Detective

Stories of the Year. *"The Problem of the Locked Caboose"*
features one of his most likeable series characters, Dr. Sam
Hawthorne, a retired New England physician who solves (and
reminisces about) incredible crimes of the Prohibition Twenties.
If you can come up with the solution to this baffling case before
Dr. Sam does, you're a smarter and more perceptive person than
I am.

"Caboose!" Dr. Sam Hawthorne exploded. "It's a wonderful
word, and we hardly hear it any more. It's a word that was
important back when trains were important—more important than
they are now, anyway. Let me fill your glass . . . another small—
ah—libation . . . and you settle back in your chair. I'll tell you
about a train trip I took in the spring of 1925, and about the
impossible theft—and impossible murder too!—that happened in
the locked caboose . . ."

The spring floods that year had washed out most of the back
roads between Northmont and the towns to the west, which is
why I was forced to take the train to Boughville in the first
place. I didn't much like train travel, but my Pierce-Arrow
Runabout couldn't forge flood-swollen streams, so I had no choice.
The doctor in Boughville, who'd done me some favors in the
past, had asked me to take over his patients while he and his
wife celebrated their 25th wedding anniversary with a cruise to
Europe on the *Mauretania*. The previous year the ship had broken
all Atlantic speed records, making the crossing from Ambrose
Channel Light Vessel to Cherbourg Breakwater in five days, one
hour, and 49 minutes. To sail on the *Mauretania* in 1925 was
the height of luxurious travel.

For me, I'd have to be content with a train ride to Boughville.

In order to arrive in time for morning appointments, it was
necessary to take the night train from Northmont. Though the
trip was less than two hours by car, the circuitous route of

the Boston & Western more than doubled that time as it stopped at every little hamlet with the morning's milk and newspapers. But there was a Pullman car on the train, so I could catch a few hours' sleep. In those days it was not uncommon for doctors to flag down trains with a lantern to board them at a nonscheduled station—and to depart at their destination by jumping off as the train slowed to five miles an hour. I'd done it just once, landing on gravel and scraping my hand so badly it pained me for weeks.

On the evening of my departure April packed an overnight bag for me and was waiting at the office door with all the solicitude of a mother hen. "Be careful now, Dr. Sam. Remember last time—no jumpin' off movin' trains!"

"Don't worry, I'll take care," I assured her.

"Mebbe if you have time you could bring me some o' that good maple syrup they make there."

"This is the time o' year for it. I'll see what I can do."

It was an hour till train time at midnight, and I stopped at the town's lunch counter for a sandwich and a little cup of bootleg Scotch before they closed. Then I went on to the depot.

"You travelin' tonight, Dr. Sam?" the stationmaster asked.

"Just as far as Boughville. Filling in for the doc while he takes a cruise to Europe."

"That's where we all should be." He glanced nervously at his big pocket watch. "Wish that ol' train would be early for once."

"What's the trouble?"

"Got a special shipment of valuables to put aboard."

"Valuables—on that old clunker? How come?"

"Most of our passenger trains don't have cabooses. This one does 'cause it hauls some freight cars too. The caboose is a paymaster's car with barred windows and a good strong safe." He glanced around and lowered his voice. "They're shippin' the Glenworth jewelry collection to Boston for appraisal and auction."

"That should bring a fancy price!" Old Mrs. Glenworth had died of pneumonia during the hard winter, leaving a small fortune in jewelry acquired during four decades of marriage to one of the state's leading industrialists. "You mean they're shipping it to Boston without a guard?"

"The family lawyer is travelin' with it. He should be here any minute now."

"Still, it's a long way around. That train won't reach Boston till midmorning, after having stopped in every village in the state. My God, the train's going west, and you want to ship it east!"

The stationmaster nodded. "I know, but it's the only train that's got a safe, you see. Parsons—that's the lawyer—don't trust himself to just carry the jewelry. He wants it locked up, protected from train robbers."

I had to chuckle at the thought of it. "You think they'll block the track and ride up on horses?"

"Men have done stranger things for a quarter of a million dollars."

I whistled softly. "That much?"

"So Parsons tells me." He glanced over at the door as it opened, and his nervousness transmitted itself to me. I almost expected to see a masked man waving a gun, but it was only the little lawyer, Jasper Parsons, whom I'd seen around town on occasion.

"Who's this?" Parsons asked, as jumpy as we had been. Then, his eyes growing accustomed to the light, he said, "Oh, it's Dr. Hawthorne, isn't it? Are you travelin' tonight, Doctor?"

"Just as far as Boughville, to see some patients. I hope to get a berth and catch a few hours' sleep."

"I'm on my way to Boston," Parsons said. "The long way around." Then, to the stationmaster, "Do you have the strongbox?"

"Right here—and glad to be rid of it!"

From somewhere far down the tracks came the mournful wail of a train whistle. "It's coming," I said.

The little lawyer slipped a small revolver from his jacket pocket. "I'm takin' no chances. I won't rest safely till this shipment is in Boston an' out of my care." He glanced at me and his face lit up with a sudden thought. "Dr. Hawthorne, you can be of assistance if you will. This strongbox won't fit in the train's safe, so I have to transfer the contents. I'd like you to witness the transfer."

"Glad to."

Presently a single glowing headlight appeared down the track, and the night train rolled into the Northmont station with a roar and a hiss of escaping steam. I felt the old thrill that everyone of that era experienced at the arrival of a train—the thrill of being suddenly dwarfed by this massive iron monster that towered above you, all smoking and alive.

We walked quickly to the rear of the train, with Parsons and the stationmaster carrying the strongbox between them. The lawyer's free hand still gripped the revolver, like some modern-day

Wells Fargo driver, and I couldn't help chuckling at the melodrama of it.

At the red-painted caboose we were met by a conductor swinging a lantern. He was a German named Fritz Schmidt, and he spoke English with a decided accent. "*Ja*, I am expecting you. Unload your strongbox while I open the safe." His youthful blond features rather surprised me.

I followed them up the steps to the caboose door, standing on the platform of the adjoining Pullman car. The conductor unlocked the door with a great deal of fanfare, and I had time to study the door itself. It was thick and firmly anchored in its casing, with a small square opening about at chest level. The opening was barred like a teller's window in a bank, and covered with glass.

"They use this car for payrolls," Schmidt explained in his thick accent. "Take it out where the workers are repairing track an' pay them right from here. *Ja*, it is safe."

To my eyes the safe did indeed seem impregnable. It was made of thick steel and bolted to the floor of the caboose. In those dingy surroundings it seemed the sturdiest thing in sight. The conductor swung the safe door wide for our inspection, then motioned for Parsons to produce the jewelry.

At that moment the train gave a sudden lurch forward, throwing us off balance, and began to creep ahead. Out the dirty window of the caboose I saw the stationmaster waving his lantern. We were under way.

"Take this list," Parsons said, thrusting a document upon me, "and check off the pieces as I hand them to the conductor." He opened the strongbox and removed a flat velvet-covered jewel case whose lid he raised for my inspection. "One emerald necklace."

I gaped at the beautiful green and gold ornament and almost forgot to check it off. A country doctor doesn't get to see many treasures like that! And what followed was even more amazing—diamonds and rubies, all in exquisite settings worthy of a queen. There were nine pieces in all, each more lovely than the others.

I wondered if the stationmaster's estimate of $250,000 hadn't been on the low side.

"All there," I confirmed as the final piece was placed in the safe and the steel door slammed shut. The conductor twirled the dial and tried the handle, making certain it was locked.

"Will there be someone in here all night?" Jasper Parsons wanted to know.

Schmidt motioned toward a bunk bed. "I will be sleeping here. It will be safe. Not to worry."

Parsons left the empty strongbox on the floor and we went out, crossing the swaying platform to the Pullman car. Behind us we heard the conductor bolt and lock the inside of the caboose door. I could see his face in the little barred window, looking just the least bit sinister.

In the Pullman car we were greeted by a conductor smoking a long curved-stem pipe while he collected fares. Unlike Schmidt, this conductor was obviously American, though with a trace of Irish heritage. "Find your berths, fellas. An' gimme your ticket to punch. Me name's O'Brian, an' I take no sass from drunks or troublemakers. We're here to sleep, an' anyone makin' a racket will find themselves off the train at trackside!"

"I'm Dr. Sam Hawthorne. Could you wake me ten minutes before we reach Boughville?"

"Sure will, Doc. You're in berth number nine."

Jasper Parsons was assigned to berth number seven, but when the little lawyer attempted to pull back the curtains and climb in, he discovered to his horror that it was already occupied. A burly bald man in paisley pajamas growled out, "What do you want?"

The Irish conductor almost dropped his pipe. "Mr. Apple! I clean forgot you was in there! Sorry to disturb yeh. Here, Mr. Parsons, you take the upper."

"I don't sleep in an upper berth," the lawyer replied with feeling.

O'Brian scratched his head. "Well," he said finally, "I guess that end berth is empty. Take that one."

The commotion brought a response from across the aisle. The curtain of number eleven was pushed aside and a young woman's blonde head appeared. "Is this going to go on all night, for heaven's sake? I'm trying to sleep!"

"My apologies," I offered, never one to ignore a pretty face. "I'm Sam Hawthorne, traveling as far as Boughville."

"That's a coincidence. I'm bound for there myself."

"I thought only doctors arrived in Boughville at four A.M."

She propped herself up on one elbow, careful to remain decently covered. "Doctors and artists. They say the spring sunrise over Boughville Pond is one of the loveliest sights in all New England."

"I hope you enjoy it," I said. "Now I'll let you get back to sleep."

I climbed into my berth and started to undress. It was always a trick in the cramped quarters of a Pullman, and I managed to bump my head twice before settling down. A glance at my watch showed it was now almost midnight.

"You all settled in, Doc?" O'Brian asked.

"Sure am." I poked my head out. Down the aisle the little lawyer was filling a paper cup with water before returning to his berth. "Do you and Schmidt change off here?"

"Not tonight. He's worked his shift, an' he's sleepin' in the caboose till we hit Boston on the return trip. Havin' a swig o' bootleg Scotch too, if I know him. Want some?"

"No thanks."

"Have a good rest. I'll wake ye in plenty of time for Boughville."

I rolled over beneath the covers, trying to get comfortable, and listened to the clicking of the wheels on the tracks.

I must have been dozing, but not really asleep, when I felt a hand shaking me awake. "What is it?" I mumbled. "Boughville already?"

O'Brian the conductor was leaning close to my head, whispering. "No, it's only two o'clock. But I think Schmidt is hurt. He needs a doctor."

I mumbled something and groped for my bag. There was no way I could walk through the car in my pajamas, so I quickly

pulled on my pants over them. Still feeling a bit naked in my
bare feet, I swung out of the berth and followed the conductor
toward the rear of the train.

I'd have guessed the train was traveling at about 20 miles an
hour, swaying just enough so it was necessary to brace myself
now and again to keep my balance. With the heavy medical bag
in one hand it was no easy chore. And crossing the platform
between cars made me jump when my bare feet touched the
cold metal.

If I'd expected to find the caboose door standing open, I was
in for a surprise. It was still closed just as we'd left it, but the
Irish conductor motioned me to peer in the little barred window.
"See him in there?"

Fritz Schmidt was sprawled on the floor of the caboose, face
down in front of the safe. Little rivulets of blood ran off in all
directions from under his body, impelled by the constant swaying
of the train. From him my eyes went immediately to the safe.
The door of the safe was standing ajar, and I knew we'd find it
empty.

"How do we get in here?" I asked, trying the door without
success.

"We don't, without breaking in. My keys don't work. He's
got it bolted from the inside."

I tapped the glass of the little barred window. "Doesn't this
thing open? You must open it for payrolls."

"It can only be opened from the inside. It's got a little
spring bolt that snaps shut when it's closed."

I ran my fingers along the edges of the door frame, but there
was not even the crack of an opening. I got down on my knees
on the cold metal platform and felt beneath the door, but there
was no space there either. I realized suddenly that a thin metal
edge ran around the door on all four sides, like a modified
ship's bulkhead, and I remembered stepping over it when I'd
entered the caboose with Parsons earlier.

"We have to reach him," I insisted. "He may be still alive.
Isn't there a trap door in the roof?"

"Sure, but ye can see from here it's bolted shut on the inside."

"Then how about the back door, to the rear platform? Can you go over the top of the car and try it? We'll never get in this way."

"All right," he agreed. "I'll try it."

He climbed up the metal ladder on our platform, and I could hear him going across the roof of the caboose to the far end. I was acutely aware of the cool night air as I stood shivering in my bare feet waiting for him to appear at the opposite end of the car. Finally I could see him through the barred window. And I could see now that the door on the far end was bolted too. But the window in it was bigger, and the bars set farther apart.

O'Brian smashed the glass and reached between the bars for the bolt. He couldn't see it, but after a few moments of feeling for it he was successful. He unbolted the back door and used his key in the lock. It swung open and he hurried over to Schmidt.

I tapped on the glass at my end, urging him to open up, and he did so. "I think it's too late," he said glumly.

I grunted and went to see for myself. One hand—the right one—was outstretched, and I could see now that Schmidt had written something on the metal floor with his own blood. A single word: *elf*.

"He's dead," I confirmed, lifting the body slightly. "There's a wound in his chest. Looks like a stab wound."

"But there's no knife! What happened to the knife?"

"The killer took it with him, obviously. Along with the Glenworth jewelry."

"But—but ye saw how the caboose was locked up! How could anyone get in?"

"Schmidt could have let them in. I'm more interested in how they got out leaving all windows and doors locked and bolted on the inside."

I walked over to the heavy door by which I'd entered and unlatched the little barred window. It opened easily, and when I pushed it shut the lock snapped. I estimated the window was about eight inches high by six inches wide.

"Not even a child could fit through there," the conductor said, "if that's what you're thinkin'."

"No," I agreed. "But maybe an elf could."

"What?"

"You'd better wake up Jasper Parsons, and tell him the jewelry is gone."

The little lawyer did not come alone. When he arrived at the caboose, fully clothed, I saw that the girl in the opposite berth had tagged along.

"You'd better stand back," I warned her. "It's not a pleasant sight."

"Is he dead? Was he murdered?" Her eyes were wide with horror.

"Yes, he's dead, and yes, we think he was murdered. Now please go back to your berth."

"I'm staying," she said firmly.

I shrugged and turned toward Parsons. He was kneeling before the empty safe and looked as if he'd just lost his closest friend. "That jewelry was in my care," he muttered, close to tears. "This will ruin me!"

"Let's see what we can do about getting it back," I said.

"Back?"

I turned to the conductor. "Am I correct that the train has made no stops since we boarded it at Northmont?"

"That's right." He consulted his watch. "First stop is Greenhaven, in fifteen minutes."

"And the train was traveling at twenty miles an hour all that time?"

"Mostly faster. We have to slow down over this stretch at night."

"Would you say anyone could jump from a train going this fast?"

"Not a chance! Especially along here—there's all rocks an' stuff. They'd batter themselves somethin' awful."

"So I think we can assume the killer-thief is still on the train. You'd better tell the engineer we'll be stopping at Greenhaven to notify the police. It might cause a delay in the trip."

The blonde girl sighed and sat down. "I just knew I wasn't going to get to Boughville in time to paint the sunrise."

"There'll be others," I assured her. "I guess I don't even know your name. Mine's Sam Hawthorne. Folks call me Dr. Sam."

She smiled and held out her hand. "I'm Dora Winter, from Boston. Please excuse the informal attire. I learned to dress properly at finishing school, but they didn't prepare me for murder."

I gave her lace-trimmed peignoir a passing glance. "Very pretty. Tell me, did you hear anything during the past hour or so?"

She shook her head. "First you awakened me when you boarded the train, and then this man was causing a fuss." She indicated Parsons.

"But you heard nothing in between?"

"No."

The lawyer had given up on the safe and was staring down at Schmidt's body. "How'd the killer get in here an' out again if the caboose was locked?"

"That's one of the problems," I admitted. "It seems impossible."

"But it happened," O'Brian said.

"Yes. Tell me something—how many people knew the combination of that safe?"

"You mean, on this train? Only two of us—Schmidt an' me. But other conductors who make the run would know it."

"So unless a passenger learned the combination from someone else, the safe must have been opened by you or the dead man. Correct?"

"It sure wasn't me!" he insisted. "How could I have gotten in an' out?"

"Schmidt would have opened the door for you."

The big Irishman looked around, searching for a companion in his misery. "Sure an' he'd've opened it for Parsons here too! They were his jewels. He'd even have opened the safe for him!"

Jasper Parsons growled and threw himself at the conductor. "You're not blamin' me, you murderin' crook!"

"Stop that!" I pulled them apart and used my best voice of authority. "Now look, we won't get anywhere fighting among ourselves. Schmidt is dead and his killer is still on this train. In a very few minutes we're going to be in Greenhaven, and then we'll have the sheriff and the state police to answer to. Let's try to straighten this out ourselves."

"Suits me," Parsons agreed. "So long as I get that jewelry back."

"I would think you'd be more concerned with the dead man," Dora Winter said. "My God, can't you at least cover him up?"

I took a blanket from the bunk bed and spread it over Schmidt's lifeless form. As I did so something stirred in the back of my mind. "This conductor's uniform he's wearing—is it the same one he had on earlier?"

"Sure is," O'Brian confirmed. "We don't bring no change o' uniform on these overnight runs. Hell, we're back home in the mornin'."

"And how many other passengers are on the train?"

"Not many tonight. One other, Mr. Apple, in the Pullman."

I'd forgotten about Apple. "How about the car ahead?"

"Empty."

"Crew?"

"The engineer an' fireman. That's all. A freight handler gets on at Greenhaven an' rides the rest o' the way."

I nodded. "Let's go see Mr. Apple."

We trooped back to the Pullman and woke him from a sound sleep. "What is it?" he asked.

"Could you get out of the bunk, sir?" I'd only seen his head, and I was anxious to know how tall he was. When he climbed out I could see I needn't have bothered. He was well over six feet— the tallest person on the train.

"Now what's the meaning of this? It's the middle of the night!"

"There's been a murder, Mr. Apple. We need everyone's cooperation."

"A murder? You mean here—on the train?"

"That's right," I confirmed. "In the caboose. Murder and robbery."

"My God, you're not safe anywhere these days! I suppose it was some of those Chicago bootleggers!"

The train began to slow down, coasting to a stop. It was 2:25 A.M. and we were coming into the Greenhaven station.

The sheriff of Greenhaven was a rotund individual named Putnam who was obviously annoyed at having had his sleep disturbed. He glanced at the body, grunted, and ordered his deputies to search the train for the stolen jewelry.

"They're in nine flat jewel cases," Parsons told him. "The largest is about ten inches by eight inches."

"If they're still in the cases," I said.

"What?"

"The thief could have tossed the cases off the train at any point and hidden the jewelry in a much smaller container."

"If they're on this train we'll find 'em," the sheriff assured us. "We'll search everything, including the passengers' luggage."

I didn't expect them to find anything and they didn't. A killer clever enough to escape from a locked caboose would be clever enough to hide the jewelry where it wouldn't be found.

"There's a great deal of money involved here," Jasper Parsons told the sheriff when the hour-long search turned up nothing. "You've got to recover that jewelry!"

"There's money involved in runnin' a railroad too," O'Brian snorted. "We gotta git rollin'."

I could see another battle brewing, so I stepped between them. "Maybe I can be of help. We all seem to be forgetting that the murdered man left us a dying message—a message obviously pointing to his killer. An elf is a dwarfish being of Teutonic mythology—the sort of myth the Germanic Schmidt would be familiar with. In fact, Schmidt would probably have used the word *elf* if he meant to say *dwarf*."

"Dwarf?"

"Is there—or has there ever been—a dwarf connected with this train? Either as a crew member or recent passenger?"

O'Brian shook his head.

The sheriff was growing impatient. "What's all this business about a dwarf?"

"The conductor," I explained, "was found murdered in a locked room, but I can show you a way in which a dwarf could have killed him."

"Go ahead."

I led them back into the caboose, where the tall Mr. Apple was studying the bloodstained floor. He looked surprised when he saw us, and I was surprised to see him. The sheriff had questioned him earlier, establishing the fact that he was a traveling salesman in plumbing supplies who often rode the night train. He'd indicated then that he had no interest in the murdered conductor or the stolen jewelry. Now he looked up at me and said, "Terrible thing—terrible way to die!"

"That it is," I agreed.

Sheriff Putnam was at my shoulder. "Let's git on with this. Show us how a midget could've killed him an' escaped from this here locked caboose."

"Well, there are a number of hiding places in here for a tiny person. Under the bed covers, behind the safe, down the other end of the car behind those boxes. None of these places would hide a normal-sized man or woman, but a midget or a very small child could go undetected there."

"An' you're sayin' this midget was already hidin' there when the caboose was locked by Schmidt?"

"That's right."

"An' was still hidin' there when you broke in?"

"No, he couldn't have still been in here, because O'Brian entered through the back door. He'd have seen anyone hiding behind the safe or those boxes. Besides, we stayed in here till the train reached Greenhaven. I did, at least. At one point I sent O'Brian out to wake Parsons."

"Then how'd the dwarf git out?" the sheriff demanded. I could see he wasn't buying a word of it.

I walked over to the solid door with its tiny barred window. "This window, unlike the others, can be opened from the inside. It's a paymaster's window. No one could fit through it except a midget or dwarf—but once through they could swing the window closed and the lock would snap shut. It's the only possible way the killer could have left the caboose locked after his departure."

Sheriff Putnam unwrapped a chew of tobacco. "How'd the midget git Schmidt to open the safe?"

"I don't know."

"By threatenin' him with the knife?"

"Maybe."

"You don't seem too sure o' things."

"I'm not. No dwarf has turned up in the case. We only have the dead man's message to hint that one even existed."

While the sheriff puzzled over this, Jasper Parsons motioned me aside. "You believe that crazy notion, Hawthorne?"

"No," I admitted. "As a matter of fact, it couldn't have happened the way I described it. If a midget went out that tiny opening, how'd he reach it? The window is chest high for a normal person. And we found no box or chair near enough for him to stand on."

"But—but if you knew it wasn't true, why'd you tell the sheriff that?"

"Just to play for time. Relax—I'm trying my damnedest to get your jewelry back."

"I think it was that other conductor—O'Brian. He knew the combination o' that safe, an' Schmidt would've opened the door for him. He left through that door at the far end o' the caboose, which he only pretended to unlock later."

I shook my head. "I watched him pull the bolt after he broke the glass. There was no way he could have tricked it up."

The little lawyer was exasperated. "Then the crime is impossible!"

"Maybe. Maybe not."

O'Brian and the engineer were arguing with the sheriff, trying to get permission to continue the interrupted journey. "We've lost an hour already!" the conductor bellowed.

"All right, all right!" Putnam agreed at last. "But I'll ride along with you as far as Boughville. That's still in my county."

Dora Winter came up to me. "Looks like I'm going to miss my sunrise," she said quietly. "But maybe I can paint a portrait of Sheriff Putnam instead."

There was no sleep to be had during the rest of the journey. We sat up in the caboose, drinking bitter coffee from a blue metal pot and speculating about the killing.

"I say it was a common ordinary train robber," the salesman named Apple insisted. "He dropped onto the roof from an over-hanging tree and came in through that trap door."

"What was Schmidt doin' all this time?" the sheriff asked, chewing on his tobacco.

"He was taken by surprise. The killer forced him to open the safe, then knifed him an' bolted the trap door so it would look like the murderer was one of us passengers."

"And how'd he leave the caboose?"

"There are tricks you can work with door bolts," Apple answered vaguely.

"But not with these doors," I pointed out. "See the metal rim around them? There's no space where a string or thin wire could be pulled through. True, a string or wire could have been pulled through this little window, but the bolt goes the other way."

"Couldn't the bolt have been pushed shut with a cane or some-thing, through the paymaster's window?"

I shook my head again. "This bolt's hard to work. Try it for yourself. A man's hand couldn't reach it through this window, and anything like a cane or a piece of pipe would probably have left scratches on the bolt—if it could move it at all from that angle. Besides, it would be a chancy, time-consuming operation. Why would the murderer risk bothering about it? Even if the door was standing open, it wouldn't implicate anybody."

"I think I've got it!" Jasper Parsons cried. "The knife wound didn't kill Schmidt instantly. We know that because he lived long 'nough to write his dying word. Suppose the killer stabbed him an' fled. Schmidt staggered to the door, closed and bolted it, and then fell back to the floor."

"Same objection, in a way," I said. "The bolt works hard, and why would he do it if he'd already been stabbed? Why not call out for help instead? After all, we were right in the next car. Besides, it was also locked by key from the inside. He'd have had to bolt the door, take out his key and lock it, then return the key to his pocket. If he lived to do all that he was quite a man—especially since there's only a drop or two of blood near the door."

"Then it's plain impossible," the lawyer said, repeating his earlier judgment.

Sheriff Putnam spit out a glob of tobacco juice. "Elves an' fairies! He was killed by elves an' fairies."

As the train rumbled on through the night, I left them and returned to the Pullman car. I wanted to inspect the door and walls for possible bloodstains, remembering how I'd had to balance myself with one hand while walking.

But there were no spots of blood.

Did that mean a killer who could keep his balance—someone like the conductor O'Brian who was used to swaying trains?

Or merely one with clean hands?

"Conway Falls," O'Brian called into the Pullman. "Coming into Conway Falls! Next stop Boughville."

"There's no one here but me," I reminded him. "The Pullman is empty."

He shrugged. "Routine."

I nodded and glanced at my pocket watch. It was already after four, and we were still a half hour away from Boughville. We'd managed to make up some of the lost time, but we were still running late.

The train had started up again, clickety-clacking along the tracks, when suddenly I heard a scream from the platform between the cars. I dashed from the Pullman, recognizing that it must be Dora Winter in some sort of trouble, and found her struggling in Apple's arms.

"What's all this?" I asked. "Let her go!"

He turned on me with a fury. "Mind your own business, Doc! This doesn't concern you!"

Though he was some inches taller than me, I figured I could take him on. Fellas my age always figure that. I aimed a blow at his jaw which he easily dodged, and before I could recover my footing on the swaying platform he countered with a blow to my solar plexus which took the wind out of me and sent me toppling off-balance. I caught myself before I fell out the door, and he quickly gave me a hand back up.

"Here, I didn't want to kill you," he said, his voice reflecting concern. He was obviously a man of moods.

"I'm okay, Apple."

He glanced at the girl and then back to me. Uncertain, he finally turned and entered the Pullman car without another word.

"Thank you," she said, brushing herself off and straightening her dress.

"Was he trying to attack you?"

She hesitated, then nodded. "He wanted me to go with him when we leave the train at Boughville."

"Don't worry, I'll stay with you to make sure you're not bothered." Silently I hoped I'd be more effective the next time.

When the train pulled into Boughville there was no sign of Apple, and I wondered if he'd decided to stay on till the following stop. Sheriff Putnam was there, though, checking those who were leaving the train. "Just an added precaution," he explained, "in case my men missed anything in their search."

I opened my medical bag, and Dora Winter opened her case of paints. He grunted and waved us on. Jasper Parsons appeared on the platform next, carrying his suitcase. "Are you leaving me, Hawthorne?"

"There's nothing more I can do," I told him.

Apple got off the train then too, accompanied by the Irish conductor. I noticed that O'Brian was counting out the Pullman tickets, licking his finger at each one.

Counting.

At my side Dora said something, but I didn't hear it. My mind was somewhere else.

Was it all as simple as that? Could it be? Could it really?

"The sun's just rising," Dora Winter said, pointing toward the glow in the eastern sky. "Maybe I can do some painting after all. Will you walk with me a bit?"

"Sure," I told her. It would be two hours before I could see my first patient. "Just a minute and I'll be with you." I took a pre-

scription blank from my bag and scribbled a brief message for
Sheriff Putnam.

"What's this?" he asked when I handed it to him.

"Just an idea I had. It might help you with the case."

O'Brian had hopped back aboard the train and signaled up to
the engineer. In a moment the iron horse was pulling out of the
station, leaving Apple and the lawyer standing with us on the
platform. "How come you got off here?" Sheriff Putnam asked
Jasper Parsons. "Weren't you goin' on to Boston?"

"Not without that jewelry I'm not! It was in my care—I'm
responsible for it."

Apple gave another glance in Dora's direction and then moved
off by himself. "Come on," I said to her. "Let's go catch your sunrise."

"Will you be back?" Parsons called after me.

"Sometime."

Dora was loaded down with her paint case and easel, so I
shifted the medical bag to my left hand and took the case from
her. We had strolled through the first morning light toward a
point overlooking a quiet country pond. It was out of sight of the
station, and in that moment we might have been the only people
for miles around.

"Do you make this trip often?" she asked, setting up her easel
so that it faced the eastern sky.

"I'm just covering for a colleague. How about you?"

She squeezed a bit of oil paint from its tube. The red of it
reminded me of blood. "No, I don't come often. Not in the middle
of the night, at least."

"What did Apple want with you?"

"The usual things."

"What made him think you'd cooperate?"

"I have no idea."

I decided it was time for a wild guess. "Was it because he'd
seen you sometime with Schmidt?"

Her hand froze in midair, holding the red-dipped brush. "What
do you mean?"

"Like so many mysteries, this one revolved around *who* rather than *how*. It baffled us because we didn't see that crucial point. We concentrated on the *how* and ignored the *who*, and that's why we couldn't solve it. The question—the pivotal question—was not how the murderer escaped, but rather who opened the safe and stole the jewelry. If we answer that question, the rest becomes obvious."

"And you know the answer?" she asked carefully.

I gazed toward the east, through the trees, shielding my eyes against the rising sun. "Forget Schmidt's death for a moment and you have the answer. He was alone in a locked caboose, one of the only two people on the train who knew the safe's combination. The safe was opened and the jewelry stolen. You see the answer now? Schmidt—and only Schmidt—could have stolen that jewelry!"

She made a mark on the virgin canvas, a slash of red that was much too deep for the color of the sky I saw. "Then who killed him? And what happened to the knife—and the jewelry?"

"He had an accomplice, of course. He told us he was going to bed, but when we found him dead he was still wearing his uniform. So he was expecting someone—not a random passenger who wouldn't have known the jewelry was aboard in the first place, but someone he'd told about it in advance, right after Parsons notified the railroad and requested the safe."

"You asked me if Apple had ever seen Schmidt and me together."

"Yes—because you were the accomplice, weren't you? Once we see Schmidt as the thief, passing the jewelry to an accomplice, the problem of the locked caboose becomes clear. He removed the jewelry from the safe and passed it out the little paymaster's window to the accomplice waiting between the cars. I don't know what phony story the two of you planned, but he never got a chance to tell it. Because you decided to keep the jewelry all for yourself.

"You stabbed him in the chest through that same little window. He staggered backward, leaving only a drop or two of blood near the door, and collapsed near the safe. Then you simply pulled the little window closed until the spring lock snapped. It wasn't a matter of the killer escaping from the caboose *because the killer was never inside the caboose!*"

"You think I did that?"

I nodded. "Schmidt named you in his dying message."

"Named me? *Elf?*"

"It came to me when I saw O'Brian counting tickets just now. Counting! As an accomplice to a robbery you wouldn't have traveled under your real name. Schmidt didn't know the name you were using, so he couldn't identify you in the usual way—by name. But he did the next best thing: he scrawled the number of your berth—*elf*, the German word for eleven. Not the figure 11, which could be mistaken for mere bloody lines, but the word itself. *Elf*—meaning number eleven, berth eleven. Your berth on the train."

Her eyes were hard now. "And the jewelry?"

"You've been using the wrong color on that canvas ever since you started. Much too dark a red! Maybe because all these tubes of oil paint don't contain what they say?"

I picked up a couple and squeezed them, feeling the hardness inside. "Empty paint tubes, opened from the bottom and then closed again. A clever hiding place, and one the sheriff's men never found. The cases and the larger jewelry pieces had to be thrown off the train of course—but most of it's right here in your tubes of paint, and the larger pieces of jewelry could be retrieved later."

And that was when she lunged at me with the knife.

"No, no, she didn't even scratch me! That note I gave the sheriff told him to follow me and be ready to arrest her. He was ready, all right—grabbed her before she could do any harm. But I'll admit it gave me a bit of a fright.

"Got to be going now? And I was just getting warmed up! Come by tomorrow night for a small—ah—libation and I'll tell you another story."

Midnight Express

By Alfred Noyes

*T*HIS *brief, terrifying excursion into the realm of madness (and into the nature of man and the universe?) is atypical of the work of British poet Alfred Noyes. The bulk of his admirable and diverse output is composed of lyrical poetry, much of it centering on the sea, as well as verse dramas such as* Robin Hood *(1927) and the epic trilogy* The Torch Bearers. *He also wrote novels and short stories—none of which approximates the mood and theme of "Midnight Express"—and published his autobiography,* Two Worlds for Memory, *in 1953, five years before his death. From 1913 to 1923 he lived in the United States and was a professor of modern English literature at Princeton University.*

"Midnight Express" is a story that demands more than one reading—and a well-lighted room, preferably with other people

*present, to read it in. I'm something of a bibliophile, but after
traveling with Mr. Noyes through the pages that follow, I wonder
if I'll ever again be inclined to pick up a battered old book bound
in red buckram. . . .*

It was a battered old book, bound in red buckram. He found
it, when he was twelve years old, on an upper shelf in his
father's library; and, against all the rules, he took it to his
bedroom to read by candlelight, when the rest of the rambling
old Elizabethan house was flooded with darkness. That was how
young Mortimer always thought of it. His own room was a little
isolated cell, in which, with stolen candle ends, he could keep
the surrounding darkness at bay, while everyone else had
surrendered to sleep and allowed the outer night to come flooding
in. By contrast with those unconscious ones, his elders, it made
him feel intensely alive in every nerve and fiber of his young
brain. The ticking of the grandfather clock in the hall below;
the beating of his own heart; the long-drawn rhythmical "ah"
of the sea on the distant coast, all filled him with a sense of
overwhelming mystery; and, as he read, the soft thud of a blinded
moth, striking the wall above the candle, would make him start
and listen like a creature of the woods at the sound of a
cracking twig.

The battered old book had the strangest fascination for him,
though he never quite grasped the thread of the story. It was
called *The Midnight Express*, and there was one illustration, on
the 50th page, at which he could never bear to look. It frightened
him.

Young Mortimer never understood the effect of that picture
on him. He was an imaginative, but not a neurotic youngster;
and he avoided the 50th page as he might have hurried past a
dark corner on the stairs when he was six years old, or as the
grown man on the lonely road, in the *Ancient Mariner*, who,
having once looked round, walks on, and turns no more his

head. There was nothing in the picture—apparently—to account
for this haunting dread. Darkness, indeed, was almost its chief
characteristic. It showed an empty railway platform—at night—
lit by a single dreary lamp; an empty railway platform that
suggested a deserted and lonely junction in some remote part of
the country. There was only one figure on the platform: the
dark figure of a man, standing almost directly under the lamp
with his face turned away toward the black mouth of a tunnel
which—for some strange reason—plunged the imagination of
the child into a pit of horror. The man seemed to be listening.
His attitude was tense, expectant, as though he were awaiting
some fearful tragedy. There was nothing in the text, so far as
the child read, and could understand, to account for this waking
nightmare. He could neither resist the fascination of the book,
nor face that picture in the stillness and loneliness of the night.
He pinned it down to the page facing it with two long pins, so
that he should not come upon it by accident. Then he determined
to read the whole story through. But, always, before he came
to page 50, he fell asleep; and the outlines of what he had read
were blurred; and the next night he had to begin again; and again,
before he came to the 50th page, he fell asleep.

He grew up, and forgot all about the book and the picture.
But halfway through his life, at that strange and critical time
when Dante entered the dark wood, leaving the direct path
behind him, he found himself, a little before midnight, waiting
for a train at a lonely junction; and, as the station-clock began
to strike 12, he remembered; remembered like a man awakening
from a long dream—

There, under the single dreary lamp, on the long glimmering
platform, was the dark and solitary figure that he knew. Its
face was turned away from him toward the black mouth of the
tunnel. It seemed to be listening, tense, expectant, just as it had
been 38 years ago.

But he was not frightened now, as he had been in childhood.
He would go up to that solitary figure, confront it, and see the
face that had so long been hidden, so long averted from him.
He would walk up quietly, and make some excuse for speaking

to it: he would ask it, for instance, if the train was going to be late. It should be easy for a grown man to do this; but his hands were clenched, when he took the first step, as if he, too, were tense and expectant. Quietly, but with the old vague instincts awaking, he went toward the dark figure under the lamp, passed it, swung round abruptly to speak to it; and saw—without speaking, without being able to speak—

It was himself—staring back at himself—as in some mocking mirror, his own eyes alive in his own white face, looking into his own eyes, alive—

The nerves of his heart tingled as though their own electric currents would paralyze it. A wave of panic went through him. He turned, gasped, stumbled, broke into a blind run, out through the deserted and echoing ticket-office, on to the long moonlit road behind the station. The whole countryside seemed to be utterly deserted. The moonbeams flooded it with the loneliness of their own deserted satellite.

He paused for a moment, and heard, like the echo of his own footsteps, the stumbling run of something that followed over the wooden floor within the ticket-office. Then he abandoned himself shamelessly to his fear; and ran, sweating like a terrified beast, down the long white road between the two endless lines of ghostly poplars each answering another, into what seemed an infinite distance. On one side of the road there was a long straight canal, in which one of the lines of poplars was again endlessly reflected. He heard the footsteps echoing behind him. They seemed to be slowly, but steadily, gaining upon him. A quarter of a mile away, he saw a small white cottage by the roadside, a white cottage with two dark windows and a door that somehow suggested a human face. He thought to himself that, if he could reach it in time, he might find shelter and security—escape.

The thin implacable footsteps, echoing his own, were still some way off when he lurched, gasping, into the little porch; rattled the latch, thrust at the door, and found it locked against him. There was no bell or knocker. He pounded on the wood with his fists until his knuckles bled. The response was horribly slow. At last, he heard heavier footsteps within the cottage. Slowly they

descended the creaking stair. Slowly the door was unlocked. A
tall shadowy figure stood before him, holding a lighted candle, in
such a way that he could see little either of the holder's face or
form; but to his dumb horror there seemed to be a cerecloth
wrapped round the face.

No words passed between them. The figure beckoned him in;
and, as he obeyed, it locked the door behind him. Then,
beckoning him again, without a word, the figure went before
him up the crooked stair, with the ghostly candle casting huge
and grotesque shadows on the whitewashed walls and ceiling.

They entered an upper room, in which there was a bright
fire burning, with an armchair on either side of it, and a small
oak table, on which there lay a battered old book, bound in dark
red buckram. It seemed as though the guest had been long
expected and all things were prepared.

The figure pointed to one of the armchairs, placed the
candlestick on the table by the book (for there was no other
light but that of the fire) and withdrew without a word, locking
the door behind him.

Mortimer looked at the candlestick. It seemed familiar. The
smell of the guttering wax brought back the little room in the
old Elizabethan house. He picked up the book with trembling
fingers. He recognized it at once, though he had long forgotten
everything about the story. He remembered the ink stain on the
title page; and then, with a shock of recollection, he came on the
50th page, which he had pinned down in childhood. The pins
were still there. He touched them again—the very pins which his
trembling childish fingers had used so long ago.

He turned back to the beginning. He was determined to read
it to the end now, and discover what it all was about. He felt
that it must all be set down there, in print; and, though in
childhood he could not understand it, he would be able to fathom
it now.

It was called *The Midnight Express;* and, as he read the first
paragraph, it began to dawn upon him slowly, fearfully,
inevitably.

It was the story of a man who, in childhood, long ago, had chanced upon a book, in which there was a picture that frightened him. He had grown up and forgotten it and one night, upon a lonely railway platform, he had found himself in the remembered scene of the picture; he had confronted the solitary figure under the lamp; recognized it, and fled in panic. He had taken shelter in a wayside cottage; had been led to an upper room, found the book awaiting him and had begun to read it right through, to the very end, at last.—And this book, too, was called The Midnight Express. *And it was the story of a man who, in childhood— It would go on thus, forever and forever, and forever. There was no escape.*

But when the story came to the wayside cottage, for the third time, a deeper suspicion began to dawn upon him, slowly, fearfully, inevitably.—Although there was no escape, he could at least try to grasp more clearly the details of the strange circle, the fearful wheel, in which he was moving.

There was nothing new about the details. They had been there all the time; but he had not grasped their significance. That was all. *The strange and dreadful being that had led him up the crooked stair—who and what was That?*

The story mentioned something that had escaped him. The strange host, who had given him shelter, was about his own height. Could it be that he also—and was this why the face was hidden?

At the very moment when he asked himself that question, he heard the click of the key in the locked door.

The strange host was entering—moving toward him from behind—casting a grotesque shadow, larger than human, on the white walls in the guttering candlelight.

It was there, seated on the other side of the fire, facing him. With a horrible nonchalance, as a woman might prepare to remove a veil, it raised his hands to unwind the cerecloth from its face. He knew to whom it would belong. But would it be dead or living?

There was no way out but one. As Mortimer plunged forward and seized the tormentor by the throat, his own throat was gripped with the same brutal force. The echoes of their strangled cry were indistinguishable; and when the last confused sounds died out together, the stillness of the room was so deep that you might have heard—the ticking of the old grandfather clock, and the long-drawn rhythmical "ah" of the sea, on a distant coast, 38 years ago.

But Mortimer had escaped at last. Perhaps, after all, he had caught the midnight express.

It was a battered old book, bound in red buckram . . .

1930–1950

Faith, Hope and Charity

By Irvin S. Cobb

*T*HERE ARE *some stories that an anthologist knows from the moment he finishes reading them are going to appeal to nearly every reader, no matter what the individual's general tastes may be. "Faith, Hope and Charity" is such a story. Not only is the writing flawless, the plot beautifully wrought, the suspense and drama powerfully extended, but the theme of grim retribution is so ironic and inexorable that it transcends pure entertainment and takes the form of a parable.*

Although only about a third of it is concerned with trains, there is an unmistakable railroad flavor to the story as a whole. The rail tracks which crisscrossed the American Southwest in 1930 seem constantly in view, so omnipresent that in a very real sense they are like walls enclosing the three criminal protagonists. What happens to each of them, as a result, seems to happen as much because of the threat of pursuit by train as because of what they do and of who and what they are.

As in the Noyes story, "Faith, Hope and Charity" is something of a departure for its author, the well-known early-twentieth-century humorist Irvin S. Cobb. Most of Cobb's prolific writings —books, columns and essays for such erstwhile publications as The Saturday Evening Post *and* Cosmopolitan; *radio and film scripts—deal with humorous topics. His most famous book (and most famous fictional character) is* Old Judge Priest, *published in 1915, which chronicles the adventures of a garrulous and immensely enjoyable Civil War veteran; Cobb also wrote a number of detective short stories featuring Judge Priest which are considered classics in the genre. His autobiography,* Exit Laughing, *appeared in 1941, three years before his death at the age of seventy.*

Just outside a sizable New Mexico town the second section of the fast through train coming from the Coast made a short halt. Entering the stretch leading to the yards, the engineer had found the signal set against him; the track ahead was temporarily blocked.

It was a small delay though. Almost at once the semaphore, like the finger of a mechanical wizard, made the warning red light vanish and a green light appear instead; so, at that, the Limited got under way and rolled on into the station for her regular stop.

But before she started up, four travelers quitted her. They got out on the off side, the side farthest away from the town, and that probably explains why none of the crew and none of the other passengers saw them getting out. It helps also to explain why they were not missed until quite some time later.

Their manner of leaving her was decidedly unusual. First, one of the vestibule doors between the third sleeping car and the fourth sleeping car opened and the trap in the floor flipped up briskly under the pressure of an impatient foot on the operating lever. A brace of the departing ones came swiftly into view, one behind the other. True, there was nothing unusual about that. But as they stepped down on the earth they faced about and received the figure of a third person whose limbs dangled and whose head lolled back as they took the dead weight of him into their arms. Next there emerged the fourth and last member of the group, he being the one who had eased the limp figure of Number Three down the car steps into the grasp of his associates.

For a fractional space their shapes made a little huddle in the lee of the vestibule. Looking on, you might have guessed that there was a momentary period of indecision touching on the next step to be taken.

However, this muddle—if that was what it was—right away straightened itself out. Acting with movements which seemed difficult and awkward, the two burden bearers carried their unconscious load down the short embankment and deposited it on the cindery underfooting close against the flank of the slightly built-up right of way.

Number Four bent over the sprawled form and fumbled at it, shoving his hands into first one pocket and then another. In half a minute or less he straightened up and spoke to the remaining pair, at the same time using both hands to shove some article inside the vent of his waistcoat.

"I have got them," he said, speaking with a foreign accent. They pressed toward him, their hands extended.

"Not here and not yet, Señores," he said sharply. "First we make sure of the rest. First you do, please, as I do."

Thereupon he hopped nimbly up the shoulder of the roadbed and headed toward the rear of the halted train, slinking well in under the overhang of the Pullmans. His mates obeyed his example. They kept on until they had passed the tail coach, which was a combination coach, and then they stepped inward between the rails, still maintaining their single-file formation. Immediately the dusk swallowed them up.

There was something peculiar about the way each one of these three plodding pedestrians bore himself. The peculiarity was this:

He bore himself like a person engaged in prayer—in a silent perambulating act of piety. His head was tucked in, his face turning neither to the right nor left; his eyes were set steadfastly forward as though upon some invisible goal, his hands clasped primly together in front of him.

Thus and so the marching three plodded on until the train, having got in motion, was out of sight beyond a curve in the approach to the station. Then they checked and came together in a clump, and then, had you been there, you would have understood the reason for their devotional pose. All three of them were wearing handcuffs.

The man who had spoken before unpalmed a key ring which he was carrying. Working swiftly even in the half-darkness, he made tests of the keys on the ring until he found the proper keys. He freed the wrists of his two fellows. Then one of them took the keys and unlocked his set of bracelets for him.

He, it would seem, was the most forethoughted of the trio. With his heel he kicked shallow gouges in the gritty soil beside the track and buried the handcuffs therein.

After that they briefly confabbed together, and the upshot of the confab was that, having matched for the possession of some object evidently held to be of great value, they separated forces.

One man set off alone on a detour to the southeast, which would carry him around the town. His late companions kept on in a general westerly direction, heading toward the desert which all that day they had been traversing. They footed it fast, as men might foot it who were fleeing for their lives and yet must conserve their strength. As a matter of fact, they were fleeing for their lives. So likewise the one from whom they had just parted was fleeing for his life.

It was partly by chance that these three had been making the transcontinental journey in company. Two of them, Lafitte the Frenchman, and Verdi the Italian who had Anglicized his name and called himself Green, met while lying in jail at San Francisco awaiting deportation to their respective countries. Within a space of a month each had been arrested as a refugee from justice; the formalities for extraditing the pair of them were swiftly completed.

So, to save trouble and expense; to kill, as it were, two birds with one stone, the authorities decided to send them together across to the eastern seaboard, where, according to arrangements made by cable, they would be surrendered to police representatives coming from abroad to receive them and transport them back overseas. For the long trip to New York a couple of city detectives had them in custody.

When the train bearing the officers and their charges reached a junction in lower California where the main line connected with a branch line running south to the Mexican border, there came aboard a special agent of the Department of Justice who had with him a prisoner.

This prisoner was one Manuel Gaza, a Spaniard. He also recently had been captured and identified; and he also was destined for return to his own land. It was not by prior agreement that he had been retransferred at this junction point to the same train which carried the Italian and the Frenchman. It just happened so.

It having happened so, the man who had Gaza in tow lost no time in getting acquainted with his San Francisco brethren. For a number of reasons it seemed expedient to all the officers that from here on they should travel as a unit. Accordingly the special agent talked with the Pullman conductor and exchanged the reservations he previously had booked for a compartment adjoining the drawing-room in which the four from the city were riding.

It was on a Friday afternoon that the parties united. Friday evening, at the first call for dinner, the three officers herded their three prisoners forward to the dining car, the passage of the sextet through the aisles causing some small commotion. Their advent into the diner created another little sensation.

Since it was difficult for the handcuffed aliens to handle knife and fork, they were given such food as might readily be eaten with a spoon or with the fingers—soups and omelets and soft vegetables and pie or rice pudding. The detectives ate fish. They shared between them a double order of imported kippers.

Presumably they were the only persons on the train who that day had chosen the kippered herrings. Shortly, the special agent was giving private thanks that his church prescribed no dietetic regulations for Friday, because within an hour or two after leaving the table, the San Francisco men were suffering from violent cramps—ptomaine poison had them helpless.

One seemed to be dangerously ill. That night near the border between California and Arizona he was taken off the train and carried to a hospital. During the wait at the station, a local physician dosed the second and lesser sufferer, whose name was McAvoy, and when he had been somewhat relieved, the doctor gave him a shot of something in the arm and said he ought to be up and about within twenty-four hours.

Through the night McAvoy slept in the lower berth of the compartment and the special agent sat up, with the communicating door open, to guard the aliens, who were bedded in the so-called drawing-room.

Their irons stayed on their wrists; their lone warden was accepting no foolish odds against himself. He had taken the precaution to transfer the keys of the Frenchman's handcuffs and the Italian's handcuffs from McAvoy's keeping to his own, slipping them on his key ring, but this had been done in case McAvoy should become seriously ill en route and it should devolve upon him to make a lap of the journey single-handed.

Next morning McAvoy was much easier, but he felt weak, he said, and drowsy. Given a full twelve hours of rest, though, he thought he would be able to go on guard when the nightfall came.

So he lay in his berth, and the special agent occupied an end of the drawing-room sofa. The trapped fugitives sat smoking cigarettes and, when the officer was not too near, talking among themselves.

Mainly they talked in English, a language which Gaza the Spaniard and Lafitte the Frenchman spoke fairly well. Verdi or Green, as the case might be, had little English at his command, but Gaza, who had spent three years in Naples, spoke Italian; and so when Verdi used his own tongue, Gaza could interpret for the Frenchman's benefit. They were allowed to quit the drawing-room only for meals.

When dinner hour came on that second evening of their trip, McAvoy was in a doze. So the Department of Justice man did not disturb him.

"Come on, boys," he said to the three aliens; "time to eat again."

He lined them up in front of him in the corridor and they started the regular processional. It was just at that moment that the train broke its rhythmic refrain and began to clack and creak and slow for that unscheduled stop outside that New Mexico town. By the time they had reached the second car on ahead, she'd almost stopped and was lurching and jerking.

In the vestibule beyond that second car the special agent was in the act of stepping across the iron floor lip of the connection when a particularly brisk joggle caused him to lose his hat. He gave a small exclamation and bent to recover it. Doing so, he jostled Gaza, the third man in the line and therefore the next to him.

The agile Spaniard was quick to seize his chance. He half turned, and bringing his chained wrists aloft, sent them down with all his might on the poll of the officer's unprotected skull. The victim of the assault never made a sound—just spraddled on his face and was dead to the world.

No outsider had been witness to the assault. No outsider came along during the few seconds which were required by the late prisoners to open an off-side car door and make their escape after the fashion which already has been described for you. Nobody missed them—for quite a while nobody did.

It wasn't until nearly nine o'clock, when McAvoy had roused up and rung for the porter and begun to ask questions, that a search was made and an alarm raised.

Penned up together through that day, the aliens had matched stories, one story against another. A common plight made them communicative; a common peril caused them each to turn with morbid reiteration to his own fatal predicament.

Said the Frenchman to the Spaniard: "He"—indicating his

recent cellmate, the Italian—"he knows how with me it stands. With him, I have talked. He speaks not so well the English but sometimes he understands it. Now you shall hear and judge for yourself how bad my situation is."

Graphically, this criminal sketched his past. He had been a Marseilles dock hand. He had killed a woman. She deserved killing, so he killed her. He had been caught, tried, convicted, condemned. While lying in prison, with execution day only a few weeks distant, he had made a getaway.

In disguise he had reached America and here had stayed three years. Then another woman, in a fit of jealousy, betrayed him to the police. He had been living with that woman; to her he had given his confidence. It would appear that women had been his undoing.

"Me, I am as good as dead already. And what a death!" A spasm of shuddering possessed him. "For me the guillotine is waiting. The devil invented it. It is so they go at you with that machine: They strap you flat upon a board. Face downward you are, but you can look up, you can see—that is the worst part. They fit your throat into a grooved shutter; they make it fast. You bring your head back; your eyes are drawn upward, fascinated. Above you, waiting, ready, poised, your eyes see the —the knife."

"But only for a moment do you see it, my friend," said the Spaniard, in the tone of one offering comfort. "Only a moment and then—*pouff*—all over!"

"A moment! I tell you it is an eternity. It must be an eternity. Lying there, you must live a hundred lives, you must die a hundred deaths. And then to have your head taken off your body, to be all at once in two pieces. Me, I am not afraid of most deaths. But that death by the guillotine—ah-h!"

The Spaniard bent forward. He was sitting alone facing the other two, who shared a seat.

"Listen, Señor," he stated. "Compared with me, you are the lucky one. True, I have not yet been tried—before they could try me I fled away out of that accursed Spain of mine."

"Not tried, eh?" broke in the Frenchman. "Then you have yet

a loophole—a chance for escape; and I have none. My trial, as I told you, is behind me."

"You do not know the Spanish courts. It is plain you do not, since you say that," declared the Spaniard. "Those courts—they are greedy for blood. With them, to my kind, there is not mercy; there is only punishment.

"And such a punishment! Wait until you hear. To me when they get me before them they will say: 'The proof is clear against you; the evidence has been thus and so. You are adjudged guilty. You took a life, so your life must be taken. It is the law.'

"Perhaps I say: 'Yes, but that life I took swiftly and in passion and for cause. For that one the end came in an instant, without pain, without lingering, yes, without warning. Since I must pay for it, why cannot I also be made to die very quickly without pain?'

"Will they listen? No, they send me to the garrote. To a great strong chair they tie you—your hands, your feet, your trunk. Your head is against a post, an upright. In that post is a collar— an iron band. They fit that collar about your neck. Then from behind you the executioner turns a screw.

"If he chooses he turns it slowly. The collar tightens, tightens, a knob presses into your spine. You begin to strangle. Oh, I have seen it myself! I know. You expire by inches! I am a brave man, Señores. When one's time comes, one dies. But oh, Señores, if it were any death but that! Better the guillotine than that! Better anything than that!"

He slumped back against the cushions, and rigors passed through him.

It was the Italian's turn. "I was tried in my absence," he explained to the Spaniard. "I was not even there to make my defense—I had thought it expedient to depart. Such is the custom of the courts in my country. They try you behind your back.

"They found me guilty, those judges. In Italy there is no capital punishment, so they sentenced me to life imprisonment. It is to that—that—I now return."

The Spaniard lifted his shoulders; the lifting was eloquent of his meaning.

"Not so fast," said the Italian. "You tell me you lived once in Italy. Have you forgotten what life imprisonment for certain acts means in Italy? It means solitary confinement. It means you are buried alive. They shut you away from everyone in a tight cell. It is a tomb, that is all. You see no one ever; you hear no voice ever. If you cry out, no one answers. Silence, darkness, darkness, silence, until you go mad or die.

"Can you picture what that means to one of my race, to an Italian who must have music, sunshine, talk with his fellows, sight of his fellows? It is in his nature—he must have these things or he is in torture, in constant and everlasting torment. Every hour becomes to him a year, every day a century, until his brain bursts asunder inside his skull.

"Oh, they knew—those fiends who devised this thing—what to an Italian is a million times worse than death—any death. I am the most unfortunate one of the three of us. My penalty is the most dreadful by far."

The others would not have it so. They argued the point with him and with each other all through the day, and twilight found their beliefs unshaken.

Then, under the Spaniard's leadership, came their deliverance out of captivity. It was he who, on the toss-up, won the revolver which they had taken from the person of the senseless special agent. Also it was he who suggested to the Italian that for the time being, at least, they stick together. To this the Italian had agreed, the Marseilles man, Lafitte, already having elected to go on his own.

After the latter, heading east by south, had left them, the Spaniard said reflectively:

"He is optimistic, that one, for all that he seemed so gloomy and downhearted today when speaking of that guillotine of his. He said he now had faith that he would yet dodge his fate. Five minutes after he is off that train he speaks of faith!"

"I cannot go quite so far," answered the Italian. "We are free, but for us there will be still a thousand dangers. So I have not much faith, but I have hope. And you, my friend?"

The Spaniard shrugged his shoulders. His shrug might mean

yes or it might mean no. Perhaps he needed his breath. He was
going at a jog-trot down the tracks, the Italian alongside him.

Take the man who had faith. Set down as he was in a country
utterly strange to him, this one of the fugitives nevertheless made
steady progress. He got safely around and by the New Mexico
town. He hid in the chaparral until daybreak, then took to a
highway running parallel with the railroad.

A "tin canner," which is what they were beginning to call an
itinerant motor tourist in those parts, overtook him soon after
sunup and gave him a lift to a small way station some forty miles
down the line. There he boarded a local train—he had some money
on him; not much money but enough—and undetected, he rode
that train clear on through to its destination a hundred miles or
so farther along.

Other local trains carried him across a corner of Colorado and
clear across Kansas. Some forty-eight hours later, he was a guest
in a third-rate hotel on a back street in Kansas City, Missouri.

He stayed in that hotel for two days and two nights, biding
most of the time in his room on the top floor of the six-story
building, going down only for his meals and for newspapers.
The food he had to have; the newspapers gave him information,
of a sort, of the hunt for the three fugitives. It was repeatedly
stated that all three were believed to be fleeing together. That
cheered Lafitte very much. It strengthened his faith.

But on the morning of his third day in his cheap hotel, when
he came out of his room and went down the hall to ring for the
elevator—there was only one passenger elevator in this hotel—he
saw something. Passing the head of the stairs, which ended
approximately midway of the stretch between the door of his room
and the wattled iron door opening on the elevator well, he saw,
out of the corner of one watchful eye, two men in civilian garb
on the steps below him.

They had halted there. Whether they were coming up or going
down there was no way of telling. It seemed to him that at sight
of him they ducked slightly and made as if to flatten themselves
back against the side wall.

He gave no sign of having seen them. He stilled an impulse to make a dash for it. Where was he to dash for, with the stairs cut off? He followed the only course open to him. Anyhow, he told himself, he might be wrong. Perhaps his nerves were misbehaving. Perhaps those two who seemed to be lurking just there behind him on those steps were not interested in him at all. He kept telling himself that, while he was ringing the bell, while he was waiting for the car to come up for him.

The car did come up and, for a wonder, promptly; an old-fashioned car, creaky, musty. Except for its shirt-sleeved attendant, it was empty. As Lafitte stepped in, he glanced sideways over his shoulder, making the movement casual—no sight of those two fellows.

He rode down, the only passenger for that trip, so there were no stops on the descent. They reached the ground floor, which was the office floor. The elevator came to a standstill, then moved up a foot or so, then joltingly down six inches or so, as the attendant, who was not expert, maneuvered to bring the sill of the car flush with the tiling of the lobby.

The delay was sufficiently prolonged for Lafitte to realize, all in a flash, he had not been wrong. Through the intervening grille of the shaft door he saw two more men who pressed close up to that door, who stared in at him, whose looks and poses were watchful, eager, prepared. Besides, Lafitte knew plainclothesmen when he saw them.

Up above and here below, he was cut off. There still was a chance for him, a poor one but the only one. If he could shoot the elevator aloft quickly enough, check it at the third floor or the fourth, say, and hop out, he might make a successful dart for the fire escape at the rear of the hotel—provided the fire escape was not guarded. In the space of time that the elevator boy was jockeying the car, he thought of this, and having thought it, acted on it.

Swinging his fist from behind with all his might, he hit that hapless fellow on the point of the jaw and deposited him, stunned and temporarily helpless, on his knees in a corner of the cage.

Lafitte grabbed the lever, shoved it over hard, and up the shaft shot the car. Before he could get control of it, being unfamiliar with such mechanisms and in a panic besides, it was at the top of the house. But then he mastered it and made it reverse its course, and returning downward he pulled the lever, bringing it toward him.

That was the proper motion, that gentler manipulation, for now the car, more obedient, was crawling abreast of the third-floor level. It crept earthward, inch by inch, and without bringing it to a dead stop he jerked up the latch of the collapsible safety gate, telescoped the metal outer door back into its folded-up self, and stooping low because the gap was diminishing, he lunged forward.

Now that elevator boy was a quick-witted, a high-tempered Irish boy. He might be half dazed but his instincts of belligerency were not asleep. He told afterward how, automatically and indignantly functioning, he grabbed at the departing assailant and caught him by one leg and for a fleeting moment, before the other kicked free, retarded him.

But by all that was good and holy he swore he did not touch the lever. Being down on all fours at the rear side of the slowly sinking car, how could he touch it? Why, just at that precise fraction of a second, the elevator should pick up full speed was a mystery to him—to everybody else, for that matter.

But pick up full speed it did. And the Irish boy cowered down and screamed an echo to a still louder scream than his, and hid his eyes from the sight of Lafitte, with his head outside and his body inside the elevator, being decapitated as completely and almost as neatly as though a great weighted knife had sheared him off at the neck.

Take the Spaniard and the Italian: Steadily they traveled westward for nearly all of that night which followed their evacuation from the Limited. It put desirable distance between them and the spot where they had dumped the special agent down. Also it kept them warm. This was summertime, but on the desert even summer nights are chilly and sometimes downright cold. Before dawn, they came on a freight train waiting on a siding. Its locomotive faced west. That suited their book.

They climbed nimbly aboard a flat and snuggled themselves down behind a barrier of farm implements. Here, breakfastless but otherwise comfortable, they rode until nearly midday. Then a brakeman found them. Harshly he ordered them to get out of there.

Immediately though, looking at them where they squatted half hidden, his tone softened, and he told them he'd changed his mind about it and they could stay aboard as long as they pleased. On top of this, he hurried forward as though he might have important news for the engine crew or somebody.

They chose to get off. They had noted the quick start of recognition which the brakeman had given. They figured—and figured rightly—that by now the chase for them was on and that their descriptions had been telegraphed back and forth along the line. The train was traveling at least twenty miles an hour, but as soon as the brakeman was out of sight, they jumped for it, tumbling like shot rabbits down the slope of the right of way and bringing up jarred and shaken in the dry ditch at the bottom.

Barring bruises and scratches, Green had taken no hurt, but Gaza landed with a badly sprained ankle. With Green to give him a helping arm, he hobbled away from the railroad.

To get away from that railroad was their prime aim now. Choosing a course at random, they went north over the undulating waste lands and through the shimmering heat, toward a range of mottled high buttes rising on beyond.

It took them until deep into the afternoon to cover a matter roughly of five miles. By now, Gaza's lower left leg was elephantine in its proportions, and every forced step he took meant a fresh stab of agony. He knew he could not go much farther. Green knew it too, and in his brain began shaping tentative plans. The law of self-preservation was one of the few laws for which he had respect. They panted from heat and from thirst and from weariness.

At the end of those five miles, having toiled laboriously up

over a fold in the land, they saw close at hand, and almost
directly below them, a 'dobe hut, and not quite so near at hand,
a big flock of sheep. At the door of the cabin, a man in overalls
was stripping the hide from a swollen dead cow.

Before they could dodge back below the sky line, he saw them
and stood up expectantly. There was nothing for them to do
except to go toward him. At their slow approach, an expression
of curiosity crept over his brown face and stayed there. He looked
like a Mexican or possibly a half-breed Indian.

When Gaza, stumbling nearer, hailed him in English, he
merely shook his head dumbly. Then Gaza tried him in Spanish
and to that he replied volubly. For minutes they palavered back
and forth; then the stranger served them with deep draughts
from a water bottle swinging in the doorway with a damp sack
over it. The water was lukewarm and bitterish-tasting, but it
was grateful to their parched throats. Then he withdrew inside
the little house, and Gaza, for Green's benefit, translated into
Italian what talk had passed.

"He says he is quite alone here, which is the better for us,"
explained the Spaniard, speaking swiftly. "He says that a week
ago he came up from Old Mexico, seeking work. A gringo—a
white man—gave him work. The white man is a sheepman. His
home ranch is miles away. In a sheep wagon he brought this
Mexican here and left him here in charge of that flock yonder,
with provisions for a month.

"It will be three weeks then before the white man, his employer,
comes again. Except for that white man he knows nobody
hereabouts. Until we came just now, he had seen no one at all.
So he is glad to see us."

"And accounting for ourselves you told him what?" asked
Green.

"I told him we were traveling across country in a car and
that going down a steepness last night the car overturned and
was wrecked and I crippled myself. I told him that, traveling
light because of my leg, we started out to find some town, some
house, and that, hoping to make a short cut, we left the road,
but that since morning and until we blundered upon this camp,

we had been quite lost in this ugly country. He believes me. He is simple, that one, an ignorant, credulous peon.

"But kind-hearted, that also is plain. For proof of it observe this." He pointed to the bloated, half-flayed carcass. "He says three days ago he found this beast—a stray from somewhere, he knows not where. So far as he knows there are no cattle droves in these parts—only sheep.

"She was sick, she staggered, she was dizzy and turned in circles as if blind, and froth ran from her mouth. There is a weed which does that to animals when they eat it, he says. So, hoping to make her well again, he put a scrap of rope on her horns and led her here. But last night she died. So to-day he has been peeling her. Now he goes to make ready some food for us. He is hospitable, also, that one."

"And when we have eaten, then what? We can't linger here."

"Wait, please, Señor. To my mind already an idea comes." His tone was authoritative, confident. "First we fill our empty stomachs to give us strength, and then we smoke a cigarette, and while we smoke, I think. And then—we see."

On frijoles and rancid bacon and thin corn cakes and bad coffee, which the herder brought them on tin platters and in tin cups, they did fill their empty stomachs. Then they smoked together, all three of them, smoking cigarettes rolled in corn-husk wrappers.

The Mexican was hunkered on his heels, making smoke rings in the still, hot air, when Gaza, getting on his feet with difficulty, limped toward the doorway, gesturing to show that he craved another swig from the water bottle. When he was behind the other two, almost touching them, he drew the special agent's pistol and fired once and their host tumbled forward on his face and spraddled his limbs and quivered a bit and was still, with a bullet hole in the back of his head.

This killing gave the Italian, seasoned killer as he was, a profound shock. It seemed so unnecessary, unless—? He started up, his features twitching, and backed away, fearing the next bullet would be for him.

"Remain tranquil, Señor," said the Spaniard, almost gayly.

"For you, my comrade, there is no danger. There is for you hope of deliverance, you who professed last night to have hope in your soul.

"Now me, I have charity in my soul—charity for you, charity for myself, charity also for this one lying here. Behold, he is now out of his troubles. He was a dolt, a clod of the earth, a creature of no refinement. He lived a hermit's life, lonely, miserable. Now he has been dispatched to a better and a brighter world. That was but kindness." With his foot he touched the sprawled corpse.

"But in dispatching him I had thought also for you—for both of us. I elucidate: First we bury him under the dirt floor of this house, taking care to leave no telltale traces of our work. Then you make a pack for your back of the food that is here. You take also the water bottle, filled. Furthermore, you take with you this pistol.

"Then, stepping lightly on rocky ground or on hard ground so that you make no tracks, you go swiftly hence and hide yourself in those mountains until—who can tell?—until those who will come presently here have ceased to search for you. With me along, lamed as I am, me to hamper you, there would be no chance for either of us. But you, going alone—you are armed, provisioned, quick of foot—you have a hope."

"But—but you? What then becomes of you?—You—you sacrifice yourself?" In his bewilderment the Italian stammered.

"Me, I stay here to greet the pursuers. It is quite simple. In peaceful solitude I await their coming. It cannot be long until they come. That man of the freight train will be guiding them back to pick up our trail. By tonight at latest I expect them."

At sight of the Italian's mystified face he broke now into a laugh.

"Still you are puzzled, eh? You think that I am magnanimous, that I am generous? Well, all that I am. But you think me also a fool and there you err. I save you perhaps, but likewise perhaps I save myself. Observe, Señor."

He stooped and lifted the dead face of his victim. "See now what I myself saw the moment I beheld this herder of ours: This man is much my shape, my height, my coloring. He spoke a corrupt Spanish such as I can speak. Put upon me the clothes which he wears, and remove from my lip this mustache which I wear, and I would pass for him even before the very eyes of that white man who hired him.

"Well, very soon I shall be wearing his clothes, my own being hidden in the same grave with him. Within ten minutes I shall be removing this mustache. He being newly shaven, as you see for yourself, it must be that in this hovel we will find a razor. I shall pass for him. I shall be this mongrel dull wit."

A light broke on the Italian. He ran and kissed the Spaniard, on both cheeks and on the mouth.

"Ah, my brother!" he cried out delightedly. "Forgive me that for a moment I thought you hard-hearted for having in seeming wantonness killed the man who fed us. I see you are brilliant—a great thinker, a great genius. But, my beloved"—and here doubt once more assailed him—"what explanation do you make when they do come?"

"That is the best of all," said Gaza. "Before you leave me you take a cord and you bind me most securely—my hands crossed behind my back—so; my feet fastened together—so. It will not be for very long that I remain so. I can endure it. Coming then, they find me thus. That I am bound makes more convincing the tale I shall tell them.

"And this is the tale that I shall tell: To them I shall say that as I sat under this shelter skinning my dead cow, there appeared suddenly two men who fell upon me without warning; that in the struggle they hurt my poor leg most grievously; then, having choked me into quietude, they tied my limbs, despoiled me of my provender and hurriedly departed, leaving me helpless. I shall describe these two brutal men—oh, most minutely I shall describe them. And my description will be accurate, for you I shall be describing as you stand now; myself I shall describe as I now am.

"The man from the train will say: 'Yes, yes, that is true; those are surely the two I saw.' He will believe me at once; that will help. Then they will inquire to know in which direction fled this pair of scoundrels, and I will tell them they went that way yonder to the south across the desert, and they will set off in that direction, seeking two who flee together, when all the while you will be gone north into those mountains which will shelter you. And that, Señor, will be a rich part of the whole joke.

"Perhaps, though, they question me further. Then I say: 'Take me before this gringo who within a week hired me to watch his sheep. Confront me with him. He will identify me, he will confirm my story.' And if they do that and he does that—as most surely he will—why, then they must turn me loose, and that, Señor, will be the very crown and peak of the joke.''

In the excess of his admiration and his gratitude, the Italian just naturally had to kiss him again.

They worked fast and they worked scientifically, carefully, overlooking nothing, providing against every contingency. But at the last minute, when the Italian was ready to resume his flight and the Spaniard, smoothly shaven and effectually disguised in the soiled shirt and messy overalls of the dead man, had turned around and submitted his wrists to be pinioned, it was discovered that there was no rope available with which to bind his legs. The one short scrap of rope about the spot had been used for tying his hands.

The Spaniard said this was just as well. Any binding that was drawn snugly enough to fetter his feet securely would certainly increase the pain in the inflamed and grossly swollen ankle joint.

However, it was apparent that he must be securely anchored, lest suspicion arise in the minds of his rescuers when they arrived. Here the Italian made a contribution to the plot. He was proud of his inspiration.

With the Mexican's butcher knife he cut long narrow strips from the fresh slick cowhide. Then the Spaniard sat down on the earth with his back against one of the slim tree trunks supporting the arbor, and the Italian took numerous turns about his waist and his arms and the upper part of his body, and tightly knotted the various ends of the skin ribbons behind the post. Unaided, no human being could escape out of that mesh. To the pressure of the prisoner's trunk, the moist, pliant lashings would give slightly, but it was certain they neither would work loose nor snap apart.

So he settled himself in his bonds, and the Italian, having shouldered his pack, once more fervently kissed his benefactor in token of gratitude, wished him success and made off with many farewells.

So far as this empty country was concerned, the Italian was a greenhorn, a tenderfoot. Nevertheless, he made excellent progress. He marched northward until dark, lay that night under a murdered man's smelly blanket behind a many-colored butte and next morning struck deeper into the broken lands. He entered what he hoped might be a gap through the mountains, treading cautiously along a narrow natural trail halfway up a dauntingly steep cliff side.

He was well into it when his foot dislodged a scrap of shaly rock which in sliding over the verge set other rocks to cascading down the slope. From above, yet larger boulders began toppling over into the scoured-out passageway thus provided, and during the next five minutes the walled-in declivity was alive and roaring with tumbling huge stones, with dislodged earth running fluid like a stream, with uprooted stunty piñons, with choking acrid dust clouds.

The Italian ran for dear life; he managed to get out of the avalanche's path. When at length he reached a safe place and looked back, he saw behind him how the landslide had choked the gorge almost to its brim. No human being—no, not even a goat, could from his side scale that jagged and overhanging parapet. Between him and pursuit was a perfect barrier.

Well content, he went on. But presently he made a discovery, a distressing discovery which took the good cheer right out of him. This was no gateway into which he had entered. It was a dead end leading nowhere—what Westerners call a box canyon. On three sides of him, right, left and on ahead, rose tremendously high walls, sheer and unclimbable. They threatened him; they seemed to be closing in on him to pinch him flat. And, of course, back of him retreat was cut off. There he was, bottled up like a fly in a corked jug, like a frog at the bottom of a well.

Frantically he explored as best he could the confines of this vast prison cell of his. He stumbled upon a spring, and its waters, while tainted lightly with alkali, were drinkable. So he had water and he had food, some food. By paring his daily portions down almost to starvation point, he might make these rations last for months. But then, what? And in the meantime, what? Why, until hunger destroyed him, he was faced with that doom which he so dreaded—the doom of solitary confinement.

He thought it all out and then he knelt down and took out his pistol and he killed himself.

In one of his calculations that smart malefactor, the Spaniard, had been wrong. By his system of deductions, the searchers should reach the 'dobe hut where he was tethered within four hours or, at most, five. But it was nearer thirty hours before they appeared.

The trouble had been that the brakeman wasn't quite sure of the particular stretch where he had seen the fugitives nestled beneath a reaping machine on that flat car. Besides, it took time to spread the word; to summon county officials; to organize an armed searching party. When at length the posse did strike the five-mile trail leading from the railroad tracks to the camp of the late sheep herder, considerably more than a day had elapsed.

The track was fairly plain—two sets of heavy footprints bearing north and only lacking where rocky outcrops broke through the surface of the desert. Having found it, they followed it fast and when they mounted the fold in the earth above the cabin, they saw the figure of a man seated in front of it, bound snugly to one of the supports of the arbor.

Hurrying toward him they saw that he was dead—that his face was blackened and horribly distorted; that his glazed eyes goggled at them and his tongue protruded; that his stiffened legs were drawn up in sharp angles of agony.

They looked closer and they saw the manner of his death and were very sorry for him. He had been bound with strands of fresh rawhide, and all through that day he had been sitting there exposed to the baking heat of the day.

Now heat, operating on damp new rawhide, has an immediate

effect. Heat causes certain substances to expand, but a green rawhide it causes to contract very fast to an ironlike stiffness and rigidity.

So in this case the sun glare had drawn tighter and tighter the lashings about this poor devil's body, squeezing him in at the stomach and the breast and the shoulders, pressing his arms tighter and tighter and yet tighter against his sides. That for him would have been a highly unpleasant procedure, but it would not have killed him.

Something else had done that. One loop of the rawhide had been twisted about his neck and made fast at the back of the post. At first it might have been no more than a loosely fitting circlet, but hour by hour it had shrunk into a choking collar, a diminishing noose, a terrible deadly yoke. Veritably it had garroted him by inches.

Dead Man

By James M. Cain

MUCH HAS BEEN WRITTEN *about the infamous train traveler known variously as the road-kid, the bindlestiff, the floater, the hobo. For more than one hundred years, young men and old, from criminals to adventurous college students, have seized the opportunity to ride free in unsealed cars and open flats or gondolas; on swaying platforms and iron coupling bumpers; or perched precariously on the long thin rods beneath freight cars. The problem became so burgeoning and widespread—as many as two or three hundred had been known to occupy a single train at one time—that railroads were forced to hire teams of detectives (known as "bulls") to police freight yards and assist brakemen on trains in transit. Perhaps the best nonfiction book on this phenomenon is Jack London's* The Road, *a collection of essays published in 1907 which deal with London's own youthful experiences as a "rider of the rails."*

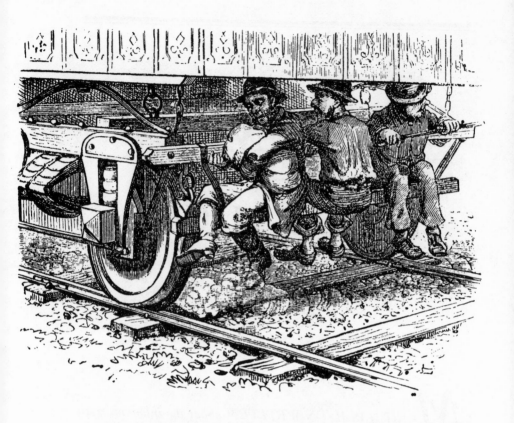

The proliferation of floaters on American rail lines reached its zenith during the Depression Thirties, when thousands of out-of-work men began to seek greener pastures elsewhere. That grim period in history has also received a great deal of literary attention, and the combination of Depression and hoboes has formed the background for dozens of sociological stories and novels. One of the most powerful of these is James M. Cain's "Dead Man"—a story which conveys the hopelessness of the era and the futility of hobo life, while at the same time probing deeply into the heart and soul of a young man who has committed the awesome crime of murder.

James M. Cain is considered by many to be the master of hard-boiled realism, a label which implies a conscious effort to be "tough" and "gritty" (to use two of reviewers' favorite terms). Personally, I doubt if Cain had any intention, when he began *writing, of producing hard-boiled realism; the style and subject matter which he employs are simply the ones that are best suited to his talents and to his vision. Those writers who have copied his style over the years are the ones producing "hard-boiled realism"—and second-rate stuff at that, because it is consciously imitative.*

Cain's most famous novel, of course, is his first: The Postman Always Rings Twice. *Another superior work is* Double Indemnity, *part of which deals with a murder plot involving a train. To the joy of his many fans (one of the more rabid of whom is myself), Cain has begun writing novels again, after a long hiatus, with* Rainbow's End *(1975) and* The Institute *(1976). The fact that he wrote both of these books while in his eighties should make all of us take heart.*

He felt the train check, knew what it meant. In a moment, from up toward the engine, came the chant of the railroad detective: "Rise and shine, boys, rise and shine." The hoboes began dropping off. He could hear them out there in the dark, cursing as the train went by. That was what they always did on these freights: let the hoboes climb on in the yards, making no effort to dislodge them there, for that would have meant a foolish game of hide-and-seek between two or three detectives and two or three hundred hoboes, with the hoboes swarming on as fast as the detectives put them off. What they did was let the hoboes alone until the train was several miles under way; then they pulled down to a speed slow enough for men to drop off, but too fast for them to climb back on. Then the detective went down the line, brushing them off like caterpillars from a twig. In two minutes they would all be ditched, a crowd of bitter men in a lonely spot; but they always cursed, always seemed surprised.

He crouched in the coal gondola and waited. He hadn't boarded a flat or a refrigerator with the others back in the Los Angeles yards, tempting though this comfort was. He wasn't long on the road, and he still didn't like to mix with the other hoboes, admit he was one of them. Also, he couldn't shake off a notion that he was sharper than they were, that playing a lone hand he might think of some magnificent trick that would defeat the detective, and thus, even at this ignoble trade, give him a sense of accomplishment, of being good at it. He had slipped into the gond not in spite of its harshness, but because of it; it was blacky and would give him a chance to hide, and the detective, not expecting him there, might pass him by. He was nineteen years old and was proud of the nickname they had given him in the poolroom back home. They called him Lucky.

"Rise and shine, boys, rise and shine."

Three dropped off the tank car ahead, and the detective climbed into the gond. The flashlight shot around, and Lucky held his breath. He had curled into one of the three chutes for unloading coal. The trick worked. These chutes were dangerous, for if you stepped into one and the bottom dropped, it would dump you under the train. The detective took no chances. He first shot the flash, then held on to the side while he climbed over the chutes. When he came to the last one, where Lucky lay, he shot the flash, but carelessly, and not squarely into the hole, so that he saw nothing. Stepping over, he went on, climbed to the boxcar behind, and resumed his chant; there were more curses, more feet sliding on ballast on the roadbed outside. Soon the train picked up speed. That meant the detective had reached the caboose, that all the hoboes were cleared.

Lucky stood up, looked around. There was nothing to see except hot-dog stands along the highway, but it was pleasant to poke your head up, let the wind whip your hair, and reflect how you had outwitted the detective. When the click of the rails slowed and station lights showed ahead, he squatted down again, dropped his feet into the chute. As soon as lights flashed alongside, he braced against the opposite side of the chute: that was one thing he had learned, the crazy way they shot the brakes on these freights. When the train jerked to a shrieking stop, he was ready, and didn't get slammed. The bell tolled; the engine pulled away; there was an interval of silence. That meant they had cut the train and would be picking up more cars. Soon they would be going on.

"Ah-ha! Hiding out on me, hey?"

The flashlight shot down from the boxcar. Lucky jumped, seized the side of the gond, scrambled up, vaulted. When he hit the roadbed his ankles stung from the impact, and he staggered for footing. The detective was on him, grappling. He broke away and ran down the track, past the caboose, into the dark. The detective followed, but he was a big man and began to lose ground. Lucky was clear, when all of a sudden his foot drove against a switch bar and he went flat on his face, panting from the hysteria of shock.

The detective didn't grapple this time. He let go with a barrage of kicks.

"Hide out on me, will you? Treat you right, give you a break, and you hide out on me. I'll learn you to hide out on me."

Lucky tried to get up, couldn't. He was jerked to his feet, rushed up the track on the run. He pulled back, but couldn't get set. He sat down, dug in with his sliding heels. The detective kicked and jerked in fury. Lucky clawed for something to hold on to; his hand caught the rail. The detective stamped on it. He pulled it back in pain, clawed again. This time his fingers closed on a spike sticking an inch or two out of the tie. The detective jerked, the spike pulled out of the hole, and Lucky resumed his unwilling run.

"Lemme go! Why don't you lemme go?"

"Come on! Hide out on me, will you? I'll learn you to hide out on Larry Nott!"

"Lemme go! Lemme—"

Lucky pulled back, braced with his heels, got himself stopped. Then his whole body coiled like a spring and let go in one convulsive, passionate lunge. The spike, still in his hand, came down on the detective's head, and he felt it crush. He stood there, looking down at something dark and formless lying across the rails.

II

Hurrying down the track, he became aware of the spike, gave it a toss, heard it splash in the ditch. Soon he realized that his steps on the ties were being telegraphed by the listening rail, and he plunged across the ditch to the highway. There he resumed his rapid walk, trying not to run. But every time a car overtook him, his heels lifted queerly, and his breath first stopped, then came in gasps as he listened for the car to stop. He came to a crossroads, turned quickly to his right. He let himself run here, for the road wasn't lighted, as the main highway was, and there weren't many cars. The running tired him, but it eased the sick feeling in his stomach. He came to a sign that told him Los Angeles was 17 miles, and to his left. He turned, walked, ran, stooped down sometimes, panting, to rest. After a while it came to him why he had to get to Los Angeles, and so soon. The soup kitchen opened at seven o'clock. He had to be there, in that same soup kitchen where he had had supper, so it would look as though he had never been away.

When the lights went off and it came broad daylight with the suddenness of Southern California, he was in the city, and a clock told him it was ten minutes after five. He thought he had time. He pressed on, exhausted, but never relaxing his rapid, half-shuffling walk.

It was ten minutes to seven when he got to the soup kitchen, and he quickly walked past it. He wanted to be clear at the end of the line, so he could have a word with Shorty, the man who dished out the soup, without impatient shoves from behind and growls to keep moving.

Shorty remembered him. "Still here, hey?"

"Still here."

"Three in a row for you. Holy smoke, they ought to be collecting for you by the month."

"Thought you'd be off."

"Who, me?"

"Sunday, ain't it?"

"Sunday? Wake up. This is Saturday."

"Saturday? You're kidding."

"Kidding my eye, this is Saturday, and a big day in this town, too."

"One day looks like another to me."

"Not this one. Parade."

"Yeah?"

"Shriners. You get that free."

"Well, that's my name, Lucky."

"My name's Shorty, but I'm over six feet."

"Nothing like that with me. I really got luck."

"You sure?"

"Like, for instance, getting a hunk of meat."

"I didn't give you no meat."

"Ain't you going to?"

"Shove your plate over quick. Don't let nobody see you."

"Thanks."

"Okay, Lucky. Don't miss the parade."

"I won't."

He sat at the rough table with the others, dipped his bread in the soup, tried to eat, but his throat kept contracting from excitement, and he made slow work of it. He had what he wanted from Shorty. He had fixed the day, and not only the day but the date, for it would be the same date as the big Shriners' parade. He had fixed his name, with a little gag. Shorty wouldn't forget him. His throat relaxed, and he wolfed the piece of meat.

Near the soup kitchen he saw signs: "Lincoln Park Pharmacy," "Lincoln Park Cafeteria."

"Which way is the park, Buddy?" If it was a big park, he might find a thicket where he could lie down, rest his aching legs.

"Straight down; you'll see it."

There was a fence around it, but he found a gate, opened it, slipped in. Ahead of him was a thicket, but the ground was wet from a stream that ran through it. He crossed a small bridge, followed a path. He came to a stable, peeped in. It was empty, but the floor was thickly covered with new hay. He went in, made for a dark corner, burrowed under the hay, closed his eyes. For a few moments everything slipped away, except warmth, relaxation, ease. But then something began to drill into the back of his mind: Where did he spend last night? Where would he tell them he spent last night? He tried to think, but nothing would come to him. He would have said that he spent it where he spent the night before, but he hadn't spent it in Los Angeles. He had spent it in Santa Barbara and come down in the morning on a truck. He had never spent a night in Los Angeles. He didn't know the places. He had no answers to the questions that were now pounding at him like sledgehammers:

"What's that? Where you say you was?"

"In a flophouse."

"Which flophouse?"

"I didn't pay no attention which flophouse. It was just a flophouse."

"Where was this flophouse at?"

"I don't know where it was. I never been to Los Angeles before. I don't know the names of no streets."

"What this flophouse look like?"

"Looked like a flophouse."

"Come on, don't give us no gags. What this flophouse look like? Ain't you got eyes? Can't you say what this here place looked like? What's the matter, can't you talk?"

Something gripped his arm, and he felt himself being lifted. Something of terrible strength had hold of him, and he was going straight up in the air. He squirmed to get loose, then was plopped on his feet and released. He turned, terrified.

An elephant was standing there, exploring his clothes with its trunk. He knew then that he had been asleep. But when he backed away, he bumped into another elephant. He slipped between the two elephants, slithered past a third to the door, which was open about a foot. Out in the sunlight, he made his way back across the little bridge, saw what he hadn't noticed before: pens with deer in them, and ostriches, and mountain sheep, that told him he had stumbled into a zoo. It was after four o'clock, so he must have slept a long time in the hay. Back on the street, he felt a sobbing laugh rise in his throat. *That* was where he had spent the night. "In the elephant house at Lincoln Park."

"*What?*"

"That's right. In the elephant house."

"What you giving us? A stall?"

"It ain't no stall. I was in the elephant house."

"With them elephants?"

"That's right."

"How you get in there?"

"Just went in. The door was open."

"Just went in there, seen the elephants, and bedded down with them?"

"I thought they was horses."

"You thought them elephants was horses?"

"It was dark. I dug in under the hay. I never knowed they was elephants till morning."

"How come you went in this place?"

"I left the soup kitchen, and in a couple of minutes I came to the park. I went in there, looking for some grass to lie down on. Then I come to this here place, looked to me like a stable, I peeped in, seen the hay, and hit it."

"And you wasn't scared of them elephants?"

"It was dark, I tell you, and I could hear them eating the hay, but I thought they was horses. I was tired, and I wanted some place to sleep."

"Then what?"

"Then when it got light, and I seen they was elephants, I run out of there, and beat it."

"Couldn't you tell them elephants by the smell?"

"I never noticed no smell."

"How many elephants was there?"

"Three."

III

He brushed wisps of hay off his denims. They had been fairly new, but now they were black with the grime of the coal gond.

Suddenly his heart stopped; a suffocating feeling swept over him.
The questions started again, hammered at him, beat into his
brain.

"Where that coal dust come from?"

"I don't know. The freights, I guess."

"Don't you know it ain't no coal ever shipped into this part
of the state? Don't you know that here all they burn is gas? Don't
you know it ain't only been one coal car shipped in here in six
months, and that come in by a misread train order? Don't you
know that car was part of the train this here detective was
riding that got killed? *Don't you know that?* Come on, out with
it: WHERE THAT COAL DUST COME FROM?"

Getting rid of the denims instantly became an obsession. He
felt that people were looking at him on the street, spying the
coal dust, waiting till he got by, then running into drugstores to
phone the police that he had just passed by. It was like those
dreams he sometimes had, where he was walking through crowds
naked, except that this was no dream, and he wasn't naked: he
was wearing these denims, these telltale denims with coal dust
all over them. He clenched his hands, had a moment of terrible
concentration, headed into a filling station.

"Hello."

"Hello."

"What's the chances on a job?"

"No chances."

"Why not?"

"Don't need anybody."

"That's not the only reason."

"There's about forty-two other reasons—one of them is I can't
even make a living myself—but it's all the reason that concerns
you. Here's a dime, kid. Better luck somewhere else."

"I don't want your dime. I want a job. If the clothes were
better, that might help, mightn't it?"

"If the clothes were good enough for Clark Gable in the swell
gambling house scene, that wouldn't help a bit. Not a bit. I just
don't need anybody, that's all."

"Suppose I got better clothes. Would you talk to me?"

"Talk to you any time, but I don't need anybody."

"I'll be back when I get the clothes."

"Just taking a walk for nothing."

"What's your name?"

"Hook's my name. Oscar Hook."

"Thanks, Mr. Hook. But I'm coming back. I just got a idea I can talk myself into a job. I'm some talker."

"You're all of that, kid. But don't waste your time. I don't need anybody."

"Okay. Just the same, I'll be back."

He headed for the center of town, asked the way to the cheap clothing stores. At Los Angeles and Temple, after an hour's trudge, he came to a succession of small stores in a Mexican quarter that were what he wanted. He went into one. The storekeeper was a Mexican, and two or three other Mexicans were standing around, smoking.

"Mister, will you trust me for a pair of white pants and a shirt?"

"No trust. Hey, scram."

"Look. I can have a job Monday morning if I can show up in that outfit. White pants and a white shirt. That's all."

"No trust. What you think this is, anyway?"

"Well, I got to get that outfit somewhere. If I get that, they'll let me go to work Monday. I'll pay you as soon as I get paid off Saturday night."

"No trust. Sell for cash."

He stood there. The Mexicans stood there, smoked, looked out at the street. Presently one of them looked at him. "What kind of job, hey? What you mean, got to have white pants a white shirt a hold a job?"

"Filling station. They got a rule you got to have white clothes before you can work there."

"Oh. Sure. Filling station."

After a while the storekeeper spoke. "Ha! Is a joke. Job in filling station, must have a white pants, white shirt. Ha! Is a joke."

"What else would I want them for? Holy smoke, these are

better for the road, ain't they? Say, a guy don't want white
pants to ride freights, does he?"

"What filling station? Tell me that?"

"Guy name of Hook, Oscar Hook, got a Acme station, Main
near Twentieth. You don't believe me, call him up."

"You go to work there, hey?"

"I'm *supposed* to go to work. I *told* him I'd get the white pants
and white shirt, somehow. Well—if I don't get them I don't go
to work."

"Why you come to me, hey?"

"Where else would I go? If it's not you, it's another guy
down the street. No place else I can dig up the stuff over
Sunday, is there?"

"Oh."

He stood around. They all stood around. Then once again the
storekeeper looked up. "What size you wear, hey?"

He had a wash at a tap in the back yard, then changed there,
between piled-up boxes and crates. The storekeeper gave him a
white shirt, white pants, necktie, a suit of thick underwear, and
a pair of shoes to replace his badly worn brogans. "Is pretty
cold, night-time, now. A thick underwear feel better."

"Okay. Much obliged."

"Can roll this other stuff up."

"I don't want it. Can you throw it away for me?"

"Is pretty dirty."

"Plenty dirty."

"You no want?"

"No."

His heart leaped as the storekeeper dropped the whole pile into
a rubbish brazier and touched a match to some papers at the
bottom of it. In a few minutes, the denims and everything else
he had worn were ashes.

He followed the storekeeper inside. "Okay, here is a bill. I
put all a stuff on a bill, no charge you more than anybody else.
Is six dollar ninety-eight cents, then is a service charge one
dollar."

All of them laughed. He took the "service charge" to be a gyp overcharge to cover the trust. He nodded. "Okay on the service charge."

The storekeeper hesitated. "Well, six ninety-eight. We no make a service charge."

"Thanks."

"See you keep a white pants clean till Monday morning."

"I'll do that. See you Saturday night."

"*Adios.*"

Out in the street, he stuck his hand in his pocket, felt something, pulled it out. It was a $1 bill. Then he understood about the "service charge," and why the Mexicans had laughed. He went back, kissed the $1 bill, waved a cheery salute into the store. They all waved back.

He rode a streetcar down to Mr. Hook's, got turned down for the job, rode a streetcar back. In his mind, he tried to check over everything. He had an alibi, fantastic and plausible. So far as he could recall, nobody on the train had seen him, not even the other hoboes, for he had stood apart from them in the yards and had done nothing to attract the attention of any of them. The denims were burned, and he had a story to account for the whites. It even looked pretty good, this thing with Mr. Hook, for anybody who had committed a murder would be most unlikely to make a serious effort to land a job.

But the questions lurked there, ready to spring at him, check and recheck as he would. He saw a sign, "5-Course Dinner, 35 Cents." He still had ninety cents, and went in, ordered steak and fried potatoes, the hungry man's dream of heaven. He ate, put a ten-cent tip under the plate. He ordered cigarettes, lit one, inhaled. He got up to go. A newspaper was lying on the table.

He froze as he saw the headline:

"L. R. NOTT, R. R. MAN, KILLED."

IV

On the street, he bought a paper, tried to open it under a street light, couldn't, tucked it under his arm. He found Highway 101, caught a hay truck bound for San Francisco. Going out Sunset

Boulevard, it unexpectedly pulled over to the curb and stopped. He looked warily around. Down a side street, about a block away, were the two red lights of a police station. He was tightening to jump and run, but the driver wasn't looking at the lights. "I told them bums that air hose was leaking. They set you nuts. Supposed to keep the stuff in shape, and all they ever do is sit around and play blackjack."

The driver fished a roll of black tape from his pocket and got out. Lucky sat where he was a few minutes, then climbed down, walked to the glare of the headlights, opened his paper. There it was:

L. R. NOTT, R. R. MAN, KILLED

The decapitated body of L. R. Nott, 1327 De Soto Street, a detective assigned to a northbound freight, was found early this morning on the track near San Fernando station. It is believed he lost his balance while the train was shunting cars at the San Fernando siding and fell beneath the wheels. Funeral services will be held tomorrow from the De Soto Street Methodist Church.

Mr. Nott is survived by a widow, formerly Miss Elsie Snowden of Mannerheim, and a son, L. R. Nott, Jr., 5.

He stared at it, refolded the paper, tucked it under his arm, walked back to where the driver was tapping the air hose. He was clear, and he knew it. "Boy, do they call you Lucky? Is your name Lucky? I'll say it is."

He leaned against the trailer, let his eye wander down the street. He saw the two red lights of the police station—glowing. He looked away quickly. A queer feeling began to stir inside him. He wished the driver would hurry up.

Presently he went back to the headlights again, found the notice, reread it. He recognized that feeling now; it was the old Sunday-night feeling that he used to have back home, when the bells would ring and he would have to stop playing hide in the twilight, go to church, and hear about the necessity for being saved. It shot through his mind, the time he had played hookey from church and hid in the livery stable; and how lonely he had felt, because there was nobody to play hide with; and how he had sneaked into church and stood in the rear to listen to the necessity for being saved.

His eyes twitched back to the red lights, and slowly, shakily, but unswervingly he found himself walking toward them.

"I want to give myself up."

"Yeah, I know, you're wanted for grand larceny in Hackensack, New Jersey."

"No, I—"

"We quit giving them rides when the New Deal come in. Beat it."

"I killed a man."

"You—?. . . When was it you done this?"

"Last night."

"Where?"

"Near here. San Fernando. It was like this—"

"Hey, wait till I get a card. . . . Okay, what's your name?"

"Ben Fuller."

"No middle name?"

"They call me Lucky."

"Lucky like in good luck?"

"Yes, sir. . . . Lucky like in good luck."

The Phantom
of the Subway

By Cornell Woolrich

*I*T SEEMS *to me that the reason why the subway train has
inspired so many suspense stories is precisely because it is sub-
terranean: it runs through the bowels of a city, through dark,
bleak, odorous tunnels without once breaking through into the
outer world. What better place for the ultimate dark deed of
murder to be perpetrated, or for grim action and excitement to be
wrought?*

*"The Phantom of the Subway," which takes place entirely on
just such a train beneath the streets of New York, is pure riveting
suspense—and little wonder, since it originated from the typewriter
of the acknowledged king of suspense fiction, Cornell Woolrich.
If there is any writer who can match Woolrich when it comes to
a narrative pace and drive that (in the horribly overworked but
nonetheless apt phrase) "holds the reader on the edge of his chair,"
I have yet to come across his or her work. Prediction: you won't*

*be able to turn the following pages quickly enough for just that
reason.*

*Woolrich, who died in 1968, was a tragic figure. (For an under-
standing of why, see Francis M. Nevins, Jr.'s incisive commentary
in the last Woolrich collection,* Nightwebs, *published post-
humously in 1971.) But his fiction is no less brilliant because of
this; in fact, it is due in part to his unhappy life and its
coloration of his outlook that his work is so powerful. His novels
include* The Bride Wore Black *and* The Black Curtain *under
his own name;* Phantom Lady *and* Deadline at Dawn *under the
pseudonym of William Irish; and* The Night Has a Thousand
Eyes, *as by George Hopley. No less than twenty-eight of Woolrich's novels and stories were made into feature-length films, and
a score more were adapted for television. Among more than two
hundred short stories is "Death in the Air," the only piece of
crime fiction to use the old and now-defunct New York Elevated
train as its background.*

———————————

Delaney boarded an empty northbound train at 125th Street
by the simple expedient of loosening a chain across the station
platform that barred his way, instead of dropping a nickel into a
turnstile. The little metal disc attached to his cap, bearing the
numerals *01629*, gave him the privilege of doing that. That disc
was his by reason of the fact that he was a subway guard.

He pulled a folded tabloid out from behind the panel in the
car-vestibule and, scorning to assume duties which were still
rightfully the night shift's, sprawled comfortably on one of the
seats, legs out before him. The pale pink news-sheet engrossed
him while the train rattled its way to the end of the line, to
start back from scratch and meet the rush hour. It was full of
topics that had very little bearing upon himself and his daily
surroundings, such as storms at sea, airplane mishaps, the shapely
limbs of a Miss Beaumont who had just flown in from Hollywood,

and also a great deal about a "phantom burglar" who was being besieged by the police in the Wadsworth Building on lower Broadway. The man had been in there ever since the small hours of the previous night, had ransacked five offices single-handed to the tune of $500,000, killed the watchman, and they still hadn't been able to lay their hands on him. A cordon had been thrown around the place, the paper said, and it was just a matter of time—time and a mere fifty or sixty floors to cover—before they caught up with him.

Delaney, reading it, felt vaguely cheated. Up above there something was always doing; down here below-ground where he was, nothing ever happened—you were like in your grave already.

As they pulled in at the end of the line, he put the paper back where he'd found it, stirred his stumps, and presented himself and his passbook to the factotum there who detailed off the personnel of the various southbound trains.

"Last section, third train out," he was told. They were all expresses this far up; the locals didn't go beyond 137th Street. The headway, during the rush hour, was a train every two minutes.

This rite—"shenanigans," Delaney termed it—attended to, he joined his mates on the benches until his own train had pulled in. It was a "ghost" train, without a soul on it so far. He stepped aboard and placed himself exactly over the coupling irons of the second and third cars from the end, one foot on each platform, like a sort of Atlas astride his own little world. The time-bell rang and he bore down on the pneumatic lever. Six doors in all, three to the left of him and three to the right, slid sibilantly closed. The train pulled out. Another damn day had begun.

One station down and the train was no longer empty. Before it dove under at Dyckman it was jammed. At 96th it was a madhouse on wheels, and at Times Square the riveted seams of the steel cars threatened to open.

That was the high-water mark, and the ebb set in. After Wall Street Delaney himself was sitting down again, reading another tabloid that someone had left behind. This was a six A.M. edition; they hadn't caught up with their "phantom" yet. They'd gotten to the top of the tower by now, but he'd miraculously slipped through them somehow, and he was on his way down. But he was still in there, and the cordon down at street level had been reinforced. They were going to keep the personnel out, and they were sending in tear-gas bombs. The police order now was to give him no quarter, shoot him on sight, for he'd chalked up his second killing: one of their own, trapped in an angle of a dead-end corridor and plugged in the back.

The strangest thing about it was that nobody knew what he looked like yet. The only two who had caught a glimpse of him were dead before they could tell—hence the "phantom" tag. Delaney doped this out laboriously for himself while his ears hummed as he plunged under the river for the first time that day and hit Brooklyn.

At the other end of the line, with a twenty-minute relief on his hands, he changed his six A.M. edition, which was stale already, for one that had just hit the streets, hadn't been born yet when he got on the train uptown. He took it upstairs with him for a smoke and a shot of fresh air. Miss Beaumont's legs were still there, but they'd lost ground; the Phantom had shoved them from the first page back to the third. He rated a scarehead now. He'd cheated the cordon of police, gotten out, loot and all. From an extension onto the roof of a church next door, as closely as they could figure it. Then down into the church through a lovely stained-glass skylight, which now lay all over the floor in pieces.

The sexton had had sense enough to duck down behind one of the pews and had gotten a good look at him and thereby also lived to spill it. He'd watched him slip out, valise and all, and duck down the steps into the Wall Street station, which was right outside the door—with two score bluecoated backs in full view a building-length away.

By the time the sexton got over to them and the stampede got started, they were just a flight of steps too late. The Wall Street West Side station is a single platform between the tracks, instead of a double one outside them like most. Break one for the Phantom. There were two trains in together, going in opposite directions, which mightn't have happened all the rest of the day.

Break two for the Phantom. By the time the cavalcade got down, they had their choice of taillights, which didn't tell them a thing.

The station agent headed the downtown one off by telephoning Clark Street, and it was held sealed when it got there and drag-netted, but the Phantom wasn't on it. They couldn't catch the uptown one in time, even by telephone, for the Fulton and Park Place Stations were too close; but when they finally stopped that train and gave it the works at Chambers Street, the Phantom didn't turn up there either. He'd had two ganged-up stations to slip off at, though none of the other passengers they quizzed remembered seeing anyone with a valise, and neither did the station agents in question.

The chase had shifted to Delaney's own domain now, and his interest was thereby whetted; a second-hand thrill was better than none at all. It was coming closer all the time.

Just before eight, the paper gave as the time the getaway into the subway had taken place. Delaney began to calculate absorbedly, sitting on an empty ginger-ale case by the station exit. He himself had made Wall Street at about eight sharp, leaving on a 7:20 headway like he had. Trains make poorer time during the rush hour on account of the gangs getting off at every stop.

"That southbound one," he told himself disappointedly, "musta been the one right ahead of me. I musta got there two minutes after he lammed. Just my luck. It wouldn't be my train he picks—but somebody else's. I must have the Indian sign on me."

He pocketed the paper disgustedly and reported downstairs for the return run. The fact that the guy was armed and had already killed two men in cold blood didn't lessen Delaney's sense of personal grievance any. He felt that he had been dished out of the little excitement there was to be had. "Just one train up, and I coulda maybe had him riding with me!"

The time bell pealed, and he slammed his section shut with a face that would have soured milk. The long haul back got under way. The outer hick-stations came and went: Church, Sterling, President, Franklin.

Then Eastern Parkway showed up. Now, at Eastern, the West

Side lines do this inbound: two branches fork together. A five-car section coming in from Flatbush Avenue, a half-train, waits there for a five-car section coming in from New Lots; they're hooked together to make a full train, ten cars, and cover the rest of the route in one. Outward-bound it's reversed: at that point they split.

Delaney's half got in, waited, and its complementary half showed up behind it on the dot, kissed it with a slight jolt. The coupling crew jumped to its duty, compressed air hissed, and the two sections were welded. The second motorman, dispensed with, went off duty. Delaney's post automatically shifted one car back, to take in what had formerly been the control car. This brought him to what had been the rear platform until now, not used by passengers getting off or on.

It was when he had stepped back from leaning out between cars to catch the signal, and they were already under way, that he first saw the thing, standing by itself in the corner of the vestibule. A dingy, dog-eared cowhide valise, flush with the door. It didn't click, didn't mean a thing at first; it was traveling *in* toward Wall Street, *not* out away from there.

Yet he couldn't understand how it could have been left where it was. That end door hadn't been in use until now, and no one had gotten on carrying a bag like that since the return trip had begun. He would have seen them. When they did bring stuff like that on, they kept it right under their feet or close to one of the doors in operation, didn't lug it all the way out of sight to the back platform.

Whatever it was, it was in the way, blocking the door. He slurred it with his foot across to the other side of the vestibule, then stood in the doorway and gave the car in general a dirty look.

"Whose suitcase is that?" he megaphoned. "Whaddya think this is, a baggage car? Clear it outa here!"

The sprinkling of passengers looked up interestedly—but blankly. They consisted of a Western Union messenger, two matrons headed for shopping, a sleepy youth who had been ladling orangeade all night, a pair of chattering Puerto Ricans, and an

old man with a long beard who believed in the second coming
of the Messiah and was dropping pamphlets on everybody
else's lap. No takers—none, that is, for the mysterious valise.

Delaney went back again to open for Grand Army Plaza; then,
when that was out of the way, stood staring at the thing, thinking
it over. Suspicion became a certainty, little by little. He'd found
it on the side that opened for Wall Street; almost all the rest, the
whole length of the line, opened on the opposite side. No one to
claim it, no one riding in with it. There was only one answer—it
didn't belong on this trip. It must have been brought on during
the run before, overlooked at the end of the line by the crew
jumping off; and now it was starting back again. It was hard to
believe, a thing that size; but maybe, with that metal partition
swinging loose in front of it, they hadn't spotted it.

He glanced up at the car number—*3334*. They shuffled the
cars around a good deal at the end of each run, he knew; coming
back he might have been assigned to what had been the train
ahead of his the last time, without knowing it. And if so, maybe
that thing in the corner over there had half a million in it this very
minute.

He went over to it, tried the two latches; but they were locked
tight. He picked it up, tested its weight—hard to say what it had
in it. Even if it was what he took it for, he still didn't get the
idea. It meant this "Phantom" had sent his loot sailing at Wall
Street and hadn't gone with it. That sounded screwy. Robbing
six offices just to give the haul a free ride by itself on the subway?
Unless he had someone working with him, waiting at the end of
the line to pick it up—like one of these pneumatic carriers that
department stores use. If he had, something had gone wrong, for
here it was on its way back again, unclaimed.

Which meant it had run the gantlet twice, not only at the end
of the line when the cars were cleared, but before that at Clark
Street when the police had halted the train and gone through it,
looking for the hijacker. It could have happened at that, incredible
as it seemed. They were looking for someone fitting the sexton's
description first of all, and the valise was only incidental. Since
they didn't find him, the suitcase itself could easily have escaped

their attention, hidden under people's legs in that milling, half-hysterical crowd. They'd had all the doors to watch, and ten packed cars to wade through, and not much time to do it in. There probably wasn't elbow-room to bend down and peer at the floor, even if they'd thought of doing so.

Delaney was beginning to understand what must have happened. The guy dove down the steps just a leap ahead of them. There were two trains in, one on each side of him. He must have had to do his thinking quick; no time to hesitate. He couldn't even count on the trains pulling out in time; they might be stopped right where they were and held there in the station.

He didn't know the sexton had glimpsed him in the church. The only give-away, he thought, was the valise. Separate himself from that, and he was safe. So he plunged it into the downtown train, spun around, and dove into the uptown one without it.

People are always running for trains; why should that have attracted any attention? And on the downtown car-vestibule they were probably crammed so close together, all with their papers up in front of their noses, that, like the police, they didn't see that he'd left something on the floor amongst them. And later, each one thought it belonged to the other fellow—until the train split up, and it became the rear platform, and there weren't any of them left any more. And the Phantom, of course, had had sense enough to lam out of his own train at Fulton, without waiting for them to overhaul it at Chambers.

So far so good, but then what? No one parts company with five hundred grand that easily, whether it means the chair or not. Delaney discarded the accomplice theory at this point; they wouldn't have had any way of getting in touch with each other in time. The Phantom hadn't intended powdering down the subway; he'd just done it instinctively—the only hole in the ground there was for him to hide in. But for him to send his haul barging off like that on its own, there must have been some connecting link in his mind, some trick play by which he could catch up with it later. Delaney refused to believe he had kissed it good-by for good, not after what he'd been through to get his hands on it.

Now just what way was there for him to connect with it

again? He certainly wasn't counting on its being turned in to the lost-and-found and then showing up later to claim it; that would be putting his head into the noose for fair. "Can you identify the contents?" "Half a million in cash and securities." And he certainly was not fool enough to think that by taking a later train from farther up he could overtake that first one in time and get his hands on it again. He'd spend the rest of the day riding back and forth, always just one train too late.

But a guy like the Phantom wouldn't work that way. . . .

No, the answer was this: he'd played a hundred-to-one shot, a thousand-to-one shot; had no other choice. He was waiting some place up the line, where this train would have to pass, waiting for that suitcase to come back to him undisturbed, overlooked! And he'd rung the bell, just this once out of a thousand times: it hadn't taken off; it was heading back to him again. It nearly made Delaney's hair stand up to think of luck like that, of nerve to take a chance like that and have it come through. This Phantom sounded like quite a guy!

But there was just one little remaining hitch to be smoothed away, at least in Delaney's own mind. How in the devil's name did he expect to know the right train, the right car, when it pulled up in front of him? They were all alike even to Delaney, and he spent his life on them. Had he marked the door in some way, so he'd know it again when it made the trip back? That was asking a lot, to expect a guy running for his life to have a stick of chalk or something all ready in his hand for just such a purpose.

Just to convince himself, though, Delaney stepped outside at the next stop and scanned all three doors of the car. There wasn't a mark on them. But the answer came to him when he got on again—so simple that he'd overlooked it until now! How did the company officials themselves, anybody at all, tell one car from another? Why, by the number, of course—stenciled in big white numerals on the blackened lower pane of each end-window. And this one was a pushover—*3334*. In that split second when the Phantom had wedged the suitcase aboard, he'd seen the number beside the door—and that was all he had to go by; that was the one slim connecting link between him and his hot half a million now.

He must have good eyes, all right, to count on glimpsing it in time, one car out of ten, as it whizzed in past whatever platform he was waiting, lurking on at this very minute. Still, it could be done.

They were coming into Clark Street now. Delaney bent down and picked up the valise. "Ain't it a shame," he mused dryly, "that I caught onto his little stunt, without nobody telling me nothing! Now all I do is just move it one car over—and where is he? All his sweat and brainwork for nothing. . . ."

Abruptly Delaney set it down again. "He'll look in first," he said to himself. "If he doesn't see it, he won't get on—figures his thousand-to-one shot muffed and it was taken off at the other end." He scratched the back of his head, displacing his cap. "I'd like to see what he looks like," he decided. "A guy as tricky and nervy as all that. Hell, I got that much coming to me, after packin' sardines in all day long."

He left the valise where it was.

He wasn't, he assured himself, endangering the money any by leaving it exposed like that. "He can get on, but he can't get it off again while I'm on the doors. I'll see to that. I just wanta watch what he does—oughta be fun, break the monotony."

A moment later, as they went under the river, he remembered that the fellow would be armed, had already killed two men who had tried to hinder him. He still left the valise where it was.

They blew into Wall Street, where the Phantom had last been seen, and nothing happened. No one at all got into Delaney's cars there, though he stretched his neck both ways; they were all going to their offices yet at that hour, not coming away from them. He spotted a pair of cops still hanging around, one at each end of the platform; that was all. As though he'd come back and show his face around there any more within the next six months!

At least it showed they hadn't nabbed him yet. Delaney decided he must have a criminal streak in himself, the satisfaction he felt at that knowledge. Almost as if he was rooting for the guy—which of course he wasn't.

As for flagging one of the bluecoats and turning the satchel over to him, there were several good reasons for not doing it. In the first place he was only surmising what it was, had no proof. Secondly and more important, no matter what it was, the regulations were that it was to be turned in at the end of the line. He was working for the company, not the police.

Wall Street dropped back, and almost immediately Fulton showed around the curve. Delaney didn't watch the platform as hard this time, was giving up hope of his theory being correct. His car hit about the center of the boat-shaped concrete "island."

There didn't seem to be anyone waiting to get on. Down at the end someone was standing shaking hell out of one of the chewing-gum slot-machines, trying to get his penny back. It looked as though he were waiting for a downtown train, made no move toward this one. Delaney incautiously turned to look up the other way; there was no one at all up there.

When he turned back again, the figure at the mirror had vanished.

Park Place ticked off, then the train slowed up for Chambers. The valise stayed where it was, unmolested. After Chambers would come a five-minute straightaway without breaks, all the way to 14th. Delaney gave Chambers a good once-over, up and down, from his vantage point. There were a couple of cops hanging around there too. A fat lady whose girth would have been the pride of any sideshow accosted him just then from the platform.

"Does it go to Times Square?" she queried.

"It does," he assured her.

She scowled and proceeded to wedge herself aboard.

The bell was pealing, and he closed the door. He hadn't calculated on how much of her there was. Most of her was on already, but not quite all. The rubber-edged door nipped her stern slightly.

A moment later, as she moved on, there was a distinct sound of rending silk. A look of alarm crossed her baby face. "Eep!" she squealed, and started revolving slowly on her axis, trying to get a look behind her.

Delaney knew the type. "Now I'm in for it," he told himself resignedly. He was.

"I'm gonna report you for this, young man—" she began indignantly, as he stepped down to the vestibule and tried to look unaware of her presence. "I'm gonna sue this company!"

This probably would have continued without a let-up all the way to 14th Street, but Delaney happened to look past her just then to where the valise had been. He snapped to attention with a jolt. The bag was gone!

It was traveling down the aisle, had already gotten half a car-length away in the minute or two his back had been turned, gripped by the same slouch-hatted figure he'd seen so harmlessly tinkering with the slot-machine at Fulton Street. Pretending to fuss about a penny while he waited to pounce on half a million dollars.

So that was their "Phantom," was it? Well, he didn't look like much from the back—just a wiry little fellow going someplace in a hurry. But Delaney wasn't letting it go at that; he was going to get a look at his face or know the reason why.

"Hey, you!" he bawled, and his voice went booming down the car. "Drop that!"

A face flashed whitely over one hurrying shoulder. Even at that distance, Delaney could see there wasn't any fright in it. There was only cold-blooded, grinning death. The fat lady was in his way, rotund, monumental, wedged in the inner doorway—and that probably saved Delaney's life.

Before he could get past her and leap after the man, as he was primed to, the answer to his hail came back—and not in words. There was a second flash over that shoulder—smaller, brighter this time—a whip-crack that topped the roar of the train. A white sworl powdered the glass of the vestibule door just behind Delaney. That door had slipped partly free with the motion of the train.

The fat lady promptly fainted, but fortunately sideways onto the nearest vacant seat. That cleared the aisle. But the figure in the loosely flapping topcoat had already bridged the platform into the next car. He banged the communicating door closed to hamper

Delaney, and the glass shattered and dribbled fluidly off it. Delaney came plunging at it, tore the frame out of the way, and opened the back of his hand in a thin red line.

The lights of Chambers Street had just fallen behind the last car—it was a long station and the whole thing had happened in a flash—and there had been two cops on the platform there. He leaped upward and sidewise in the second vestibule, gave the emergency cord a yank that buckled it into a long loop. If they backed up a few yards, they could get help aboard from the station.

The fugitive had increased his lead to a whole car-length now. He seemed to glide between the scattering of frozen, stunned passengers, immune to touch. It was Delaney following after, capless now, with his grim face and bleeding hand, who sowed panic. Women jumped up on the seats with both feet, screaming— then herded toward the back of the train, all trying to get out of the car at once.

The express slurred to a crazy, jolting stop as the signal reached the motorman. Some of the passengers were thrown to the floor.

"Get out on the rear platform," Delaney shouted over his shoulder. "Sing out for help—they may hear you back at the station!" Whether they understood or not he couldn't tell; he didn't wait to find out.

The fugitive was a car and a half ahead now, satchel or no satchel. Half a million can weigh very little when it's going to be all yours. The man was out of Delaney's section by this time. A weird silence had overtaken the stalled cars the minute the motion went out of them—all but the chirping at the rear. Delaney, without slowing up, megaphoned his hands and boomed ahead: "Sullivan! Stop that man! The guy with the bag!" It carried like a trumpet call through the still cars.

A minute later he cursed himself for doing it. There was another of those whip-cracks, and the smoke from it was still lazing over-head when he got to the next guard's platform. Sullivan was sprawled on his back, a hole over his eye that had just begun to bleed. Delaney jumped over him, swore like a mad dog as the sight registered, went ploughing on. The hysterical passengers scattered like leaves in front of him, pushed out windows with their elbows, clawed their way out the other end of the car.

The distant figure with the grip, all that he had eyes for now, had hit the first car at last, couldn't go any farther. Delaney heard himself bellowing out loud like a vindictive bull. He'd never known a guy could want to kill another guy so much, until now. He was in such a red rage that the thought of the gun was actually a come-on instead of a deterrent. A bullet right through the heart, he felt, wouldn't have been able to slow him up now.

The front car came into focus before his smouldering eyes—and the killer had vanished, wasn't in front of him any more. Just as he leaped the platform-gap, the train gave a jerk forward, then plunged into full motion again.

Damn that motorman, why did he ignore the signal like that? He was cutting them off from help at Chambers Street—with 14th Street a full five-minute run ahead! The train picked up speed like it never did under the eyes of a station timekeeper; it was in full careening flight already, rocking from side to side.

There had only been a single Negro in the first car. He was crouched down at seat-level now, pointing terrifiedly. "He went in there! He got a gun; watch y'self, man!" Then he slithered out of the way.

Delaney had known already he was in there, in the booth with the motorman. It was the only place left for him to go, unless he took a jump down forward under the whistling wheels. Delaney lunged at the metal door with his shoulder, heaved. It held fast. He must have wedged his body against it, since there was no way of locking it on the inside.

Delaney roared through the crack, "Stop the train, you fool! Cut the switch! What're you doing anyway?"

It wasn't the motorman's voice that answered from the other side of the partition, cold, distinct above the tunnel roar: "Get away from that door or I'll let him have it! You'll be on a train *without* a driver!"

And then the old fellow's voice, crazed with fear, "Delaney, for God's sake, do what he says—he's got a gun at the back of my neck!"

A green all-clear signal winked by beside the track outside.

They'd have a few more of those, Delaney knew, but in a minute or two they'd be getting red ones as they overtook the train ahead. And they were bound to if they didn't stop. The headway was longer now than during the rush hour, but the rate they were going would use it up in no time.

He tried to warn the maniac in there of what would happen, continuing to heave at the door while he panted, "You can't get away with it, you mad dog! You'll pile us up on the train ahead!"

The panel gave slightly and the killer's voice sounded from the inside, "Show me how it works! Come on, show me how it works—and I'll do the handling!"

The train slowed momentarily as the contact broke, then picked up speed again as it was resumed.

There was an insane laugh that froze Delaney. "That's all I need to know!" The panel fell all the way back in a flash, and as Delaney crouched to rush the opening, the old motorman toppled out into his arms, blood threading down by his ear. The booth banged shut again behind him, and the train seemed to rear forward.

Delaney eased the overalled figure to the floor, dragged it back out of the way. "Pop! What'd he do, shoot you?"

But it wasn't a bullet-wound, it was a vicious blow with the butt of the gun that had knocked him out. Meaning, probably, that the skunk was running low on cartridges, wanted to hang on to the few he had left.

Delaney didn't know much about guns, but he remembered that that fellow was carrying a revolver, and that six slugs was all one packed. He'd shot two off in the Wadsworth Building and two just now in the train. Unless he had a second gun or a pocket full of refills, he had only two left. But a hell of a lot of good knowing that did, with the lights of Canal Street cometing by and then another double green track-light right after that. Red was due any minute.

Delaney leaned across the prostrate motorman, huddled length-wise on the seat now, and stuck his head out the open upper half of one of the windows. And there it was, still way up the track, but already visible. Two midget dots of warning, one above the other, at right angles to the tunnel wall. And beyond that, almost invisible in the gloom, a cluster of even tinier ruby pinpoints, where their predecessor was slowing up as it neared 14th Street. Two, maybe three local stops away yet, but they'd be on top of it before it could pull out again.

He let the impregnable booth go hang, turned and fled down the deserted aisle toward the back, as all the passengers had done before him. But he wasn't thinking of his own skin. The second car was empty too, but at the end of that the bolder and more curious among them were huddled, peering up ahead with blanched, tense faces. They started to scatter again as he bore down on them.

"Metal!" he shrieked. "One of you—gimme something made of metal—anything, to throw a short-circuit!"

They didn't understand him or were too frightened. Another local stop gleamed by, and beyond it the two red stop-signals were already the size of dimes.

The fat lady who had involuntarily already saved his life once was huddled there, shaking and sniffling between faints. He clawed at her generous throat and she gave a screech of terror, tried to waddle away. The long silk scarf she wore tucked about her whipped off in his hand, yards and yards of it. He ran back toward the first car, trailing it after him. The red light came abreast, shot past them.

He rolled the thing up into a big loose ball, ducked past the control-booth with it, and dropped flat on his stomach over the lip of the open front platform. His head hung down over the edge. Up ahead, the taillights of the next train were four-square now and expanding every minute. Either the guy deliberately intended to commit suicide rather than be caught, or he didn't know how to stop any more.

But right while Delaney lay there with the big fluffy bunch of silk poised in his hand to pitch at the "shoe" that gripped the third rail, and stall them, the Phantom gave him the answer. He broke out of the booth just in back of Delaney, bag still in one hand, something else now in the other. The control-key that shut off contact. He'd brought it out with him.

He pitched it at one of the windows. There was a crash, and it vanished. They couldn't stop now; there was no way—not from the control-room, anyhow.

He streaked toward the back, gun out again to replace the key he'd thrown away. He was going to let it happen, callously sending dozens of people to death or painful injury, simply to better his chance of escaping in the resulting chaos. That was the idea, another of those thousand-to-one shots of his. To beat the crash to the end of the train before it came, toss his suitcase off the rear platform, drop off after it himself and, if he survived the fall, make good his escape up through the nearest emergency exit.

And survive he probably would, at that; it was just the kind of freak luck he'd been running in for twelve hours straight now. What would a few lacerations or bruises mean to him, living on borrowed time like he was?

Delaney dropped his head downward again, concentrated on the shoe gliding along the third rail, below and off to the side of him. One thing at a time—there were human lives on this train, and on that other one up front there, and they counted for more than even half a million dollars.

Three times, Delaney swung his arm out ahead of him with the rumpled mass of silk, that excellent conductor, foaming out of his hand, and three times swung it under and downward—without letting go. If the rush of air deflected it, carried it harmlessly past the shoe straight down the middle of the trackbed . . .

But there wasn't any more time left, not even enough to hesitate by. The taillights ahead were only a train-length away by now. He could look up the aisle of the end-car already; it was like a small lighted tunnel telescoped within a bigger black one. Let the gods of luck give somebody else a break for a change.

He opened his hand and let go, with just a fillip to the right to carry the silk off-center. It streamed out and downward, opening as it went. It hit the third rail just inches ahead of the shoe, whipped from sight and seemed to be sucked in under the rail-guard as the former caught it.

Then there was a warning spatter of sparks. The whole tunnel turned blue as though a giant flashlight picture had just been taken down there under the car-truck. And then a report like heavy artillery that put the Phantom's puny pistol-cracks to shame.

The blue glare went out again as suddenly as it had flared up, but the cars were already jarring to a sickening halt. Delaney had been given his break. He had short-circuited the train.

He nearly went sailing off on his stomach through the open platform door with the suddenness of the lurch. He caught the single chain that laced it with one upflung arm and dangled there, half in and half out. He managed to squirm back in again, scrambled to his feet, and plunged down a car aisle that had turned dark now and was filled with a thin layer of acrid smoke drifting lazily rearward. The train-lights had gone with the power, but a single automatic emergency bulb gleamed dully just above the vestibule of each car. He thanked God for them, for the passengers' sake if not his own.

They'd all been thrown down by the halt, and they'd reached a pitch of terror by now, some of them anyway, that was almost animal. But he wasn't concerned with them just now. He raced down the clear lane between their prone, jabbering forms that someone else had opened just ahead of him, with the wave of that deadly little gun.

He was in mid-car, out of reach of the levers, when all the doors silently swung back around him. He knew who'd done it! The fellow was getting out the side instead of going all the way to the back. He must have remembered that there'd be a guard down at the end-section who might tangle with him. And now that the train had stalled, it was no longer suicide to jump off at the side; in fact, easier and quicker than the other way.

Delaney spurted for the nearest controls to try to reverse them again before the fellow had time to slip through, but by the time he'd done it, he knew it was too late. Leaning out at nearly a forty-five-degree angle between cars, trying to pierce the tunnel gloom down that way, only proved the assumption to be correct. It was just the next car down that he'd made his getaway from, and the feeble radius of light from the bulb down at that vestibule momentarily outlined something moving away from it that instantly lost itself in the murk. But Delaney had seen that it was a figure holding onto a square shape and hopping awkwardly athwart the local tracks to the two-foot emergency runway niched into the side of the tunnel. And that led far down to where a blue and a white light, one above the other, and a puff of gray daylight marked an exit.

Well, he wasn't there yet. And he'd shot, maybe killed Sullivan, banged the old man on the conk, and tied up the whole line into a knot. Delaney reversed the controls a second time and jumped down to the tracks himself. The tunnel was black, but it looked red to him just then.

Two long jumps cleared the local rails for him, and he caught the single hand-guard that hemmed the causeway on the fly, hoisted himself up onto the little narrow foot-path. It was at about train-level. Instantly the blue and white light up ahead vanished. Something was between him and it.

Delaney sprinted along the straight, two-foot cement ribbon of foothold, pushing himself in toward the wall constantly with one hand on the rail that paralleled it. It was hard to make time along a place that narrow and tricky, but it was even harder if you had a valise to pack, he told himself. You'd have to scuttle along crabwise in that case, so it wouldn't trip you. He himself tripped once, went down face-forward, and all but fell down to the tracks three feet below. He picked himself up and bolted on, knees and palms stinging.

The exit lights ahead slowly rose in perspective as they drew nearer, cleared the top of the silhouette that had obscured them, and hit him in the eye like two moons. For the first time, then, he saw how close he and his quarry were. There was only about ten yards between them. The thumping and slapping of the suitcase as it was borne along were clearly audible. The cars of his own motionless train were far in back of him by now; he was traversing the pitch-black empty stretch between it and the one behind, a local, also stalled and semi-lighted. Just ahead of that, though, were the exit lights and the gush of daylight that marked safety for the killer.

But Delaney already knew he'd beat him to it, wasn't worried any more. That grip was hampering the fellow something fierce. The ten yards were down to about seven now, and the man's hoarse, strangled breathing seemed to fill the tunnel.

Delaney made himself audible at last, though the other must have known all along someone was after him. "Come on, you! Give up! I've got you now!"

A second later, he'd paid for his over-confidence. One foot somehow got in front of the other, and he went down a second time. He managed to stay on the runway but was flat as a mat.

Just as the floor came up and smacked him, the figure ahead whirled. There was a bang, a flash, and a thin whistle past where Delaney's head should have been.

One bullet left, and five yards between them. They were both motionless for a minute, half-strangling for air. Delaney crouched, leaped at the man from scratch in a sort of long, rising tackle that brought him up to shoulder-level by the time they connected. The gun exploded a second time, but straight at the ceiling like a sprint signal this time, but with one of Delaney's hands at the wrist that wielded it, the other at the fellow's neck, pulling it together into a flesh-necktie. It clicked harmlessly twice more in the air, then dropped to the runway with a crash and bounced down to the tracks below.

Delaney took away his open hand from the fellow's throat, only to bring it back again hardened into a meteorite of a fist that drove between the other's eyes as though it had come all the way from another planet.

If any consciousness survived the impact, there was no sign of it, only reflex action. The wrist Delaney had been gripping jerked from his grasp; the other's body went down flat over the valise that had been standing just behind him. The head missed the edge of the runway, dropped from sight, and pulled all the rest of him down to the tracks after it with a sort of acrobat's half-turn and back-flip, under the hand-rail. The valise stayed on the ledge; but the Phantom stayed down below there in an indistinguishable heap.

Delaney, about to jump down after him and get him, was

suddenly conscious of lights flaring all around him, like an abrupt aurora borealis there in the tunnel. That local, not far down, was all at once blazing with electricity again, bleaching the tunnel walls. So was his own train, far up the other way. They'd ironed out the short-circuit, and the power had come on again.

A puff of black, acrid smoke seemed to spurt from under the mound of clothes that lay on the tracks just beneath him, as though they were on fire. He turned his head away and leaned sickly up against the tunnel wall for a minute.

Later, trudging away from there, hauling the recovered valise slowly after him, the professional came to the surface in Delaney again. "Two shorts in a row," he mused despondently. "They'll can me sure when they find out it was me caused the first one."

"And did they?" asked his blindfolded train mate Sullivan from the hospital cot that evening.

"I didn't let on it was me done it," answered Delaney, "but somebody must have tipped them off. They seemed to know it, anyway. They didn't dock me, though. Instead, all the higher-ups come around shaking hands with me, trying to make a monkey outa me! They said something about promoting me. . . ."

"Well, what're you kicking about?" the other asked. "You sound like—"

"It was bad enough before, riding the platforms," complained Delaney. "Now it'll be twice as slow, stuck behind some signal-board keeping tabs on the lights all day long! That's what a guy gets. He don't know when he's well off!"

The Man on B-17

By August Derleth

*A*NOTHER *almost legendary figure in railroading is the
engineer—the man who stands at the throttle of the big steam
locomotives; the man who is responsible for bringing his train in
on time; the highballer, the tough, grizzled veteran whose only
love, several tons of iron and steel, whispers to him and sometimes screams for him in the night. . . .*

*"The Man on B-17" is about a latter-day member of this
fraternity, and about what happens to him during several of his
highballing runs from Rexford's Crossing to Hungerford, in the
back country of Wisconsin. If you can read it without feeling a
chill, and without hearing in your mind the mournful wail of a
locomotive's whistle, you might be a fine person, but you're
probably not a train buff.*

*Until his death in 1972, August Derleth was Wisconsin's fore-
most regional writer, having published an impressive number of
fiction and nonfiction works about his home state. He was the*

creator of Solar Pons, perhaps the most successful pastiche of Sherlock Holmes; and among his many short stories are several more dealing with trains, including a spoof of Orient Express intrigue (see the Bibliography). A lifelong student and writer of macabre and supernatural fiction, he founded Arkham House in 1939—a publishing company which specializes in the prose and poetry of such writers as H. P. Lovecraft—and thereby offered other aficionados the only steady source of this type of literature.

Like many of Derleth's best stories, "The Man on B-17" originally appeared in the most famous of the pulp magazines, Weird Tales.

Okeh, I'll go over it again from the beginning.

The way it happened was like this. I was bringing Number Twelve down toward Hungerford; you highball from Rexford's Crossing—that's about thirty miles back—but you have to wheel in toward B-Seventeen sort of easy on account of that curve there. The trestle is on a curve, and the gorge below, with the river running deep and swift there. That night . . .

No, that wasn't the night it happened. I'm telling you this because it began before that—quite a while. This was a night in the beginning of winter—maybe three months ago. Late November. Snow falling. Yes, the first night of snow. Okeh—then it was the eighteenth. I don't fix the date, but if you say that was the first night of snow, then that was it.

Well, that night I wheeled around toward B-Seventeen, and I saw this fella standing there. I thought it was Bart Hinch. Bart had a shack this side of the trestle; he walked it out of Hungerford regular about that time of night. But this guy wasn't Bart; he was a slim guy, not Bart's build much, and he was just standing there on the trestle—along about the middle. The headlight caught him, and I hit the whistle hard. I couldn't stop, and I didn't see how he was going to cut out in time. But he did it somehow. Never hit a thing, just went on smooth as you please. And then there at the other end, I could have sworn I saw a woman, just standing there, waiting—probably for that guy on B-Seventeen.

Well, sir, that was the beginning.

After that, I saw him again. I saw him fairly regular. And one night coming down toward town, I was wheeling in extra-slow—oh, that was around Christmas; we'd had a deep snow, and it was blowing some, white gusts of snow over the trestle, and I thought I'd better take her slow around that curve; that's a tricky one—and there he was again, but closer to the end of the trestle; so I leaned out of the cab and I hollered at him.

"Lightfooted?" I yelled at him.

He looked at me. I thought he smiled.

No, I couldn't be sure. The snow was blowing, and there he was, standing beside the track at the bank—not two feet from the trestle; and I said to Carroll—he was in the cab with me that night—I said, "That guy's looking for trouble," I said, "and if he keeps up that way, he'll find it. Head on."

Carroll can tell you. Carroll said, "Who is he?" and I said, "Hanged if I know!"

Very next night we saw him again, Carroll and me both. This time he was square in the middle of the trestle, and I swear before God I thought we were going to hit him. I said to Carroll, "We're going to hit him!" I said, and I was bearing down on that whistle for all she had. He was there in the middle of the bridge, and the snow falling all around him. I didn't see him till just before we hit him.

At least, I thought we hit him.

We started slowing down at the other end of the trestle. No, I didn't feel a thing. Most of the time you can tell. I didn't know what to do, but then I figured it wasn't much use stopping; the snow was that thick you couldn't see anything anyway, and if we knocked him off the trestle, why, he'd be way down somewhere in the gorge, maybe swept along in the water, God knows where. There was no use in it; we could report it in Hungerford.

No, I didn't report it. Reason was when we stopped at

Hungerford, Mr. Kenyon, the conductor, came up alongside from the last coach. "You see that fellow on B-Seventeen?" he asked. I started to explain that I couldn't stop, and then I began to wonder how *he'd* seen him. I said yes, I'd seen him, and with this and that, it came out he saw him *after* we passed over the trestle. Saw the woman, too. She was on the other side that night. Carroll's side, but Carroll wasn't looking that way. I don't know how he did it. Lightfooted is hardly the word. That bridge is narrow—narrower'n most. About the only way he could do it is to hang down off the side, and I don't know how he could do it that night, what with the snow and the ice underneath. Be bound to slip off and go right down. But Mr. Kenyon saw him right smack in the middle of the trestle; he must have bounded right back up from wherever he went.

"What was he doing?" I asked.

"Looked to be waiting for somebody," said Mr. Kenyon.

Well, that was the way I took it from the first. Maybe the woman. But then, the woman seemed to be waiting for someone, too. It didn't figure out right; it didn't add up. After that, I wasn't quite so nervous when I saw him again.

Sure, I saw him again. About a week later, that was. He was walking the trestle. Just walking. I saw him sort of rise up just behind the marker for the bridge—they're all numbered the way they should be, and the last bridge before Hungerford is that one—B-Seventeen. He rose up and started walking toward town. If I hadn't known better I'd have sworn that he climbed up out of the gorge along the wall there.

No, he couldn't have done it. Wall's almost sheer on that side for twenty feet or so down before it gets craggy enough to climb. Ain't a man alive could do it on a night like that one, a winter night with snow and ice. It was like glass along that side of the gorge, and I don't see that there was any way it could be done. But as I said, there he was. I turned to Carroll and I said, "There he is again."

"Damn his eyes!" said Carroll. "Old Twelve's going to get him one of these nights."

Those were his very words. I couldn't argue with him about

that. I figured then it was just a matter of time before we hit
him. I didn't care how good he was at ducking out of the way.
I've seen 'em beat that game just so long, and then they get caught.
A train highballing along that way ain't something anybody in his
right mind's going to take and fight. You can tell by the feeling
you get in one of those steam-wagons, in your hands and all
through you when you're pushing her down—and Number
Twelve's no hay-burner, no, nor no tramp, either; Number
Twelve's an old girl you can count on, a real battleship—and you
get the feeling she wouldn't like it when a guy keeps daring her,
and sooner or later she'd take him.

Well, it was the same that night. Saw him on the trestle, and
then somehow he was on the other side; he must have run
pretty fast. I opened the window and leaned out and hollered at
him.

"Don't you believe in signs?" I hollered, meaning he should
take notice where it says at both ends of B-Seventeen that
trespassing is forbidden and so on. He didn't pay me no more
attention than as if I'd been the wind. But that time I saw his
face. Young fellow. Not like Bart at all. Had on a tassel-cap and
a mackinaw. Looked fair—light-haired. Couldn't have weighed
more'n a hundred-seventy-five. Okeh, I thought, I'll turn you in.

So I did. I waited till we hit Elroy and gave his description
to the cinder-bull there, and the cinder-bull went out—it was clear
that night, with a moon showing, and not cold; he went out right
away. Number Twelve's the night owl through Hungerford and
Elroy. He went out that night and the next night and the next.
That guy was on the trestle every night. But the cinder-bull
didn't see hide nor hair of him. Or the woman, either. And she
was there at least two out of those three times. Because Carroll
saw her once, and I saw her the second time, and we probably
just missed her the other time. She was probably there, all right,
just like the other times. So the cinder-bull gave up. He wouldn't
argue. "I'm the Casey Jones," I said, "and Carroll's an old raw-
hider, and the ticket snatcher, Mr. Kenyon—all three of us saw
him," I said. But I might as well have talked to the wind. So
I ran in my report to the Super and let it go at that.

We kept on seeing him and the woman, sometimes regular, sometimes after a week or so when we didn't see either one. It went that way all through the winter. It went on that way until that night early this month, first week in March, when it happened—and since then neither of us has seen a thing, not a solitary thing.

Well, just like I said before, we bore down on B-Seventeen that night with the snow blowing thick as smoke all around us. Carroll saw him first—and he let out a yell. "There he is again!" And I looked, and sure enough—there he was, a-kneeling in the middle of the trestle. Kneeling—yes, sir! Right smack in the middle, and I knew we were going to get him, I knew the old girl was going to take and pitch him off into the gorge. I wanted to close my eyes, but I couldn't. And a good thing, maybe, I couldn't.

"Three of 'em!" Carroll hollered out.

And sure enough, there was three. That guy in the tassel-cap and the mackinaw was at this end, and the woman was at the other end. The headlight showed 'em all three just as plain. The guy in the mackinaw was braked, seemed like, to keep anyone coming from the bridge; and the woman on the other end. She looked—well, no, I wouldn't say *mean*, just *grim*—and he looked *terrible*, like as if he was angry and cold and set to kill. The one in the middle—that one—well, we saw him before we hit him, and we knew him; that one was Bart Hinch.

We hit him. There's no more to say about that. He was there and we couldn't stop, and whatfor in God's name he was kneeling there in the middle of the trestle, praying or whatever it was he was doing, nobody'll ever know. It wasn't our fault; we couldn't throw Number Twelve off the trestle just to save him. So we hit him, and I felt it when the old girl knocked him off into the gorge, and it near made me sick to know we'd done it.

We stopped at Hungerford. That was two miles away, maybe a little better. You could see where we hit him. There was nothing we could do but report it, and let them go back, come daylight, to find what they could. . . .

Sure, I talked with Bart Hinch a good many times.

No, never heard him say anything about somebody waiting for him on B-Seventeen. I don't know what he said in his cups in town, and he never said anything to me about hating to walk home at night. Could be that's how come he didn't go out much after dark; but me—I wouldn't know.

No, I never knew Tod Benning. All I know about him is that he ran off somewhere before he was to marry Lois Malone and that it killed her or she killed herself or something like that. Never heard that Bart owed him money and that he set out to collect it and never came back. Talk's cheap.

What did it look like on the trestle that night? Well, it looked to me as if the fella in the mackinaw was holding down one end of the bridge and the woman was holding down the other so's Bart couldn't get off either way. I don't care how it sounds—you asked me, and I'm telling you. Carroll'll tell you the same thing. That's the way it looked. Sure, it was snowing. Sure, I might be mistaken. But the old girl's light cut right through that snow, and I saw those faces—and Bart Hinch's was mortal afraid, and it didn't look like he was seeing Number Twelve, either, but just those two, that fella in the mackinaw and the woman.

No, sir, we hit only once, only one thing. That was Bart Hinch. I saw it. I saw how the old girl just tossed him out of the way, out into the gorge. Then he was gone into the blackness and the snow underneath. I felt it where I sat. So did Carroll. He'll tell you the same. Only once.

How do I account for there being two bodies down there? I don't account for it. Bart was killed by Number Twelve. I said that. I saw it happen. The other one, the one you say is Tod Benning, you said yourself was dead a long time, two years or so, maybe more. I've been in Number Twelve seven years, and this is the first time we ever hit a man. Anyway, they say there's no bone broken—and the old girl would have broken him up some. So maybe he fell or was flung off the trestle—I can't say.

Yes, I can identify the man on B-Seventeen if you show him to me. Or his picture. The woman, too. It'll be the same as last time. You put those pictures down in front of me, and it'll be the same.

The man is number five, there, and the woman's number thirteen.

No mistake. At least, *I'm* not making the mistake, and Carroll's not making it. So it must be yours. If the woman's picture is one of Lois Malone—well, the woman on the trestle that night looked enough like her to be her twin sister, even if she never had one. But you don't fool me on that man, number five there. I saw him as plain as I see you, more than once. That's the man. And if you say that's a picture of Tod Benning, then that body you dug up out of the river isn't Tod Benning's, no matter what the doctor and the dentist have got to say, because that's the man Carroll and Mr. Kenyon and I saw on B-Seventeen. . . .

The Three Good Witnesses

By Harold Lamb

WORLD WAR II, with all its complex intrigue and espionage, has been a favorite background of suspense-fiction writers; but relatively little of their work in this area makes use of trains. One novel which comes immediately to mind is David Westheimer's Von Ryan's Express, *and there are a number of other books which deal with prewar activities (Eric Ambler's* Background to Danger *is one) and postwar cabal (Robert Parker's* Passport to Peril*). The only short piece I know of, though doubtless there are others, which concerns itself directly with the European conflict is Harold Lamb's "The Three Good Witnesses"—a pure old-fashioned adventure/suspense story involving spies, secret documents, and sudden death on board an express bound from Istanbul to Greece in 1945.*

Its author, the late Harold Lamb, is best known for his minutely researched historical novels, among them Genghis Khan (1927), The Crusades *and* The March of the Barbarians.

Much of his short adventure fiction is concerned with ancient history as well, and first appeared in such quality pulp magazines as Blue Book. His attention to background detail is evident in "The Three Good Witnesses" and serves to involve the reader strongly in the events happening on the train and in Europe during those dark days of global strife.

The last thing you read at night sticks in your mind. Or it might be your subconscious mind. Either way, you keep thinking about it all night, and you never forget it.

Somewhere Humphrey Ward had seen that in a book, and it made sense to him.

What he read last on that second night out of Istanbul on the Taurus Express was a small dog-eared volume entitled *Customs of the Medieval Arabs*, and Humphrey Ward had come to a line that said: *A man's guilt shall be established by the evidence of three independent and trustworthy witnesses.*

Why three? he thought. *And only three?*

It didn't make sense, and when a thing didn't make sense, Hump chewed at it until he got around to an answer. He liked to do the intelligence quizzes in the magazines. He did them on the quiet, because his average, carefully calculated, was 58.7, which was a little less than good. But the tougher the quizzes were, the better he liked them.

In this case he hit on an answer. Two witnesses to a crime might tell the same lie, or they might imagine they had seen something that never happened—by coincidence! But if three trustworthy gents told the same story, that story would be fact. The odds against three people imagining the same thing were something like one in a thousand. Satisfied that he had the right answer, he put the little volume down on top of one of his bags and methodically checked the fastenings of his first-class compartment, Number Seven.

The slide catch was locked on the connecting door; the chain was caught across the corridor door. This *wagon-lit* car was an ancient number—exactly the type he had known in France in '18 and just as crowded, although he was now leaving Turkey in the year '44. The only new thing about the *wagon-lit* car was a brass sign that said in Turkish: *Do not lean out the window because of danger.*

Switching off the bright reading-light, he switched on the blue dome sleeping-light. It made him feel at home, like in '18. Thereupon Hump's conscious mind switched off the three-witnesses puzzle.

Humphrey Ward was sorry to be leaving Turkey. Overage and overweight for this war, Hump would have liked to get something done in Turkey, where, at the urging of his State Department, he had arrived to aid the Turks to test-drill for oil, only to discover that Turkey had no oilfields—or so he had been told. And he would have liked to see a battlefront somewhere, instead of only the fine new American airfields across Africa, where small monkeys skipped around the mechanics, and good canned beer was passed across the PX counters. Even in Turkey, which everyone assured him was a hotbed of espionage, he had spotted not one Axis agent. He had dined at Rejans on *pilaf* and Turkish coffee without having any Balkan undercover guy breathing down his neck; he had visited all the mosques around the Golden Horn without seeing one Viennese blonde drop a scented handkerchief across his path. He had seen, in short, nothing of this enormous war.

The last war had been much simpler than this. You went forward in one direction, blasting out the Jerries. . . . Hump had volunteered to establish contact with a wandering patrol at night in what became notorious later as the Argonne Forest. The patrol he found had been Jerries. . . .

Hump woke up suddenly with the feeling that he had something to do. It was a queer feeling, cold and bewildering, because he didn't know anything he had to do. Snapping on the reading-light, he glanced at his wrist watch and found that it was ten minutes to five.

He felt as if he had to get off that train quick.

"Not me," he assured himself drowsily.

The cold made him cough. Outside, he knew it was still snowing, and probably they were climbing the heights of the Bolkhar Dagh. The jerking of the car had disturbed him. Yet they wouldn't reach the frontier, the Syrian customs, for an hour or so. And George, the *wagon-lit* conductor, had his passport and statement of the money on him. Hump called the conductor George because he found the name Haig Kevorkian hard to pronounce.

Hump felt the familiar bulges of his money-belt, checking with his fingers the wad of assorted foreign paper, the square of the express checks, and the fold of his letters of identification. They were all there. No one had been monkeying with his things—no one *could* have got into the first-class compartment.

Nevertheless Hump felt as if the sergeant had been bawling, *All out, you guys!*

Mechanically, Hump pulled on his shoes and reached for his coat. Then he laughed. What he was doing didn't make sense. Because this *wagon-lit* car was so familiar, he had been thinking about France when he went to sleep.

Awake now, he remembered who had to get up and leave the train at five o'clock: Tom Hatfield, the other American—the hard-boiled twenty-six-year-old A.T.C. pilot, once a parachute-tester and Panamerican flyer, who hadn't seen his own country for five years.

Tom had to get off at five, at a place called Adana, to change to a plane that would take him swiftly to Cairo, because Tom, who came from Frankfort, Kentucky, was carrying dispatches from the American embassy at Ankara to the U.S.F.I.M.E. at Cairo; and since Turkey was a neutral country, he had to travel by Taurus Express to the frontier line, where he could board the plane waiting for him. Tom had told Hump that much over the bottles of beer in the *wagon-restaurante* the evening before—not saying much, except in answer to Hump's questions, and always keeping that locked briefcase under his arm, or propped up against him, apparently not trusting Hump any more than the others on the train.

Wide-awake now and dressed, Hump lit a cigarette and un-hooked the chain from the door to go to the corridor. It was still dark, with only a small light going at the end.

Down there the conductor's bed had been pulled down—the narrow wooden shelf. Only, Mary the Deadhead was stretched out on the shelf instead of Kevorkian. She was lying on her sheepskin jacket, with Kevorkian's coat over her, and Hump thought she had been talking to Kevorkian, the conductor, when he came out.

"It's almighty cold," he said by way of good morning.

They only stared at him, surprised.

The girl's thin face looked pinched and blue under the light. Tom called her Mary the Deadhead because her name was hard to pronounce. Also Mary had no place on this car; she slept on Kevorkian's makeshift bed; she sat around the corridor on the small push-down seats or in the dining-car, and she ate bread and cheese or *kebabs* at the stands when the Taurus Express stopped at a station.

Hump had offered her a seat on the couch in his compartment. But she said it was *avval mevki*, first-class—although she was willing enough to sit in Tom's first-class compartment.

"It's hard to teach these Turkish girls to talk, mostly," Tom had explained. "But Mary knows some real American."

Tom seemed to learn a lot about Mary in those two days. According to him, she was only sixteen, and had been to school before the war at the American Farm School in Thessalonica, which Hump knew as Salonica. No, Mary wasn't Greek—she was Macedonian, and proud as hell, and trying to get to the United States to learn to be a real nurse.

"She has as much chance of that," Tom had elucidated, "as I have of getting into the Kremlin. She hasn't money, or an Egyptian visa, or transportation through the war zones. She walked out of Macedonia, but she says God could send transportation. She has been reading in the Bible how Paul walked to Rome from some place."

How Tom got all that out of Mary, Hump did not know. Tom

had been around, and he seemed to figure out what these people were thinking, which Hump could not do. Then Mr. Chiniara had also explained Mary. Mr. Chiniara knew the answers, too— having explained how he had escaped from Greece in a *caïque* only a week ago.

"It is that all *wagon-lit* passengers," Mr. Chiniara had explained in his excellent French, "on this express are of the refugees from the Axis. And all would pay much to be *en route* to the United States, because where else is there security for Rumanians, for Slovak men of affairs, except in the United States? It is what you call a migration out of the dying Old World, toward the New World. It is formidable. Except, that you, monsieur, and that other American have already the security. Where you go," he had added wistfully, "always you are safe. But it is not so with us."

Just then a light showed, blurred, in the hard-driving snow, and the Taurus Express jolted, as if changing pace. The old car creaked.

"We're getting in to Adana, George?" Hump called out.

The conductor, hunched up in his chocolate tan uniform, only nodded. He looked weary. He looked like a sunburned brigand, or a banker, who did not like to be bothered. And then Hump stepped from the cold familiar corridor into unknown darkness and complete uncertainty.

Remembering that it was Tom's station, and that the courier had not put in an appearance, he knocked at the door of Number Ten. When he tried the door, it opened into darkness, and Hump wondered if Hatfield had left. When he switched on the light, he saw the other American lying on the bed, and he said:

"Hey, you—rise and shine!"

Tom did not move. On the small table an alarm clock ticked; Hump remembered that Tom had said he carried it to be sure of getting up.

Hump could not wake the boy. Snapping on the reading-light, he peered at Tom. He was breathing, but shaking did not stir him. Then Hump noticed a streak of dried blood on the pillow; and when he felt the boy's head, a bit of blood came off on his fingers.

"I'll be—" said Hump, and sat down on the bed. After a

second he closed the door. He had noticed then that the briefcase containing the dispatches was gone. Only Tom's clothes and a small open bag with shirts and a carton of cigarettes remained. Hump thought about that, while he was aware that the train had slowed and stopped.

As sure as shooting, he thought, Tom would have had that briefcase in bed with him. When Hump felt around along the mattress, he turned up a .45 automatic, with a clip of cartridges in it, and the safety-catch on—but no briefcase.

Whoever had taken the briefcase laid Tom out, asleep. Whoever had come in from the corridor . . . Hump swore softly. He was *certain* that Tom would have locked the corridor door, and hitched on the chain, just as he himself had done. But now it was open.

For a moment Hump figured on that, his hands feeling cold with excitement. When he tried the handle of the connecting door into the adjoining compartment, he found it locked. Then Hump felt mad, clear through. It didn't make sense, anyone getting into a locked compartment unless he had a key.

Seeing that the train was starting again he rushed in a near run toward Mary at the end of the corridor. Out the window he glimpsed soldiers in their long flapping greatcoats moving under a light, swinging their arms.

"Did you see anyone go into Number Ten?" he demanded of the girl. He pointed at Tom's compartment.

She shook her head without saying anything. Kevorkian lurched in, like a bodyguard, standing over the Macedonian girl.

"Look," Hump snarled at him, "you have a key to the doors?"

Kevorkian shook his head. The slide locks and the chains, he explained, would not open to a key. He looked suspicious and angry.

No one else was moving in the corridor at that hour. After thinking for a minute, Hump went back to Number Ten. His mind raced now, without any clear idea. *American dispatches had been stolen!* Maybe something that meant a lot. And Hatfield was out—maybe with concussion, after that blow on the head.

Five years overseas—ninety parachute jumps—and now knocked out like this in a train! That train, to Hump, seemed to be hostile and secret, covering up the wrong done to Tom. "When the folks write to me now," Tom had said, "I don't know the people they tell me about, any more. They're all like strangers." That was how Tom felt, who was tired of strange lands and hungry for his own. And here was Hump, going home, easy, first-class.

He knew Tom would have locked that corridor door. Then why was it open now? Unless somebody had wanted to leave evidence that anyone in the corridor could have got in.

"That doesn't make sense," Hump muttered, fingering the pistol. "Unless that somebody got in another way."

It was like an intelligence quiz. The only other door was the connecting one, locked. But at this point Hump looked carefully at the connecting door, and tingled with excitement. Locked, it certainly was. Yet the catch on his side *had not been pushed home.* That meant it had been locked by the catch on the other side. That meant somebody might have worked the connecting door open in the night, and had gone back the same way, after unhitching the corridor door.

Before Hump reasoned any more, he felt so angry he began to rap his fist against the door. The compartment beyond would be Number Eight and Nine, second-class, with two men in it. He had glimpsed two men playing backgammon there during the day.

The door swung open, away from Hump. He saw Mr. Chiniara putting on his coat, his neat hair, smelling of oil, mussed up. In the shadow of the lower berth lay another man in a woolen undershirt, staring at him.

"What is it," cried Mr. Chiniara, "that you have?"

His broad face twisted in surprise. He pointed at Hump's hand. It held the .45, but Hump wasn't thinking of that. He felt sure these two had the missing briefcase, although he couldn't see any sign of it.

In his excitement, he found it hard to speak French at all.

"*Le portmanteau,*" he muttered. "The bag of my friend—it is here."

Mr. Chiniara still stared. "Here we have only our valises."

Naturally, he was upset at seeing the pistol. Hump hesitated, while they watched him.

"If you have lost anything," said Mr. Chiniara, "I pray you to look. I know nothing of it."

When he moved aside, Hump stepped into the room, his eyes questing over the upper berth. Close to him he felt a movement, and turned instinctively. Then his head felt numb, and lights flared across his sight. He was conscious that he had been hit over the eyes, and that his arms reached out as he fell, and other arms caught him. While he was so held, he kept trying to support himself on one knee. He heard a familiar rushing sound, like wind. It was icy cold, and it stung his mind. . . .

He couldn't see into the darkness, but he felt the beat of hard snow on his wet face. Then, under the shock of the cold and the wind, he realized that the arms were pushing him through the window. His head and shoulders were out in the storm.

When the hands shoved him again, he kicked out savagely, back. His foot drove a man's body back, and Hump rolled to one side, pulling himself out of the grip of the other man, falling back into the compartment. Something hard smashed against his shoulder, numbing one arm.

He swept his other arm around, caught a man's legs and pulled. His head knocked against metal lying loose on the floor. Instantly he freed his hand and caught at it, feeling the steel shape of his pistol. The compartment was dark, and when he fired the first shot from the .45, the flash picked out the shapes of two men lunging at him.

Flame exploded against him; the blast of the explosion turned him around. Feeling the berth against his back, he rolled over on it, lashing out with one foot. Another shot slammed into the wood under him.

Hump kept shoving back, swinging his .45 around. His head seemed to split between the eyes. He was hanging on to the automatic, loosing off the full clip until the hammer clicked and no shot came.

Then he heard a man breathing hard, like a tired animal. Something bumped against the berth. After that, he couldn't

hear anything except the rattle and roar of the train. He thought,
*Maybe Tom has another clip—but I haven't, and there's nothing
to do.*

Cautiously the corridor door opened. A hand came in and
felt for the switch. Kevorkian stood there, his face a mask, his
eyes hard.

On the floor Mr. Chiniara lay, with his hair rumpled, on top
of the man in the undershirt. Watching them, Hump noticed
that they didn't move.

Quietly, Kevorkian shut the door behind him. Somehow Mary
was with him now, leaning down, and touching the throats of
the men. When she pulled down Mr. Chiniara's eyelid, Kevorkian
cracked his thumb. "Finish," he said.

Then they both looked at Hump, leaning on his elbow on the
berth, with one leg hanging over. He didn't feel like moving. He
was thinking how he had finished Mr. Chiniara and the other
guy, and he hadn't been dreaming when he did it. Their outlines
were blurry because he couldn't see well. But the two standing
there expected him to say something, so he said:

"They took the briefcase. I'm sure they did."

Kevorkian and Mary looked at each other; then the conductor
snapped the lock on the door, because people were moving and
talking out in the corridor. They heard a man swearing. In the
dark square of the connecting door Tom Hatfield appeared,
holding on to the door.

"Who the hell," he said pleasantly, "is shooting up this place?"
He saw the two on the floor. "Jonah and the whale's guts!" he
murmured.

Mary looked at his hard young face, and she made him sit
down on the berth. There was dried blood ringing his ear.

Hump found himself on his feet, trying to poke around for the
briefcase. He couldn't move very well, the compartment was so
crowded, and his knees kept caving in, but he was thinking that
he ought to find the briefcase, and the briefcase couldn't be
found. After two or three moments, he knew it wasn't in that
compartment, and he sat down beside Tom because his knees
felt weak.

"He wants some whisky, Mary," said Hatfield. "You'll find a pint in my bag. Bring it here."

When the bag came, Tom fished in it and brought out the cigarette carton. Then he produced a bottle, and Kevorkian handed over a glass from the water-stand, after rinsing it. Hump drank down the glassful and found that he could see all right.

"They got your papers," he explained.

"They did?"

"In the briefcase. And it—it isn't here."

The Kentuckian whistled softly and glanced at the empty glass. "Mr. Ward," he urged, "suppose you let us in on what actually happened. The first thing I remember is hearing slugs busting up my berth."

Carefully, then, Hump recounted his discovery, his reasoning, and what had happened to him. Mary looked pretty white and excited while she listened. But the other two might have been wooden Indians handing out cigars.

When he had finished, Tom looked at the open window. "If they got that dispatch-case, they probably heaved it out there." He hesitated briefly. "There wasn't anything in the case but some copies of the *Cumhurriet*—that morning paper. Back at Haidar Pasha, a Britisher I know told me to be careful this trip. I put the papers some other place."

Hump thought that place would be the cigarette carton. And he thought how he had shot two men, without having one particle of evidence to back up his story.

When he told the three of them that, Tom said suddenly, "But you guessed right, Mr. Ward. I sure *locked* that door last night."

Kevorkian pointed at Hump. "A mild gentleman like you—to kill *two* in the dark!" He spoke quietly now, with respect.

"But he did not!" The girl Mary stamped her foot and went off into a flood of Macedonian or Armenian or something foreign.

Kevorkian listened, shaking his head and nodding, and making gestures like a man trying to think and play the piano at the same time. Finally he waved his hand. "Quick!" he muttered. "Ah, how we waste time. Who is dead, here?"

He caught hold of Mr. Chiniara. At the same time, Mary led Hump into the other compartment, saying that he couldn't feel good enough to help.

Kevorkian and Tom were in the act of heaving the man in the undershirt out the open window, into the driving snow. After that they threw out the bags and clothes and began to rip up the rug from the floor. Hump, watching through the door, gasped, but he felt better when he saw a knife lying on the floor by the revolver that had been shot at him.

"Think not of it, please," the girl said. "Because Haig Kevorkian, he is Macedonian. When he fought the Gairmans at Thessalonica, he threw bodies over the cliffs, two-three years ago."

"Did he?"

Mary the Macedonian nodded, thinking. "Yes, I saw him." She looked at Hump, as if pondering about him. "You also are a very brave man even if you are not Macedonian. But we 'ave not left Turkey yet, and you would be judgment-tried for two-three years in spite of your age and innocence. It is better to have no bodies."

By then compartment Number Eight and Nine was clear of all signs of occupancy—Kevorkian being engaged in shoving the berths back into the daytime couch. Then a rap of sharp authority sounded on the door.

When the door was opened, a slender man in uniform stepped in. He wore khaki wool with brass insignia; he was no older than Tom, and Kevorkian eyed him as if beholding a ghost arise.

"Chiniara," said the soldier. "Drikar?" And he glanced at Tom, puzzled. Under his arm he had a wad of passports, and in his hand he held two open, studying the photographs.

"The Syrian passport control," breathed Mary, holding hard to Hump's hand. "Moses in the bulrushes, how I forgot!"

Until then, Hump also had forgotten how his passport, along with the others—except for Tom's—had been turned over to the conductor, to present to the Syrian authorities. The soldier, who carried a small sword-bayonet, had the two passports of the late occupants of Eight-Nine. Tom said nothing. Kevorkian looked

at Mary. Hump felt his pulse beating in his throat. The girl let
go of his hand.

She got up and stepped in front of the Syrian officials.
Shaking her tawny hair, she disclaimed in another language,
her eyes snapping, her hand indicating the driving snow outside.
The Syrian listened with interest.

"She's something to look at," said Tom, coming in, "when
she's like that."

Kevorkian sidled over to them, listening. He nudged Hump.
"She says you are General of United States American Secret
Service. At Adana you put Chiniara and Drikar off the Taurus
Ekspressi with a small-arm pistol."

"But he'll want proof. He'll make a report—"

"Him?" Kevorkian gestured widely, as if thrusting away the
troubles of the world. "Why shall he? He is Arab. We are not
yet at Ekbesse, where the frontier is. What does he care what
happens in Turkey?" Kevorkian thought about that. "He has the
passports, but— Have you any Syrian money?"

Hurriedly, Hump reached for his money-belt and pulled out a
blue-pink wad of foreign paper money. Taking it, Kevorkian
went into the next compartment and silenced Mary the Deadhead.
He passed the Syrian money to the frontier control—possibly,
Hump thought, not *all* the Syrian money—and took in exchange
the two passports. These he tossed out the window.

"Finish!" said Kevorkian.

"It's teamwork," Tom observed, taking a cigarette out of his
pocket but not opening the carton. Thoughtfully, he nodded. "I
saw it, because I was watching that little lady, thinking she might
be drawing down an Axis pay-check. You see, her family starved
in Greece, up near that Thessalonica place. Yuh, Mary was doling
out the half-cans of milk with the Red Cross at Athens, and
she didn't hear about her family for some time. And this Kevorkian
has his pop and kid brother shot by the Jerries. Well, having
no families, the girl and he teamed up on this here express. He
let her ride deadhead, and told the Turkish frontier police she
was his only daughter. They let her ride."

Outside, gray mist swirled past the window. Through the mist white mountain peaks and gray rocks showed—old pinnacle rocks.

"That's why," explained Tom, "they don't want any show-down inspection on this train."

Sun struck through the mist, a low sun, making a rainbow around the snow crest, like jewels hung in the sky.

Tom eyed the window without interest. "We're out of Turkey now, fellow. But this Mary the Deadhead will have her a time to get by the British control. You can't," added Tom, aggrieved, "smuggle a pack of cigarettes past the British. Try to smuggle a girl, and they'll blow their top."

He was just talking, thought Hump, to make things seem all right. Although the warm sun touched the window, Hump felt still cold and numb. Although Tom kept saying how those two must have been a pair of two-pound espionage free agents, grabbing papers to make a small profit, the voice of Hump's sub-conscious mind would not have it so.

Mr. Chiniara and Mr. Drikar were still there, in the next compartment, right with him, their white faces showing red in the flashes. They still had their hands on him. He hadn't one shred of evidence or one witness to show how he'd figured them to be guilty, and how they had tried to kill him without a trace by shoving him out into the storm from the speeding Taurus Express.

He was still sitting by Tom, and the sky was jet blue over red clay hills when the train stopped beside a long station that had a sign: *Aleppo*.

When the young Kentuckian started to pull down the window and hand out his bag, a voice said in English, "One minute, please, sir."

Outside, in the glare of sunlight, a British sergeant stood looking up at the windows. "Everyone will remain in his place in this car," he said.

"Okay," said Tom, sitting down.

Hump had looked at his watch three times before the corridor door opened and a sunburned young officer came, wearing a Major's insignia, with Kevorkian showing behind him.

"Good morning," he remarked. "I'm Radcliffe." He began to

leaf through some passports, among which Hump recognized his own.

Mary came in, with her hair combed back, and carrying her old sheepskin jacket. Now that she was warm, and her face flushed, Hump thought she did look pretty. What had Tom said about her? "I thought I had had plenty of grief, but Mary the Deadhead is sixteen, and she has been through three years of it already."

Major Radcliffe was speaking, casually, as if remarking it was a warm day. "I'm looking for two missing passengers, identified as Greeks, Chiniara and Drikar by name."

For once Mary had nothing to say. Tom began to whistle softly. Suddenly the Major opened the connecting door behind him. The empty compartment seemed to interest him, especially the bare wooden floor.

He glanced up at Tom. "What became of the two passengers in Number Eight?"

"Were there two?" said Tom, seeming surprised.

The Major turned his attention to Mary. "Young lady," he murmured, "you weren't in Number Eight, were you? You don't seem to have any other place—or a Syrian entrance visa. I'm afraid—"

Mary shook her head vigorously. "Please—I sat down in the corridor."

"Quite." The Major lifted an eyebrow at Kevorkian. "Don't you remember two passengers booked through to Aleppo? One was quite stout, a book dealer who escaped from Greece ten days ago? The other—"

Kevorkian's thumb cracked; then his lined face cleared. "Ah, those! They descended from the car at Adana. Yes, the one who was fat and the other." He waved a hand.

"Really?" Radcliffe seemed interested in the partition above Hump, and Hump remembered very well how a bullet had splintered the wood there. No, Mr. Chiniara was still to be accounted for, and he, Hump, was guilty.

"How did you hurt your forehead, sir?" the Britisher asked pleasantly.

Hump's voice croaked. "Accident. Bumped into—"

"Quite. I should tell you that the Rumanian family in Number Fourteen heard shots just *after* passing Adana. They were so frightened they locked themselves in until now."

Yes, Hump had known how it would be. He did not try to figure it out, any more. "I shot them—both of them," he said calmly. "They hit me first."

The effect upon Major Radcliffe was not what he had expected. The officer's blue eyes fastened on him as if over the sights of a gun. "Please realize that I am not joking. My orders are to find those two pseudo-Greeks, wherever they may be."

Hump sat still. It was worse than he had figured on. It didn't make sense, this young Britisher being hard as steel.

Tom stirred. "What might *pseudo* be, Major?"

Mary's eyes flickered, as if beholding a new vista opening up. "Major—you want to *find* them?"

"And how, as the Americans say."

"But, why?"

Radcliffe was still cold, inexorable. Carefully he looked at Mary. "Because we were advised by our people in Istanbul that certain Axis agents had been working out of the Balkans with identification as refugees. These two, Chiniara and Drikar—to give their passport names—were on this train in this sleeping-compartment. Our man on the train noticed that they threw something out of their window at Adana. But they hardly threw themselves out the window."

"Uh-uh," said Tom. "*We* did that."

Something inside Hump relaxed, and he blinked at the hot sunlight.

"The rats," Tom observed. "Your man tipped me off to expect trouble."

"Certainly," barked Kevorkian. "No Greek would be fat like Chiniara after only one week escaped from Greece."

"No Greek would have hair oil from Paris," put in Mary excitedly.

"That being the case," said Radcliffe, "will somebody tell me the truth, now?"

Mary chirped up first, rubbing one foot against the other,

almost falling down in trying to say everything at once in American English. "All right, Butch. This mild Victorian gentleman knowing nothing of this war, he drops your two men in a gun-fight like nobody's business. And now, please, he is still suffering from shock, so will you give him a place on a plane direct to Cairo, where he can rest.

"Also, this American courier, he is late with dispatches, and he must have a place in the plane, the first B.O.A.C. plane. And"—she faltered under the officer's scrutiny—"since I can't enter Syria, will you please put me also on the plane, because in Cairo I can get a job as nurse with the Ela Greeks from Macedonia who are being fed there. And"—her dark eyes swept Tom Hatfield—"maybe God will give a way to go to America, like He passed Saint Paul through the Taurus Gates. Is it a deal, Major? Three places on the first plane, and you have your men like the Royal Canadian Whoosis, only dead."

To Hump's surprise, the officer voiced no shocked protest. Apparently he was accustomed to dark and devious methods of travel at this war frontier. "The plane can be arranged, of course," he said. "If—"

Mary flashed him only one glance, like the Queen of Sheba giving the eye to Solomon. "Do your stuff," she cried at Hump.

Because he was relaxed and warm inside, Hump could relate clearly now how he had figured out the sliding catch on the door, and what he stepped into. Now that the compartment door stood open, behind Radcliffe, those constant images of Chiniara and Drikar were gone.

The Major made a note in a small memorandum book. Then he looked at Hump, while the others kept silent.

"That story of yours, Mr. Ward," the Major remarked cheerfully, "has not one bit of evidence to support it. By your own statement, the evidence is buried in the snow down the slopes of the Taurus mountains."

"Nuts," put in Tom. "I tell you I helped chuck it out."

"I examined the two men," cried Mary the Deadhead, "and I am a trained nurse. They were corpses."

"And for identification," boomed Kevorkian, waving his long

arm, "I, a soldier of Macedonia, can swear their passports were the men you say."

Radcliffe scribbled a word in his memorandum book and closed it.

"The evidence of three independent witnesses," he said, "is sufficient. I'll ring the airdrome."

Snowball in July

By Ellery Queen

*"S*NOWBALL IN JULY" is another "impossible crime" story—not a railroading locked-room this time, but the account of an entire passenger train in upstate New York that seems, incredibly, to have vanished as if by magic. (To my knowledge, the only other detective story to use this challenging premise is Sir Arthur Conan Doyle's "The Lost Special." Ellery Queen's solution, however, is much less complicated and much more credible.)*

In the formal mystery story, just as in stage magic acts, illusion is everything. What you see happening is exactly what the author wants you to see, no more and no less; the result, of course, is that the reader is baffled—until the truth behind the illusion is revealed to him, at which time he is likely to say, as I did the first time I read this tale, "Of course. How simple. I should have known." Queen has few peers in preparing and presenting this special brand of legerdemain.

EQ, the pseudonym of the writing team of Frederick Dannay and the late Manfred B. Lee, is universally recognized as the preeminent authority on mystery and detective fiction; similarly, Ellery Queen's Mystery Magazine, which the team founded in 1943, is recognized as the preeminent showcase for the best short work of crime writers throughout the world. The character of Ellery Queen has appeared in dozens of novels, hundreds of short stories, several theatrical films in the 1940s, a long-running radio show, and most recently the network TV series starring Jim Hutton (now lamentably canceled). Which leaves only stage plays, and I wouldn't be surprised to hear any day now that one is scheduled to open on Broadway. I wonder if anthologists are entitled to free tickets. . . .

At playful moments Diamond Jim Grady liked to refer to himself as a magician, a claim no one disputed—least of all the police. Grady's specialty was jewel robbery at gunpoint, a branch of felonious vaudeville which he had elevated to an art form. His heists were miracles of advance information, timing, teamwork, and deception. And once he got his hands on the loot it vanished with the speed of light, to be seen no more in the shape the manufacturing jeweler had wrought.

Grady's most spectacular trick was keeping himself and his fellow artists out of jail. He would drill his small company without mercy in the wisdom of keeping their mugs covered, their mitts gloved, and their traps shut while on stage. There was rarely a slip in his performances; when one occurred, the slipping assistant disappeared. As Diamond Jim reasonably pointed out, "What witness can identify a slob that ain't here?"

Grady might have gone on forever collecting other people's pretties and driving the law and insurance companies mad, but he pulled one trick too many.

In explanation it is necessary to peep into Diamond Jim's love life. Lizbet had been his big moment for two years and ten months—a slim eyestopper as golden and glittery as any choice piece in his collection. Now, in underworld society a romantic attachment of almost three years' duration is equivalent to an epic passion, and Lizbet may be forgiven the folly of having developed delusions of permanence. Unfortunately, that was not all she developed; include an appetite for pizza pies and French ice cream, and along with it her figure. So when one night Grady's bloated eye cased the dainty anatomy of Maybellene, pivot girl of the Club Swahili line, that was all for Lizbet.

One of Grady's staff, a lovelorn lapidary who could grind an ax as well as a diamond, tipped Lizbet the bad news from a phone booth in the Swahili men's room even as Diamond Jim prepared toothily to escort Maybellene home.

Lizbet was revolted at the perfidy of man. She also realized that unless she lammed with great rapidity her life was not worth the crummiest bangle on the junk counter of the nearest Five-and-Dime. She knew far, far too many of Diamond Jim's professional secrets; she even knew where a couple of bodies—of ex-slobs—were buried.

So Lizbet took barely the time to grab an old summer mink and a fistful of unaltered mementoes from Grady's latest personal appearance before she did an impromptu vanishing act of her own.

Immediately Lizbet became the most popular girl in town. Everybody wanted her, especially the police and Grady. The smart money, doping past performances strictly, was on Grady, but this time the smart money took a pratfall. Lizbet was not in town at all. She was in Canada, where—according to every Royal Northwest movie Lizbet had ever seen—the Mounties were large and incorruptible and a girl could think without worrying about stopping a shiv with her back. Having thought, Lizbet hung the summer mink about her plump shoulders, taxied to the nearest police station, and demanded protection and immunity in exchange for a pledge to take the witness stand back home and talk herself, if need be, into lockjaw.

And she insisted on being ushered into a cell while Montreal got in touch with New York.

The long-distance negotiations took twenty-four hours. Just long enough for the news to leak out and inundate the front pages of the New York newspapers.

"So now Grady knows where she is," fumed Inspector Queen. He was on special assignment in charge of the case. "He'll go for her sure. She told Piggott and Hesse when they flew up to Montreal that she can even drape a first-degree murder rap around Grady's fat neck."

"Me," said Sergeant Velie gloomily, "I wouldn't give a plugged horse car token for that broad's chances of getting back to New York with a whole hide."

"What is Grady, a jet pilot?" asked Ellery. "Fly her down."

"She won't fly—has a fear of heights," snapped his father. "It's on the level, Ellery. Lizbet's the only girl friend Grady ever had who turned down a penthouse."

"Train or car, then," said Ellery. "What's the hassle?"

"A train he'd make hash out of," said Sergeant Velie, "and a car he'd hijack some truck to run off the road into a nice thousand-foot hole."

"You're romancing."

"Maestro, you don't know Grady!"

"Then you're tackling this hind end to," said Ellery negligently. "Dad, have Grady and his gang picked up on some charge and locked in a cell. By the time they're sprung, this woman can be safe on ice somewhere in Manhattan."

"On ice is where she'll wind up," said Sergeant Velie. "And speaking of ice, who's for a bucket of Thomas Collins?"

When Ellery found that Diamond Jim had anticipated interference and disappeared with his entire company, including Maybellene, a respectful glint came into his eye.

"Let's pull a trick or two of our own. Grady will assume that you'll get Lizbet to New York as quickly as possible. He knows she won't fly and that you wouldn't risk the long trip by car. So he'll figure she'll be brought down by rail. Since the fastest way by rail is through express, it's the crack Montreal train he'll be gunning for. Does he know Piggott and Hesse by sight?"

"Let's say he does," said Inspector Queen, perking up notwithstanding the heat, "and I see what you mean. I'll fly Johnson and Goldberg up there along with a policewoman of Lizbet's build and general appearance. Piggott and Hesse take the policewoman onto the Special, heavily veiled, while Goldie and Johnson hustle Lizbet onto a slow train—"

"You think this Houdini plays with potsies?" demanded Sergeant Velie. "You got to do better than that."

"Oh, come, Sergeant, he's only flesh and blood," said Ellery soothingly. "Anyway, we're going to do better than that. To befuddle him completely, somewhere along the route we'll have her taken off and complete the trip by automobile. In fact, Dad, we'll take her off ourselves. Feel better, Velie?"

But the Sergeant shook his head. "You don't know Grady."

So Detectives Goldberg and Johnson and an ex-chorus girl named Policewoman Bruusgaard flew to Montreal, and at the zero hour Detectives Piggott and Hesse ostentatiously spirited Policewoman Bruusgaard—veiled and sweltering in Lizbet's mink—into a drawing room on the Canadian Limited. Thirty minutes after the Limited rolled out of the terminal Detectives Johnson and Goldberg, attired as North Country backwoodsmen and lugging battered suitcases, swaggered behind Lizbet into the smoking car of a sooty, suffocating all-coach local express entitled laughingly in the timetables The Snowball. Lizbet was in dowdy clothes, her coiffure was now blue-black, and her streaming face—scrubbed clean of heavy makeup—seemed a sucker's bet to fool even Grady, so many wrinkles and crow's-feet showed.

And the game was en route.

For on a sizzling hot morning in July two unmarked squad cars set out from Center Street, Manhattan, for upstate New York. In one rode the Queens and Sergeant Velie, in the other six large detectives.

The Sergeant drove lugubriously. "It won't work," he predicted. "He operates practically by radar. And he can spot and grease an itchy palm from nine miles up. I tell you Grady's got this up his sleeve right now."

"You croak like a witch doctor with bellyache," remarked Inspector Queen, squirming in his damp clothes. "Just remember, Velie, if we don't get to Wapaug with time to spare—"

Wapaug was a whistlestop on the C. & N. Y. Railroad. It consisted of several simmering coal piles, a straggly single street, and a roasted-looking cubby of a station. The two cars drove up to the brown little building, and the Inspector and Ellery went inside. No one was in the hotbox of a waiting room but an elderly man wearing sleeve garters and an eyeshade who was poking viciously at the innards of a paralyzed electric fan.

"What's with The Snowball?"

"Number 113? On time, mister."

"And she's due—?"

"10:18."

"Three minutes," said Ellery. "Let's go."

The cars had drawn up close, one to each end of the platform. Two of the six detectives were leaning exhaustedly against an empty handtruck. Otherwise, the baked platform was deserted.

They all squinted north.

10:18 came.

10:18 went.

At 10:20 they were still squinting north.

The stationmaster was in the doorway now, also squinting north.

"Hey!" rasped Inspector Queen, swatting a mosquito. "Where was that train on time? In Vermont?"

"At Grove Junction." The stationmaster peered up the tracks, which looked as if they had just come out of a blast furnace. "Where the yards and roundhouse are. It's the all-train stop two stations north."

"Train 113 stops at the next station north, too, doesn't she? Marmion? Did you get a report on her from Marmion?"

"I was just gonna check, mister."

They followed him back into the hotbox, and the elderly man put on his slippery headphones and got busy with the telegraph key. "Marmion stationmaster says she pulled in and out on time. Left Marmion 10:12."

"On time at Marmion," said Ellery, "and it's only a six-minute run from Marmion to Wapaug—" He wiped his neck.

"Funny," fretted his father. It was now 10:22. "How could she lose four minutes on a six-minute run? Even on this railroad?"

"Somethin's wrong," said the stationmaster, blowing the sweat off his eyeshade band. He turned suddenly to his key.

The Queens returned to the platform to stare up the local track toward Marmion. After a moment Ellery hurried back into the waiting room.

"Stationmaster, could she have switched to the express track at Marmion and gone right through Wapaug without stopping?" He knew the answer in advance, since they had driven along the railroad for miles in their approach to Wapaug; but his brains were frying.

"Nothin's gone through southbound on these tracks since 7:38 this mornin'."

Ellery hurried out again, fingering his collar. His father was sprinting up the platform toward the squad car. The two detectives had already rejoined their mates in the other car and it was roaring up the highway, headed north.

"Come on!" shouted Inspector Queen. Ellery barely made it before Sergeant Velie sent the car rocketing toward the road. "Somehow Grady got onto the trick—a smear, a leak at headquarters! He's waylaid The Snowball between here and Marmion—wrecked it!"

They kept watching the ties. The automobile road paralleled the railroad at a distance of barely twenty feet, with nothing between but gravel.

And there was no sign of a passenger train, in motion or standing still, wrecked or whole. Or of a freight, or even a handcar. Headed south—or, for that matter, headed north.

They almost zoomed through Marmion before they realized that they had covered the entire distance between the two stations. The other car was parked below the weathered eaves of an even smaller shed than the one at Wapaug. As they shot back in reverse, four of the detectives burst out of the little station.

"She left Marmion at 10:12, all right, Inspector!" yelled one.

"Stationmaster says we're crazy. We must have missed it!"
The two cars rocked about and raced back toward Wapaug.
Inspector Queen glared at the rails flashing alongside. "Missed
it? A whole passenger train? Velie, slow down—!"

"That Grady," moaned Sergeant Velie.

Ellery devoured a knuckle and said nothing. He kept staring
at the glittering rails. They winked back, jeering. It was
remarkable how straight this stretch of track between Marmion
and Wapaug was, how uncluttered by scenery. Not a tree or
building beside the right of way. No water anywhere; not so much
as a rain puddle. No curves, no grades; no siding, spur line,
tunnel, bridge. Not a gully, gorge, or ravine. And no sign of
wreckage. . . . The rails stretched, perfect and unburdened, along
the hellish floor of the valley. For all the concealment or trickery
possible, they might have been a series of parallel lines drawn
with a ruler on a sheet of blank paper.

And there was Wapaug's roasted little station again.

And no Snowball.

The Inspector's voice cracked. "She pulls into Grove Junction
on time. She gets to Marmion on time. She pulls out of Marmion
on time. But she doesn't show up at Wapaug. Then she's got to
be between Marmion and Wapaug! What's wrong with that?"
He challenged them, hopefully, to find something wrong with it.

Sergeant Velie accepted. "Only one thing," he said in a hollow
voice. "She ain't."

That did it. "I suppose Grady's palmed it!" screamed his
superior. "That train's between Marmion and Wapaug somewhere, and I'm going to find it or—or buy me a ouija board!"

So back they went to Marmion, driving along the railroad at
ten miles per hour. And then they turned around and crept
Wapaugward again, to shuffle into the waiting room and look
piteously at the stationmaster. But that railroad man was sitting
in his private oven mopping his chafed forehead and blinking at
the shimmering valley through his north window.

And no one said a word for some time.

When the word came, everyone leaped. "Stationmaster!"
said Ellery. "Get your Marmion man on that key again. Find

out if, after leaving Marmion at 10:12, The Snowball didn't turn back."

"Back?" The elderly man brightened. "Sure!" He seized his telegraph key.

"That's it, Ellery!" cried Inspector Queen. "She left Marmion southbound all right, but then she backed up north *past* Marmion again for a repair, and I'll bet she's in the Grove Junction yards or roundhouse right now!"

"Grove Junction says," whispered the stationmaster, "that she ain't in their yards or roundhouse and never was—just went through on time. And Marmion says 113 pulled out southbound and she didn't come back."

And all were silent once more.

But then the Inspector slapped at a dive-bombing squadron of bluebottle flies, hopping on one foot and howling. "But how can a whole train disappear? Snowball! Snowball in July! What did Grady do, melt her down for ice water?"

"And drank her," said Sergeant Velie, licking his lips.

"Wait," said Ellery. "Wait . . . I know where The Snowball is!" He scuttled toward the door. "And if I'm right we'd better make tracks—or kiss Lizbet goodbye!"

"But *where?*" implored Inspector Queen as the two cars flashed north again, toward Marmion.

"Down Grady's gullet," shouted the Sergeant, wrestling his wheel.

"That's what he wanted us to think," shouted Ellery in reply. "Faster, Sergeant! Train leaves Marmion and never shows up at the next station south, where we're waiting to take Lizbet off. Vanishes without a trace. Between Marmion and Wapaugh there's nothing at all to explain what could have happened to her—no bridge to fall from, no water or ravine to fall into, no tunnel to hide in, no anything—just a straight line on flat bare country. Marvelous illusion. Only the same facts that give it the appearance of magic explain it. . . . No, Velie, don't slow down," Ellery yelled as the dreary little Marmion station came into view. "Keep going north—past Marmion!"

"North past Marmion?" said his father, bewildered. "But the train came *through* Marmion, Ellery, headed south. . . ."

"The Snowball's nowhere south of Marmion, is it? And from the facts it's a physical impossibility for her to be anywhere south of Marmion. So she *isn't* south of Marmion, Dad. *She never went through Marmion at all.*"

"But the Marmion stationmaster said—"

"What Grady bribed him to say! It was all a trick to keep us running around in circles between Marmion and Wapaug, while Grady and his gang held up the train between Marmion and Grove Junction! Isn't that gunfire up ahead? We're still in time!"

And there, four miles north of Marmion, where the valley entered the foothills, cowered The Snowball, frozen to the spot. A huge trailer-truck dumped athwart the local tracks had stopped her, and judging from the gun flashes, she was under bombardment of half a dozen bandits hidden in the woods nearby.

Two figures, one lying still and the other crawling toward the woods dragging a leg, told them that the battle was not one-sided. From two of the shattered windows of a railroad car a stream of bullets poured into the woods. What Grady & Co. had not known was that Northwoodsmen Goldberg and Johnson had carried in their battered suitcases two submachine guns and a large supply of ammunition.

When the carful of New York detectives broke out their arsenal and cut loose on the run, the Grady gang dropped their weapons and trudged out dejectedly with their arms up. . . .

Ellery and the Inspector found Lizbet huddled on the floor of the smoking car with assorted recumbent passengers, in a litter of hot cartridge shells, while Detectives Johnson and Goldberg prepared rather shakily to enjoy a couple of stained cigarets.

"You all right, young woman?" asked the Inspector anxiously. "Anything I can get you?"

Lizbet looked up out of a mess of dyed hair, gunsmoke, sweat, and tears. "You said it, pop," she hissed. "That witness chair!"

All of
God's Children
Got Shoes

By Howard Schoenfeld

*A*LTHOUGH *"All of God's Children Got Shoes" is about hoboes, it deals with a wholly different breed of the species than James M. Cain's story earlier (a third tale involving floaters which appears later in these pages is yet again different). Nor is it a murder story, or even a crime story except in a certain sociological sense. What it is is a beautifully underplayed, straightforward account of two men in the postwar South who would rather be called thieves than bums, and whose cavalier attitude toward life and the law masks a frightening truth. The suspense here is a product not so much of the events described as of characterization and dialogue (what is said and what is not said)—a crackling undercurrent of menace as effective as that which is more apparent and direct.*

Howard Schoenfeld has published but a handful of short stories and one very good softcover private-eye novel, Let Them Eat Bullets, *all of which appeared in the 1950s and all of which are*

memorable for the above-mentioned virtues of realistic dialogue,
understatement, and careful character development. He lives in
New York City, where, I'm pleased to report, he is at work on a
new book.

We headed south on our way to Florida, but only got as far
as Georgia before it got too cold. In Georgia we were picked up
and put in jail as vagrants. We worked on the road gang for two
months until it began getting warm again, and they let us go.
They gave us 50 cents a day for every day we worked on the
road gang, and we had $30 apiece when they turned us loose,
and had had warm beds all winter and been fairly comfortable,
but it had been a long time to go without a drink.

We took our money and went to the first bar we could find
in Macon, and left it there. By then it was warm enough to go
back on the road, so we managed a wine jug, went down to the
Macon railroad yards, and grabbed a freight going toward
Birmingham. It was one of those local freights that stop everywhere and are always backing up and maneuvering around. This
one had a yard engine on it and was twice as slow as it should
have been, even for a local. We opened an empty boxcar and
crawled in, leaving the door open so sunlight could get in. There
were some empty toesacks on the floor, and we sat on them while
the train started moving. Then we hit the wine jug.

Carl, sitting with his back against the wall, pulled his foot
up to his knee and tried to do something about the sole of his
shoe. The sole was coming off.

"These shoes are all shot to pieces. I've got to get a new pair
somewhere," he said.

"You should have bought a pair when we had the money to
pay for them," I said.

"Yeah," Carl said. "I guess so."

"You could get a pair for nothing if you weren't so stubborn."

"Where?" Carl asked.

"At the Salvation Army in Birmingham."

"Not me. You'll never catch me in one of those places. I'm no bum," Carl said.

"You can't go around barefooted."

"Don't worry. I'll get shoes all right."

"How? You going to start stealing again?" I asked.

"What if I do? It's nothing to you."

"You'd rather be a thief than bum a pair of shoes."

"I'm no bum. You're not either," Carl said.

"Yes, I am. We're both bums."

"You make me sick talking like that. We aren't bums and you know it," Carl said.

"Yeah, I know."

"Then shut up, will you?"

"O.K. Don't get excited."

"O.K."

We sat there a few minutes, the train now going at full speed, and sunlight streaming in on the floor of the boxcar.

"Sometimes you forget," I said.

"What're you talking about?" Carl asked.

"Laws. They don't apply to us any more. We know they don't, but sometimes we start acting as if they do," I said.

"Yeah. You're right about that. Laws don't apply to us. We're just a couple of thieves," Carl said, grinning.

"No. We're a couple of 'gentlemen of the open road,' " I said.

"Alcoholic gentlemen," Carl corrected, passing me the jug.

"Very, very alcoholic," I said, taking it. We both laughed.

The train slowed down and stopped, cars bumping together. Up front they were taking on coal and water. Where we were we could see two or three farmhouses, trees in their front yards, and cows in the back. As soon as the train got watered and coaled and started off slowly again, a boy came out of one of the houses carrying a grip. He ran to the boxcar we were in and threw his grip inside. Then he crawled in. His grip had a college sticker on it, so we knew he was a college boy.

"Howdy, fellows," the college boy said.

"Morning, bud," Carl said.

The college boy sat down and dangled his feet out of the door of the boxcar as the train got going. He was a tall, stout fellow with red hair. His face muscles were thick.

"Better not sit like that. You're liable to lose a foot," Carl said.

The college boy got up and found a toesack. He sat on it the way we were, with his back against the wall, feet stretched out straight on the floor in front of him.

"It's dangerous riding with your feet out. You might hit a cow guard. They'll knock your legs off, shoes and everything, just like that," Carl said. He snapped his fingers to show how.

"Thanks for telling me," the college boy said.

"That's all right. What size shoe do you wear?" Carl asked, politely.

"Why, uh, nine and a half, I guess. Why?"

"That's too big. Nothing."

"Shut up, Carl," I said.

"Where you bound for?" Carl asked.

"Tupelo, Mississippi. I go to college there."

"You don't want to ride this train. You want to get off at the next town and wait for a hot shot. You'll never get anywhere on this train," Carl said.

"Why?"

"This is a local. It stops everywhere. Takes its time."

"Oh."

"What do you study at Tupelo?" I asked.

"Economics, sociology, philosophy—stuff like that."

"I went to college once," Carl said.

"Did you play football?" the college boy asked.

"No. I got the Phi Beta Kappa key."

"Aw, I don't believe that! You wouldn't be doing this if you had the key."

Carl took the key out of his watch pocket.

"Here it is. I've never pawned it," he said proudly.

"That's the key all right, but it's pretty hard to believe. Why don't you go to work?"

Carl laughed. "I'm too delicate for work."

I caught the college boy's eye and nodded at the jug. The college boy stared at it, then at Carl, and then at me. He was goggle-eyed.

"Cripes," he said, "when I get back to Tupelo I'll write an article for the local papers about you guys."

"Thank you," Carl said. "You don't know how much that means to me."

"Why don't you spend an entire day with us? You could write a whole novel about us then," I said.

"No, I have to go back to school."

"I'd like to read a novel about us," Carl said.

"You could call it *Gentlemen of the Open Road*," I urged.

"Or *Alcoholic Gentlemen of the Open Road*," Carl suggested.

"Or *Very, Very Alcoholic Gentlemen of the Open Road*," I said.

"No," the college boy decided. "But I saw a movie about people like you a couple of years ago. Ray Milland played the lead. Parts of it were almost poetic."

"I feel poetic sometimes," Carl said.

"So do I. Would you like to hear me recite *The Shooting of Dan McGrew*?" I asked.

"The hero of the movie became a bowery bum because he couldn't stop drinking. He even pawned his typewriter," the college boy said.

"That's very tragic. I wouldn't want to lose a typewriter that way, would you, chum?" Carl asked.

"No. I can't imagine anything more tragic that pawning a typewriter," I said.

"How did you fellows become tramps?" the college boy asked.

"We're not tramps. We're thieves," Carl said.

"Don't pay any attention to him. He's half nuts," I said.

After that we didn't talk much until we got to Gurdon. The train stopped at Gurdon, where there was a depot, ten or twelve frame houses, a gas station, and a general store. When the train stopped, Carl turned to the college boy.

"Here's where you get off," he said.

"I think I'll stay on this train awhile," the college boy said.

"You thought we were bums. We don't like you, kid. You'll have to get off here," Carl said.

"Why?"

"I said here's where you get off. You going to make trouble?"

"Not if that's the way you feel about it."

"That's the way we feel about it. Get out."

"All right," the college boy said.

He picked up his grip and got out of the boxcar and walked away toward the gas station at Gurdon. There were hitchhikers standing at the station.

Carl got up and looked out.

"That was a nice pair of shoes he had on," he said.

"Yeah. Cordovan," I said.

"They were too big for me," Carl said.

A woman came over to our car from the gas station and started to get in. She was wearing overalls and was young and had a hard face. I could see her from where I was sitting.

"You can't get on here," Carl said.

"Why not?" the woman in overalls asked.

"We don't want you. Get off."

"I will not. I've got as much right here as you have," she said.

She was trying to get in the boxcar, hunching on her elbows on the edge of the door at Carl's feet. She was halfway on and halfway off, her legs dangling.

"All right, you asked for it," Carl said.

He put his foot on her shoulder and pushed. The woman in the overalls fell back on the ground with a thud, in a sitting position.

She sat there cursing as the train started moving slowly, Carl standing at the door.

"What did you do that for?" I asked.

"I got to get a pair of shoes. How many people you think I want around?"

The train was going a little faster. We had left the woman in overalls behind. A hitchhiker came out of the gas station and ran over to the boxcar we were in, carrying a grip. The hitchhiker trotted alongside the open door and tossed his grip in.

Carl got a hold on an upright and leaned out.

"Here you are, pal. Take my hand," he said. He pulled the hitchhiker in.

"Thanks."

"That's all right." Carl sat down again.

The hitchhiker picked up his grip and sat down, too, with the grip near him. He was a dark-haired man of medium height, with eyes of an odd amber color. His clothes were good. He wore a brown gabardine suit and had on brown shoes. He looked out of place in a boxcar.

The train was going fast now. The hitchhiker was lucky to have been able to get on after he threw his grip inside.

"Those are nice shoes you're wearing," Carl said.

"Yeah," the hitchhiker said. "They ought to be. They cost enough."

"They look like a rich man's shoes. You must be rich," I said.

"What size are they?" Carl asked.

"Size eight. I'm not rich."

"You dress like you're rich," I said.

"I'm a reporter. I work for a living."

"I've always wanted to meet a reporter," Carl said. "Who do you report for?"

"A newspaper in New York. You probably never heard of it."

"Probably not."

"That's why I'm on the bum. I'm writing a series of articles on what's happening to the underprivileged during the current boom. We still have our underprivileged with us, you know. Even now."

"So I've heard," Carl said. He was eyeing the hitchhiker's expensive shoes.

"You don't look like you've been bumming," I said.

"No. I've only been on the road two days. I sleep in hotels at night."

"How long will it take you to get the information you want?"

"Three more days."

"That will make five days you've spent on the road. Will you know enough to write the articles then?" I asked.

"Yes. I knew enough before I started."

"How?"

"Reading things. Statistics, among other things."

"I see."

"You ought to do some reading yourself. You wouldn't stand for this situation."

"What situation?"

"This situation where some people have everything and others have nothing."

"I don't know why you're complaining. You're wearing a fine pair of shoes," Carl said.

"That isn't the point. It isn't right that I have a pair of good shoes and you don't."

"I should like to have your shoes," Carl said.

"Then you agree with me."

"No. I only want your shoes. Will you give them to me?"

"No. Why should I?"

"You won't give me your shoes?"

"No."

"You believe in some kind of a cause?"

"In a way. Yes."

"Would you die for it?"

"I'd like to think I would."

"Would you be a martyr?"

"If I had to be," the hitchhiker said nervously. "Yes."

"You shall," Carl said.

"What do you mean?" the hitchhiker asked, alarmed.

Carl pulled his knife out of his pocket and stood up. He pressed the handle of the knife, and the blade shot out, long, slim, and dangerous-looking.

The hitchhiker licked his lips.

"You shall die a martyr to my cause. My cause is a pair of shoes," Carl explained.

The hitchhiker went into a funk, his amber eyes darting in their sockets quickly. He took his shoes off in a hurry.

"You can have the shoes. I don't want them. Here, take them."

He held out the shoes. They had come off in record-breaking time. He was in a funk, his hands shaking and his eyes rolling. He looked at me. I was having a fine time. So was Carl.

Carl walked toward the hitchhiker, the knife in his hand. The reporter dropped the shoes. Carl reached down and grabbed him by the arm.

"It's too late now. You should have given them to me when I asked for them. You might go to the cops. It's too bad, but I'll have to kill you."

The hitchhiker, looking at the knife in Carl's hand and then at me, started screaming.

"I won't go to the cops. I don't want to die," he screamed. "Oh, God."

"Pray," Carl said. He lifted his knife hand and touched the man's neck with the point of the blade.

"Oh, God—"

Suddenly he broke into a screech, jerked loose from Carl, ran in his stocking feet to the door of the boxcar, and jumped out of the moving train.

Carl ran over to the door of the boxcar and stared out. I ran over too. The train was going through level country, and we could see back pretty well. I leaned out as far as possible, holding onto the door. Backward nothing could be seen for a couple of minutes except farmhouses, and fields under cultivation. Then we saw the hitchhiker get up slowly and brush himself off. He stood there awhile, brushing and getting his bearings. He limped away from the tracks, walking gingerly over the ground in his stocking feet, toward a nearby farmhouse.

"Whew," Carl said. "That was a dumb trick. It's a wonder he wasn't killed."

"It's a good thing he took a running jump. He might have fallen under the wheels."

"What did he want to jump off for? I wasn't going to hurt him. I wouldn't kill anybody," Carl said.

"He didn't figure it that way."

"Well, to hell with him. Look at these shoes." Carl was looking at the soles. "They aren't bad."

He handed me the shoes. They were a pretty good pair.

"See if you can get me a pair like these," I said. "You've got good taste for a thief."

Carl grinned. He liked being called a thief. He was afraid somebody might think he was a bum.

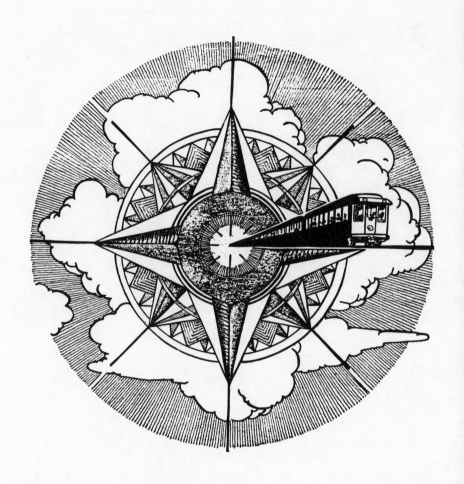

1951 – Today – and Tomorrow...

The Sound
of Murder

By
William P. McGivern

*W*HEN *the terms "intrigue," "espionage" and "mystery"*
are mentioned in connection with trains, two words come instantly
to everyone's mind: Orient Express. The mystique surrounding
this late-lamented (born, 1883; died, 1962) trans-European
passenger train, the first and long-reigning monarch of its kind, is
due in part to a series of fantastic true adventures in which it
was involved—and in part to such brilliant novels as Graham
Greene's Stamboul Train *and Agatha Christie's* Murder on the
Calais Coach, *as well as such films as Alfred Hitchcock's* The
Lady Vanishes *and Carol Reed's* The Night Train. *More*
fictional murders (and a couple of factual ones) have been
committed in its wagons-lits cars between Paris and Istanbul
than on any other type of public conveyance.

But there is even more to the mystique than that. In order to
fully understand it, I think one has to have been fortunate enough
to ride either the "Magic Carpet to the East" itself or a similar

189

*old-fashioned European express. Late in 1971 my wife and I
occupied a compartment on just such a train traveling by night
from Munich to Vienna and then, without us, to Budapest. We
hurtled through darkness and unfamiliar countryside, toward a
place I had never been and things I had never seen; we were
surrounded by strangers, most of whom spoke languages I did
not understand. The steady rattling throb-and-sway of those old
trains assaults the senses, so that one hears and sees and feels
things more acutely; and it heightens the imagination as well,
making anyone with a scowl look a bit sinister, any attractive
woman look secretive and alluring. This is no exaggeration. The
experience was stimulating, fascinating—just as it must have been
for countless other romantically inclined travelers. It is such
stimulation, such fascination, that helps to inspire both the
creation of entertainment and the nurturing of legends.*

*"The Sound of Murder," one of the best and more restrained
of the shorter works about the Express d'Orient, captures some
of the flavor of the great train without dwelling on melo-
dramatic stereotypes. It is also a first-rate crime story, as
evidenced by at least two magazine reprintings since its original
appearance in 1952. Its creator, William P. McGivern, is well
known in suspense-fiction circles as the author of several fine
novels, including* The Savage Streets, Odds Against Tomorrow,
and the award-winning But Death Runs Faster; *he has also
written a number of screenplays. His most recent book,* Night
of the Juggler *(1975), is slated for production as a major film.*

The Orient Express stops for an hour or more at the Yugoslav-
Trieste border. Customs are a formality as a rule, but the changing
of foreign currencies into dinars takes quite a bit of time.

Knowing this, Adam James yawned slightly as the train pulled
into Sesana. He wasn't really bored; he merely wished he were
in Belgrade, at work, instead of here at the frontier. He rubbed
the window of his compartment with the palm of his hand. There

was little to see outside—uniformed customs officials waiting to board the train, an oiler walking down the opposite track, and beyond the wooden station, white foothills under a dark sky. It was a cheerless prospect; the hills were huddled together, as if the earth had hunched its shoulders against the bitter weather.

The customs officer knocked and entered, bringing in a touch of coldness on his clothes and breath. He was cordial and efficient, and bowed himself out with a smile a few minutes later. The money-control officer was equally cordial, but his work took more time. Finally he too went away, and Adam sat down with his book, a dull but important one on Yugoslavian politics, and lit his pipe.

However, his moment of peace was brief. The argument between the couple in the adjoining compartment flared up again, and he closed his book with a sigh. They had been at it, off and on, since the Express had left Trieste an hour or so ago, and the partition between the compartments was so thin that Adam could hardly ignore the noise. They spoke Croatian or Serbian, neither of which he understood, but the anger in their voices was unmistakable—no matter what the language.

He had noticed them in Trieste where they had boarded the train. The woman was very attractive, with light blond hair, clear fresh skin, and the slender, gracefully muscled legs of a dancer. She was in her early thirties, Adam had guessed, and wore a plum-colored tweed suit under a good fur coat. The man was stout and florid, with small alert eyes and a manner of petulant importance. He was fastidiously turned out in a black overcoat with a fur-trimmed collar, a black Homburg, and, rather inevitably Adam had thought, carried a cane. His gray flannel trousers were sharply creased, and his spats gleamed whitely against his glossy black shoes.

There was something about them, some constraint in their manner, that had caught Adam's attention. They said little to each other as they waited to board the train, but there was a quality in the set of their shoulders which indicated they had plenty to say and were only waiting for the chance to say it.

Unfortunately for himself, Adam thought, they got their chance when they were finally alone in their compartment. At first he'd been mildly interested in their bickering; but as they became angrier and louder, he had become bored and irritated.

There was a knock on the door, and the conductor entered. He was a small, neatly built man with quick intelligent eyes, and had a tiny black mustache above a generous but cautious mouth.

"Your passport, sir," he said, handing Adam the slim green gold-lettered booklet. "Everything is in order. You will not be disturbed again until we arrive in Belgrade."

"Thanks, but I haven't been disturbed," Adam said.

The conductor raised his eyebrows. "That's an unusual reaction for an American. Most of you are—well, impulsive. You have no patience."

"Oh, there are all types of Americans," Adam said with a smile. "Also, there are all types of French, British, and even Yugoslavians, I imagine."

"No, you are wrong. Here in Yugoslavia we grow up with the land, and become like it, slow and patient. You Americans are different. Excitable, I mean. You leap at things. That is desirable in some matters, but it can also cause trouble."

"Well, that may be," Adam said. He had spent fifteen years of his life as a foreign correspondent, and his job, reduced to an oversimplification, was to find out what people thought, and why they thought it. He was interested in the conductor's opinions, and he wanted to put the man at ease. He raised a hand as the argument in the next compartment broke out again. "Are they Americans?" he asked innocently.

"No, of course not."

"Well, *they* seem pretty excitable."

The conductor looked blank. Then he smiled good-humoredly. "I asked for that, as you say. No, they are Yugoslavians. The Duvecs—she is a dancer, and he is an actor." The conductor listened to the argument with a little smile. "The artistic temperament," he said. "Well, I must go on with my work. I have not offended you with my directness, eh?"

"Certainly not. Stop by when you get a minute and we'll finish our talk."

"Thank you, I shall try."

The conductor went away and Adam returned to his book. He was grateful, a chapter later, when the train began to move. Sesana was behind them now. They would pass Zagreb sometime after dinner and be in Belgrade the following morning. He would have been almost cheerful if it weren't for the argument in the next compartment.

The couple had reached a new and higher pitch after a few moments of blessed silence. The woman's voice was shrill now, where before it had been somewhat controlled. The man shouted at her whenever she ceased speaking. This continued for a few moments, and then Adam heard the door of the compartment jerked open energetically. The man shouted a last sentence or two; then the door was banged shut with angry finality. Adam heard the man's heavy footsteps pass his door and fade away in the direction of the dining-car.

"Well, well," he thought, "peace at last!" There was nothing quite like a door-slamming exit to put an end to an argument. Perversely, however, now that everything was quiet, he lost interest in his book. He decided to have dinner and finish his reading later—though probably by then the argument would be on again, he thought wryly, and he'd berate himself for missing the present opportunity.

He washed his face, combed his hair, and walked through the lurching train to the dining-car. There were two third-class coaches connected to the *wagon-lit*, filled with stolid, impassive soldiers who endured the unheated compartments with the stoic acceptance of domestic animals.

There was no menu on the Express, just the one *préfixe* dinner: soup, roast veal and vegetables served with a theoretically white but in fact orange-colored Dalmatian wine. This was followed by stewed prunes and thick sweet Turkish coffee.

The man in the fur-trimmed overcoat, Duvec, was seated at the far end of the diner, hungrily and belligerently attacking a bowl of soup. He wore an angrily righteous look, Adam thought, and was probably reviewing the argument with his wife in the most favorable possible light. Duvec wore his overcoat buttoned up to the throat, and occasionally put down his spoon and rubbed his plump hands together to warm them, though the diner wasn't cold; Adam was comfortable enough in his suit-coat.

The sleeping-car conductor entered the diner a few moments later, looking pale and agitated. He glanced about quickly; then, striding to Duvec's table, he bent and whispered a few words. Their effect was electric. Duvec sprang to his feet, almost overturning his table, and his mouth opened and closed soundlessly.

"Please come with me," the conductor said in a firm voice.

The two men hurried from the car, the other diners staring after them curiously. Adam frowned at the tablecloth for a moment or so, oddly disturbed. Finally, obeying a compulsion he didn't quite understand, he rose and started back through the train for the sleeping-car. But at the vestibule he was stopped by a blue-uniformed mail-car guard. The man put a hand against Adam's chest.

"You must not enter," he said in slow, laborious English.

"But this is my car," Adam said.

"You must not come in."

"Has something happened?"

The guard merely shook his round head stubbornly.

At this point the sleeping-car conductor appeared in the opposite vestibule. He opened the door and spoke a few words to the mail-car guard, and the man took his hand from Adam's chest.

"You may come in," the conductor said.

"What has happened?" Adam asked.

"A great tragedy, a great tragedy," the conductor said, rubbing his mustache nervously. Adam became aware that the train was slowing down.

"We're stopping?" he asked.

"Yes, yes. Please come inside."

Adam followed him into the sleeping-car and turned the corner into the aisle. Duvec stood before the open door of his compartment, sobbing terribly. Beyond him, held by two mail-car guards, was a stocky Yugoslavian soldier in a patched and dirty uniform. Duvec turned away from his compartment and sagged weakly against the wall. He beat a fist slowly against his forehead, and his lips opened and closed as if he were praying.

Adam stepped forward and glanced into Duvec's compartment. He knew what he would see. Somehow he had anticipated this; but it was still a jarring, shocking sight. Mrs. Duvec lay on the floor in the careless, undignified sprawl of death. One slender leg was doubled under her body, and a lock of blond hair lay across her pale throat. The bronze handle of a letter-opener—or a knife—protruded from between her breasts.

The train had come to a full stop. There was no sound as Adam stepped back from the compartment except Duvec's hoarse, strangled sobs.

The conductor touched Adam's arm. "You will be good enough to remain in your compartment, please. I have sent a messenger back to the police at Sesana. We will wait until they arrive."

"Naturally," Adam rejoined. "But what happened?"

"It was the soldier. He thought all the passengers were in the dining-car. He came in to pilfer what he could, I imagine. He was surprised when he found the woman here; he lost his head—" The conductor shrugged eloquently. "It is a great tragedy."

The soldier seemed to understand what was being said. His eyes were wild and frightened. He suddenly shouted, *"Nil! Nil!"* and chattered out a stream of words which Adam didn't understand.

"He protests his innocence," the conductor said matter-of-factly. "That is to be expected."

"He lies, he lies!" Duvec said in a ragged voice. "He killed my wife, and he must die for it."

"There is no doubt he is guilty," the conductor agreed. "We can establish that easily. Your wife was alive when you left her?"

"Yes, yes! My God, yes!" Duvec cried. He began to sob again, hopelessly, piteously. "We had a quarrel, a silly, stupid quarrel, and I left in anger. But she was alive, alive as we are now." He glanced at Adam, as if noticing him for the first time. "But *you* must have heard our quarrel."

"Yes, I heard it," Adam said.

"Then you heard our voices until the moment I left."

Adam nodded. "Yes, I heard you."

The conductor shrugged. "Then there is proof that she was alive when her husband left. The soldier admits going into her compartment—but at that point he loses his love for the truth."

"What's his story?" Adam asked.

"He says that Mrs. Duvec was already dead. This is why he attempted to flee, he tells us."

"Who caught him?"

"I had appointed a guard for this car while I worked out space plans with the attendant in the next car," the conductor said. "We get a crowd at Zagreb, and it is necessary to prepare for them in advance, you see. I appointed a guard because the sleeping-car is empty during the dinner hour, and the soldiers— well, you understand how it is with soldiers. The guard, a man from the mail-car, was at the opposite vestibule—that is, he was at the other end of the car from where we now stand. Something caused him to turn and glance down the aisle. He saw the soldier backing out of the Duvecs' compartment. He shouted, and the soldier attempted to run back to his own car. But the guard caught him, fortunately."

"What caused the guard to look down the aisle?"

The conductor raised his eyebrows. "Who can tell? The good Lord, perhaps; it was an impulse—and it apprehended a murderer. The guard will be officially congratulated."

"Yes, yes, of course," Adam muttered. "Catching murderers is always a cause for congratulations. Whose knife did the soldier use, by the way?"

The conductor looked blank. He turned to Duvec, who said, "It was my wife's letter-opener. Perhaps she was using it when the soldier burst in on her."

"That is logical," the conductor said, nodding. "We will get the truth from him, all of it; you will see."

Suddenly the soldier shouted wildly and broke away from his two guards. He ran down the narrow aisle, jerked open the door at the end of the car, and disappeared. The guards lumbered after him, and Duvec screamed, "Get him, get him, the murderer!"

The conductor remained calm. "He cannot leave the train,"

he said. "The vestibule doors are secured from the outside. That was my first order. He will be caught, never fear."

Adam glanced at Duvec and the conductor, frowning. Finally he said, "Excuse me, please," and entered his own compartment. He sat down and lit his pipe.

Something was wrong about all this, wrong as the very devil, and he could feel it in his bones. But how could he prove it? He stretched his long legs out in front of him and rested his head against the back of the seat. Proof . . . where was it? He puffed on his pipe, trying to recall everything that had happened since the Express left Trieste. He sorted out all the details he could remember, and juggled them into different relationships, turned them upside down and inside out, trying desperately to justify his conviction.

The conductor appeared in his doorway ten minutes later, wearing a small pleased smile. "It is finished," he said. "We have caught him. He sought to hide in the coal-car, but was found."

Adam stood up and began knocking the dottle from his pipe. "That's fine," he said. "The only thing is, you've got the wrong man."

"The wrong man? Impossible! His guilt is proven by his attempt to escape."

"Nonsense. He's simply scared out of his wits. Bring everyone here, and I'll show you the murderer," Adam said, marveling slightly at the ring of confidence in his voice.

The conductor squared his shoulders stubbornly. "This is a police matter, I must remind you."

"Yes, but it won't redound to your credit to present them with an innocent suspect when they arrive."

The conductor rubbed his thin black mustache. "Very well," he said at last. "I am not afraid to test your opinion against mine. I have reached my conclusions logically. I am not in error."

"We'll see," Adam said.

The soldier was brought back down the aisle, securely held by two mail-car guards. He was not more than eighteen, Adam saw, a strongly built youth with a dull face and blank hopeless eyes; obviously he had resigned himself to his fate. Duvec, who still wore his fur-trimmed overcoat, stood at the end of the aisle, occasionally rubbing a hand despairingly over his broad forehead.

Adam was in the doorway of his compartment. The soldier and his guards were at his left, Duvec and the conductor on his right. They all watched him expectantly.

"This soldier did not kill Mrs. Duvec," Adam said quietly.

"What do you know about it?" Duvec shouted.

"If you will listen, you will find out."

"I will not listen. You have no authority here."

"Silence!" the conductor said in a sharp voice. "I am in charge until the police arrive. I have given the American permission to speak."

"Thank you," said Adam. "I'll continue. As I have said, the soldier did not kill Mrs. Duvec. I think I can prove that to everyone's satisfaction. First of all, has it not struck you as odd that the guard in this car did not hear Mrs. Duvec scream?"

For an instant there was silence. Then the conductor said, "She was struck down before she could cry out." However, Adam's question brought a tiny frown to his face.

"I think that's an unlikely explanation," Adam said. "Let's reconstruct what must have happened if the soldier is the murderer. First, he opened the door of the compartment. Mrs. Duvec looked up at him, startled and probably frightened. What would one expect her to do? Scream, of course."

"My wife was no silly maiden," Duvec snapped. "She would not scream at the sight of a man; she would have ordered him from the compartment. That is unquestionably what happened. She asked him to leave, ordered him to leave. He took advantage of that moment to seize the letter-opener from her and plunge it into her heart. Yes, he silenced her before she could scream."

The conductor nodded, looking somewhat relieved. "Yes, certainly that is it," he said.

"No, that isn't it," Adam said. "Why would a strong, agile young man use a knife on a woman? If he wanted to silence her, he would use his hands. In the time it would take him to grasp the knife away from her, and strike her down with it, she might have screamed half a dozen times. And yet, I repeat, the guard in this car heard no sound at all from Mrs. Duvec."

The conductor shook his head impatiently. "You are making up theories. We are dealing with facts. According to your own testimony, Mrs. Duvec was alive when her husband left the compartment. She was dead when the soldier left the compartment. Those are the facts. No one but the soldier could have killed her."

"You're wrong, but it's partly my fault," Adam said. "I've misled you. However, I'll clear things up now. There's the murderer," he said—and he pointed at Duvec.

"Monstrous!" Duvec shouted. "I will not stand for these slanders."

"Let me ask you this," Adam said. "Why are you wearing a heavy overcoat in a comfortably heated train? What is under it, Duvec? Or, more to the point, what *isn't* under it?"

"I don't know what you're talking about," Duvec snapped.

"I'll tell you, then," Adam said. "What *isn't* under that overcoat is your suit-coat—the suit-coat which was bloodied when you murdered your wife. When I saw you in the diner I knew something was odd. You wouldn't have worn an overcoat all the way from Trieste, so you must have put it on before leaving your compartment. However, the emotional fireworks accompanying your departure made it seem unlikely that you would have stopped to put on an overcoat. That routine bit of business would have shattered the effect of your exit. But why wear the coat at all? The train isn't cold. Therefore, I decided, it was worn not for comfort but for camouflage. And what was it you were so eager to camouflage?"

"You are talking like a madman," Duvec said. "My wife was alive when I left her. You know that is true. You said you heard us."

"I said I heard *you*," Adam corrected him. "Duvec, you killed your wife in a moment of rage. This puts you in a tough predicament. There was a witness of sorts to the crime—an auditory witness, in the next compartment—myself, of course. But I could be used to your advantage. You could create the illusion that your wife was alive when you left her by taking both parts of the dialogue for a moment or so before banging out of the compartment. This was no trick for an actor. Meanwhile, as you imitated your wife's voice, you removed your bloodstained suit-coat and got into your overcoat. Then you left the compartment with a final artistic bellow at your wife. The suit-coat, I'll bet, you either hid in your compartment or threw off the train on the way to the diner. In either event, a search will produce it."

"Talk, talk, talk!" Duvec cried.

"Take off your overcoat," said Adam.

"This is childish nonsense," Duvec said angrily. He unbuttoned his overcoat and flung it open. He wore a gray tweed jacket above gray flannel trousers. There was a little silence in which Adam felt his stomach contract unpleasantly. "Are you satisfied now?" Duvec said contemptuously.

The conductor had unconsciously placed a hand on Duvec's arm as Adam had talked. Now he removed it hastily. "Forgive me," he said.

"Wait a minute," Adam said, frowning. He had noticed that Duvec wore ruby cuff-links. What was wrong with that?

"No—enough," the conductor said angrily. "There will be no more of these wild accusations."

"No, I'm right," Adam snapped. "He wouldn't wear cuff links with a tweed jacket, any more than he'd wear black shoes with a brown suit. Of course! He changed into the tweed jacket and hid the bloodstained suit-coat underneath the overcoat. He threw the suit-coat out one of the vestibule doors. He was fairly safe then; at least he had an alibi. But luck joined forces with him and provided the crime with a reasonable suspect. The soldier blundered onto the scene and put Duvec completely into the clear. But it won't work. I'll bet one hundred dollars to a dinar that the police will find a bloodstained flannel jacket within ten miles of this spot."

Duvec began to weep. "I can stand no more!" he cried. "My wife is dead, and I hear myself called her murderer!" He turned aside, still sobbing, and put a hand to the vestibule door for support. The gesture was so natural that no one noticed him reach for the doorknob. He jerked open the door and was into the vestibule before anyone could move. The conductor shouted at the mail-car guards who still held the soldier. They plunged out of the car after Duvec, with the conductor on their heels.

They caught him in the next coach and dragged him back to the sleeping-car. Duvec offered no resistance. He stared straight ahead with shoulders slumped, and there was an expression of terrible anguish on his face. Adam realized that for the first time since the murder of his wife Duvec had ceased to act.

In a low, trembling voice he said, "She was going to leave me, you see. I—couldn't stand that. I—couldn't."

Half an hour later the conductor came to Adam's compartment. "You must excuse me," he said rather sheepishly. "I think of what I said about the excitable Americans, and my face becomes hot with shame. I must apologize."

"Please don't worry about that," Adam said.

"But I do not understand completely. Your proof was not overwhelming, I do not think. And yet you seemed so *sure*."

"I was sure," Adam said. "You see, in the classic tradition, Duvec made one mistake which I didn't bother to mention. When he acted out the scene with his dead wife, he engineered the dialogue badly. He shouted a few last words at her, you will remember, and then banged the door."

The conductor looked blank. Finally he rubbed his mustache and smiled slowly.

"You understand, of course," Adam said. "In Yugoslavia or America, anywhere for that matter, arguments between husbands and wives very seldom end that way. When I realized that, I knew Duvec was guilty. Mrs. Duvec wouldn't have let him get away with the last word—if she were alive, that is."

"But of course," the conductor agreed, nodding gravely.

The Train

By Charles Beaumont

ADULTS HAVE *various reactions to trains and train travel, ranging from indifference to fascination; but how does an inventive child react to them? Do his sensitivity and imagination make of them something they are not? Or, conversely, do this same sensitivity and imagination perhaps give him a truer understanding of them than our own? The theme of Charles Beaumont's "The Train" is centered around these questions and around that terrible moment in one's life when he loses forever his innocence and becomes something less than he might have been.*

The considerable suspense here does not depend for its effects on conventional topics—murder, intrigue, personal peril from another human being. Rather, it builds through a series of simple events and circumstances which are made terrifying primarily because they are seen through the eyes of a little boy. Few authors are able to write effectively from the point of view of a child;

Beaumont's story is all the more remarkable for his ability to do so with depth, feeling and insight.

Charles Beaumont, who died tragically in the early 1960s, was a consummate craftsman of the modern "popular market" short story—perhaps the finest writer of this type of fiction to publish in the 50s. He wrote extensively for Playboy, *and his strongest work for this and other magazines appears in two superior collections,* The Hunger and Other Stories *(1958) and* Night Ride and Other Journeys *(1960). Much of his writing is concerned with the bizarre and/or the psychological; all of it is as effective as it is entertaining.*

Neely was the little hand on a clock; he was the mercury in a thermometer: he moved and he didn't move. Hours it had taken just to pull off the bedclothes, because Mother slept quietly and the train had stopped lurching—*hours*—and now he must push his body up and swing his legs over the side of the berth.

He lay barely breathing, his toes strained against the cool hardness of the metal. How long since they turned the lights off? From the corner of his eye he looked at Mother, and even from the back he could tell she had not yet fallen into a deep sleep. Any little thing woke her up when she was like this. Sometimes she sat right up when the train passed over a rough track section. So he knew he couldn't move any farther. Because then she would wake and turn over and ask him what was the matter.

Neely thought of excuses rapidly, rejected rapidly. Say that he had to go to the bathroom? No; she'd want to help him and that would be terrible. Besides, he'd already been—twice, in fact. That he was turning over? No; she'd want to know why the covers were off. Ill, his stomach hurt—no, no, that would spoil everything. There would be the pills that he couldn't swallow and the porters running to telegraph doctors and everything in a mess.

There was no excuse. He'd have to wait, for—something.

Soft light from the moon and moving stars streamed in through the half-shaded windows, making the small bed cool and blue. The heavy green curtains were black now, and the light made the sheets crisp. Neely loved the coolness and the comfort of the berth, and he knew that tomorrow night he would sleep. He would slide in between the clean linen, press it tight, watch Mother load up the green net, take one look around him before the overhead lamp snapped off and then relax and let the gentle swaying put him to sleep. He looked forward to tomorrow night. But it had been almost a year since the last time, and there was much to do, much to see and feel. . . . So he had gone to bed promptly and without a fuss and waited.

Neely clenched his teeth and tried not to listen to the wheels. He kept his eyes open, fighting all the seductive sensations. He *had* to stay awake! For the Trip.

The train groaned and swayed and rocked and clicked and far ahead it cried mournfully, hot steam rushing out of its iron throat like dragon's breath in the dark unfriendly night.

Clicketa-clicketa-clacketa-clicketa . . . go-to-sleep-go-to-sleep . . . clicketa-clicketa . . .

Neely fought so hard he almost didn't hear the snore. It was a soft snore, but sharp, like a cough, and when he did hear, his heart began to pain him. He waited, praying. The sound came again, and now he could tell: it had happened. Mother was really asleep—sound asleep. She wouldn't hear him now. She wouldn't wake and ask him questions and scold him.

He could leave now.

Quickly then, synchronizing each short move with each considerable noise or jar, Neely climbed out of the berth. He stopped when his feet touched the rough floor-carpet and watched Mother. She had not stirred. The snores became regular and deeper. Neely smiled and pulled the black suitcase out from under the berth and took from it his old terrycloth bathrobe and leather slippers. Then he carefully pulled the curtains together and buttoned them.

The car was dark and silent: only a dim blue light at the end and the sound of the distant iron wheels. The heavy curtains were all drawn shut, some bulging with the weight of restive bodies, some falling over regularly set shoes. The quiet green hall of sleep.

Neely grinned and thrilled. Things started to come back. It was the same Train he loved and thought about all the time, the same. And he could spend hours going through it, all by himself this time, with no one to direct him or stop him. It was here, right before him, what he'd dreamed about during the long dull days at school and in the ugly house where Mother and Father lived.

He held his robe and slippers and tiptoed past the sealed berths into the narrow rocking hall. He stopped for a moment before the brown-painted case with its ominous brown ax, thought briefly of breaking the glass and grabbing the ax and screaming "Fire! Fire!" and shrugged and went into the room with the curtain for a door.

It glistened with five spotless white sinks and a maze of silver tubes. It was the room Neely loved best, next to the Phantom Car, so he stood on the cold floor for a time, playing with every delicious memory. And thinking, Nothing has changed—it won't ever change!

In the tiny light, he tried out the smells first. The strong smells of iron and soap and stale cigar smoke, of good leather and bright spittoons—more fragrant than the blood of every vanquished giant who ever lived. Then the sign, which started in serious dignity: IT WOULD BE APPRECIATED IF PASSENGERS— He tried out each experience, one by one. . . .

The full-length mirror held the image of the small boy and flattered him. Neely ran a hand through his blond hair and made several hideous faces and then adjusted his robe until it was perfect. He thought of going into the watercloset and reading the sign there, but that took time and there was much to see. There was the Phantom Car, waiting, miles ahead.

He did not see the face peering out from the opening in the corner curtains, the big friendly face with the laughing eyes.

"Hey, young fella, you goin' in or what?"

The voice was an explosion, a rumbling exploded nightmare, before it became familiar.

It was the porter. And he slept where car porters sleep.

"Hello," Neely said, feeling caught.

The man laughed and shook his head. "Boy, your mama know you up this late?"

"Yes sir, she does. . . ."

"Well, okay, all right, get on with what you doin'. Don't let *me* disturb you!"

The curtains closed again and Neely could hear the chuckling.

He walked out of the room back into the hall and let the air go out of his lungs. Then he went to the heavy door and pushed hard and got it open.

The air was cold between cars: he could feel it blowing through all the sections and giggled as he fell and had to grab the rail.

It was all the same! But better, infinitely better, because he was alone, all by himself to see it. The necklace of stars moving slowly out the window, the moaning iron-rubbing-iron and the great wonderful comfort of even the dangerous sliding plates.

He knew he'd have to hurry. It must be very late—hadn't the porter said so? Maybe almost morning. But he had to sort out things, and this seemed the best place to get it over with.

Mother had asked him once why he loved the Train, and he hadn't been able to answer her. She explained that a train was just a way of getting from one place to another, just like a car or a bus or an airplane, and she said she was worried about him always talking about trains.

Why *did* he feel the way he did? Why did he call the train his World, from the beginning?

Looking out the window at the terrible, desolate and unknown night, with all its lonely fears and terrors, he saw, suddenly, one of the reasons. It was—that he was being safe and in danger, at the same time. All the ugly things were whistling by, and he was going right through them. And none of them touched him. He could laugh at them!

The train went over a soft spot in the bed, and the track began another curve. Out the platform window the tiny head of this hollow iron snake could presently be seen, gasping silent orange fire.

Neely balanced himself again and thought about how different it was in an automobile. There you could only sit, and Mother and Father and other people would talk and argue, and you smelled their breath and felt their heavy nearness and you wanted all the time to stretch out your legs, far, always, and you could only sit. And the airplane was no better; just a big automobile in the sky, nothing to do but sit, nothing to see but air. . . .

Neely stopped thinking of reasons. Who cared, anyway? They didn't matter. What mattered was seeing the Train again.

He walked from *Tecumseh* into *Chief Powhatan*, through *Pocahontas* and *Larimie* and *Thundercloud*. And with every step, the other life faded. When he came to *Mt. Rainier* he had forgotten what Mother looked like. At *General Robt. E. Lee* all memories of Father vanished. With each step, the other life peeled away.

When Neely came at last to *Montclair*, there was only the Train. The green walls and the fuzzy rough seat arms and the MEN room and rolling rocking through night. He wasn't a ten-year-old boy any more, but a part—a living part—of the Train.

What was it Mother had said about everything being different this time—about his growing up and facing life?

Neely pushed hard on the handle, his throat tight, mouth dry, wondering vaguely why the last car was always the hardest to open.

He walked into *Montclair*.

There were no lamps, but he could see clearly now. It was the last thrill. No curtains in this car, no line of shoes or friendly porter sleeping. But strange chairs, unattached to the floor, sitting by tables, silver ashtrays leading to the very end. And everything peculiar, somehow . . . as though nobody had ever, ever been here before. Except, perhaps, ghosts.

The Phantom Car, where he was always—even with Mother— most excited and thrilled and delightfully frightened.

The sounds of the Train were loudest here. The metal ashtrays bobbled on their heavy foundations and the leather-covered magazines shifted slightly. And there was the big glass door at the rear . . .

Neely tiptoed slowly down the hall of chairs, looking forward to every moment and despising every moment that slipped into the past. He walked, sure that the car had some sort of meaning for him—for it was really his destination: he had never wanted to walk toward the engine.

The moon slid behind clouds, and it was dark except for small ribbons of glow which fell faintly across the fixtures.

Neely walked.

The door to the observation platform stuck, and for a moment he was terrified, because the moon was still behind clouds. But he tugged and managed to get it open.

Listen, Neely! Listen to the big sharp wind now, how it screams all around you! And see into the night, into the million fear-filled shadows, the cold and lifeless night. Feel the strong iron wheels bump and pound, carrying you through it all. And most important—he went to the railing and put his small hands about the metal—most important, Neely, let it come true. Let it come true!

"Take him by plane, Dora, for God's sake. Don't let him get disappointed. It's the least we can do."

It was as if he only now heard the words: they whispered deep inside his ears, inside his head.

"Or let me drive you up this time. You know what he's made of this thing. Let the kid have that pleasure!"

Strange words that didn't make any sense. . . . But Father had used them. And then Mother had said:

"If you think I'm going to let my child grow up to be a schizophrene, you're wrong, Jeff Fransen. Any psychologist will tell you—children have got to get out of their worlds, and the sooner they do, the better. Do you think we'd be able to keep him off trains the rest of his life?"

"But, honey, he's only ten!"

"Ten-year-old kids write books on sex these days."

"He'll hate us—I'm telling you. If you take him into his

'train' this time and let him get disappointed, he'll hate us."

"Nonsense. You're—honestly, Jeff, you're talking like a first grade pupil, not a college professor."

"All right, all right. You'll be taking him; it's you he'll hate most!"

Neely shook his head of all the crazy words and let the cindery wind claw at his face. He was alone now, in the Train. Everyone else was sleeping and he had seen the Train again.

He stood, holding the rail, feeling the movement, laughing at the night whirling by.

Time was now the little hand on a clock and the mercury in a thermometer. It almost stopped: Neely stood on the platform, holding it all motionless within himself.

He didn't know how many hours were passing, or days, or minutes, maybe. For he had the thought that was the most wonderful of all: the thought of everything staying just like it was. He could stand forever on the platform of his World and never go back. Mother would sleep forever in the faraway berth and Father would be forever waiting and Time would suspend itself as it was now. . . .

The sudden slowing and jogging and voices filled the air, but not Neely's mind. He had thought of all eternity in the Train, so for now his mind was filled and there was not room for more.

"Pull 'er on up ahead to the tank," said a voice. "We'll keep this one here."

"Hotbox on 916—I already told MacCready it'd take about half an hour," said another voice.

"Pull 'er up anyways. We're running late," a third voice called.

The buzz of words, close by. Violet flares. The sound of feet running and then the mile of green cars disconnecting and rumbling ahead, far ahead up the track and out of sight, leaving the last car in the dark, alone.

Then—stillness.

Neely felt the rush of years deliriously, and it was not until he knelt his head to swallow that he saw. The moon had come from

behind its layer of clouds and he saw—that the ground no longer
moved. The cross-ties were not blurred, but stationary, each one
distinct. And the wind had ceased.

He rubbed his eyes, turned and ran the length of the car to
the door. He opened it savagely, strained to see, looked out
into—

The night.

Excitement gathered as he tried to think. He looked again.
Nothing. Just a track leading into blackness, nothing else, no
train; and around him, the hills and trees and . . .

He remembered. His wish! It—had come true! Now he
couldn't go back down the halls of the cars, back to Mother.
And he couldn't ever see the other life again. It was a miracle,
but the Train itself had been a miracle, and this was what he
had wished, above all else.

Neely felt his heart about to explode. He raced back to the
platform and saw the empty tracks.

The tears rushed up, suddenly. What had happened? His wish
had come true: what had happened, *why was he crying*?

He had what he wanted and now was crying, afraid. He was
afraid, afraid. *Why*?

"Please!" Neely screamed. "Please! Make—oh, make it come
back. Make it come back. I don't want to be alone here, I don't
want to be alone in the Train. Please, God!"

He shut his eyes tight, waited and opened them again. Then
he stumbled and fell into a corner and sobbed hysterically,
until he realized what he had been saying: That he hated the
Train, that he really wanted the other life. No, not that—had
to have it. And the strange words began to mold clearly, the
words Father had said to Mother. *"Don't let him get disappointed . . ."*

The Train melted, even as Neely understood. The Room of
Happiness became a washroom; the Train became iron; the
wheels wheels. It all became, slowly, a way to get from one
place to another, a machine invented by somebody years and
years ago, put together by men, used by people.

Neely screamed out his confusion, sobbed until his throat could make no sound.

Then the black darkness came and entered his mind. . . .

The bridge of black was long—it stretched far across Time. Things happened, they had happened, they were happening; people appeared, talking and exclaiming; and Mother, excited, nervous. Neely felt himself lifted and carried by strong hands, carried through illimitable cars gently while the worried words droned louder, louder in consciousness. . . . The bridge ascended when he thought of the empty tracks, so he stopped thinking and pulled the blackness about him as a quilt to keep out the cold.

But the words came through: he could not cover them over. The important ones came like quick fishes, barbed fishes with the big mouths and sharp white teeth.

What's the matter, lady, don't you know better than to leave your kid run all over?. . .

Sorry, ma'am—he probably just got scared is all, maybe just too scared to do anything when he seen we was adding that other car. Thought he was being left behind or something, maybe. . . .

Can you hear us, sonny? You all right? Now now, there's nothing to worry about. It's all over now, all over. See, son, we had what they call a hotbox—that means when something goes wrong, like on a car, you know?—and, see, what we had to do, we had to put on another car. That's all there was to it. . . .

Don't suppose he got sick, do you? . . .

No, that doctor'd of said so, wouldn't he? Kid just got panicky when he seen he was alone. . . .

You think it's all right now, ma'am? You think we ought to get him anything? Or just put him to bed; yeah, that's it, best thing in the world for him. . . .

Neely waited until the pool was clear and all the words had gone away; then he let Mother tuck him in and pull down the shades and pat him with her nervous shaking hands.

"Neely, Neely . . ."

He was tired, so he tried to sleep now. But—the noise disturbed him. And the berth was too narrow. And all the shaking and rocking hurt his head.

He tried only once to remember.

Then he lay back and began to wonder when they would finally get to wherever they were going.

That Hell-Bound Train

By Robert Bloch

ROBERT BLOCH EARNED a considerable measure of fame (if not fortune) from the publication of his novel Psycho and Alfred Hitchcock's subsequent classic film based on the book. But his other credits are even more impressive: hundreds of mystery, science-fiction and fantasy/horror stories; a score of high-quality novels such as The Scarf, Dead Beat, Nightworld, and American Gothic; numerous film and television scripts; a good deal of critical and reader acclaim; and a couple of professional and fan writing awards. "That Hell-Bound Train," in fact, is an award winner; in 1959 it received the coveted Hugo, which is presented by science-fiction fandom in honor of the best long and short works in the genre each year.

One of Bloch's virtues as a writer is his ability to combine suspense and irony with an impish humor that sometimes runs to outrageous puns, and other times, as is the case here, takes the form of tongue-in-cheek whimsy. Another writer said to me

213

recently that "*That Hell-Bound Train*" is the deal-with-the-devil fantasy to end all deal-with-the-devil fantasies; she may well be right. One thing is certain: the story is wholly delightful, with an ending that is fitting and perfect in every way.

When Martin was a little boy, his Daddy was a Railroad Man. He never rode the high iron, but he walked the tracks for the CB&Q, and he was proud of his job. And when he got drunk (which was every night) he sang this old song about *That Hell-Bound Train*.

Martin didn't quite remember any of the words, but he couldn't forget the way his Daddy sang them out. And when Daddy made the mistake of getting drunk in the afternoon and got squeezed between a Pennsy tank-car and an AT&SF gondola, Martin sort of wondered why the Brotherhood didn't sing the song at his funeral.

After that, things didn't go so good for Martin, but somehow he always recalled Daddy's song. When Mom up and ran off with a traveling salesman from Keokuk (Daddy must have turned over in his grave, knowing she'd done such a thing, and with a *passenger*, too!), Martin hummed the tune to himself every night in the Orphan Home. And after Martin himself ran away, he used to whistle the song at night in the jungles, after the other bindlestiffs were asleep.

Martin was on the road for four-five years before he realized he wasn't getting anyplace. Of course he'd tried his hand at a lot of things—picking fruit in Oregon, washing dishes in a Montana hash house—but he just wasn't cut out for seasonal labor or pearl-diving, either. Then he graduated to stealing hub-caps in Denver, and for a while he did pretty well with tires in Oklahoma City, but by the time he'd put in six months on the chain-gang down in Alabama he knew he had no future drifting around this way on his own.

So he tried to get on the railroad like his Daddy had, but they told him times were bad; and between the truckers and the airlines and those fancy new fintails General Motors was making, it looked as if the days of the highballers were just about over.

But Martin couldn't keep away from the railroads. Wherever he traveled, he rode the rods; he'd rather hop a freight heading north in sub-zero weather than lift his thumb to hitch a ride with a Cadillac headed for Florida. Because Martin was loyal to the memory of his Daddy, and he wanted to be as much like him as possible, come what may. Of course, he couldn't get drunk every night, but whenever he did manage to get hold of a can of Sterno, he'd sit there under a nice warm culvert and think about the old days.

Often as not, he'd hum the song about *That Hell-Bound Train*. That was the train the drunks and sinners rode; the gambling men and the grifters, the big-time spenders, the skirt chasers, and all the jolly crew. It would be fun to take a trip in such good company, but Martin didn't like to think of what happened when that train finally pulled into the Depot Way Down Yonder. He didn't figure on spending eternity stoking boilers in Hell, without even a company union to protect him. Still, it would be a lovely ride. If there *was* such a thing as a Hell-Bound Train. Which, of course, there wasn't.

At least Martin didn't *think* there was, until that evening when he found himself walking the tracks heading south, just outside of Appleton Junction. The night was cold and dark, the way November nights are in the Fox River Valley, and he knew he'd have to work his way down to New Orleans for the winter, or maybe even Texas. Somehow he didn't much feel like going, even though he'd heard tell that a lot of those Texans' automobiles had solid gold hub-caps.

No sir, he just wasn't cut out for petty larceny. It was worse than a sin—it was unprofitable, too. Bad enough to do the Devil's work, but then to get such miserable pay on top of it! Maybe he'd better let the Salvation Army convert him.

Martin trudged along, humming Daddy's song, waiting for a rattler to pull out of the Junction behind him. He'd have to catch it—there was nothing else for him to do.

Too bad there wasn't a chance to make a better deal for himself, somewhere. Might as well be a rich sinner as a poor sinner. Besides, he had a notion that he could strike a pretty shrewd bargain. He'd thought about it a lot, these past few years, particularly when the Sterno was working. Then his ideas would come on strong, and he could figure a way to rig the setup. But that was all nonsense, of course. He might as well join the gospel-shouters and turn into a working-stiff like all the rest of the world. No use dreaming dreams; a song was only a song and there was no Hell-Bound Train.

There was only *this* train, rumbling out of the night, roaring towards him along the track from the south.

Martin peered ahead, but his eyes couldn't match his ears, and so far all he could recognize was the sound. It *was* a train, though; he felt the steel shudder and sing beneath his feet.

And yet, how could it be? The next station south was Neenah-Menasha, and there was nothing due out of there for hours.

The clouds were thick overhead, and the field-mists rolled like a cold fog in a November midnight. Even so, Martin should have been able to see the headlights as the train rushed on. But there were no lights.

There was only the whistle, screaming out of the black throat of the night. Martin could recognize the equipment of just about any locomotive ever built, but he'd never heard a whistle that sounded like this one. It wasn't signaling; it was screaming like a lost soul.

He stepped to one side, for the train was almost on top of him now, and suddenly there it was, looming along the tracks and grinding to a stop in less time than he'd ever believed possible. The wheels hadn't been oiled, because they screamed too, screamed like the damned. But the train slid to a halt and the screams died away into a series of low, groaning sounds, and Martin looked up and saw that this was a passenger train. It was big and black, without a single light shining in the engine cab or any of the long string of cars, and Martin couldn't read any lettering on the sides, but he was pretty sure this train didn't belong on the Northwestern Road.

He was even more sure when he saw the man clamber down out of the forward car. There was something wrong about the way he walked, as though one of his feet dragged. And there was something even more disturbing about the lantern he carried, and what he did with it. The lantern was dark, and when the man alighted, he held it up to his mouth and blew. Instantly the lantern glowed redly. You don't have to be a member of the Railway Brotherhood to know that this is a mighty peculiar way of lighting a lantern.

As the figure approached, Martin recognized the conductor's cap perched on his head, and this made him feel a little better for a moment—until he noticed that it was worn a bit too high, as though there might be something sticking up on the forehead underneath it.

Still, Martin knew his manners, and when the man smiled at him, he said, "Good evening, Mr. Conductor."

"Good evening, Martin."

"How did you know my name?"

The man shrugged. "How did you know I was the conductor?"

"You *are*, aren't you?"

"To you, yes. Although other people, in other walks of life, may recognize me in different roles. For instance, you ought to see what I look like to the folks out in Hollywood." The man grinned. "I travel a great deal," he explained.

"What brings you here?" Martin asked.

"Why, you ought to know the answer to that, Martin. I came because you needed me."

"I did?"

"Don't play the innocent. Ordinarily, I seldom bother with single individuals any more. The way the world is going, I can expect to carry a full load of passengers without soliciting business. Your name has been down on the list for several years already—I reserved a seat for you as a matter of course. But then, tonight, I suddenly realized you were backsliding. Thinking of joining the Salvation Army, weren't you?"

"Well—" Martin hesitated.

"Don't be ashamed. To err is human, as somebody-or-other once said. *Reader's Digest*, wasn't it? Never mind. The point is, I felt you needed me. So I switched over and came your way."

"What for?"

"Why, to offer you a ride, of course. Isn't it better to travel comfortably by train than to march along the cold streets behind a Salvation Army band? Hard on the feet, they tell me, and even harder on the eardrums."

"I'm not sure I'd care to ride your train, sir," Martin said. "Considering where I'm likely to end up."

"Ah, yes. The old argument." The conductor sighed. "I suppose you'd prefer some sort of bargain, is that it?"

"Exactly," Martin answered.

"Well, I'm afraid I'm all through with that sort of thing. As I mentioned before, times have changed. There's no shortage of prospective passengers any more. Why should I offer you any special inducements?"

"You must want me, or else you wouldn't have bothered to go out of your way to find me."

The conductor sighed again. "There you have a point. Pride was always my besetting weakness, I admit. And somehow I'd hate to lose you to the competition, after thinking of you as my own all these years." He hesitated. "Yes, I'm prepared to deal with you on your own terms, if you insist."

"The terms?" Martin asked.

"Standard proposition. Anything you want."

"Ah," said Martin.

"But I warn you in advance, there'll be no tricks. I'll grant you any wish you can name—but in return, you must promise to ride the train when the time comes."

"Suppose it never comes?"

"It will."

"Suppose I've got the kind of wish that will keep me off forever?"

"There is no such wish."

"Don't be too sure."

"Let me worry about that," the conductor told him. "No matter what you have in mind, I warn you that I'll collect in the end. And there'll be none of this last-minute hocus-pocus, either. No last-hour repentances, no blonde *frauleins* or fancy lawyers showing up to get you off. I offer a clean deal. That is to say, you'll get what you want, and I'll get what I want."

"I've heard you trick people. They say you're worse than a used-car salesman."

"Now wait a minute—"

"I apologize," Martin said hastily. "But it *is* supposed to be a fact that you can't be trusted."

"I admit it. On the other hand, you seem to think you have found a way out."

"A sure-fire proposition."

"Sure-fire? Very funny!" The man began to chuckle, then halted. "But we waste valuable time, Martin. Let's get down to cases. What do you want from me?"

"A single wish."

"Name it and I shall grant it."

"Anything, you said?"

"Anything at all."

"Very well, then." Martin took a deep breath. "I want to be able to stop Time."

"Right now?"

"No. Not yet. And not for everybody. I realize that would be impossible, of course. But I want to be able to stop Time for myself. Just once, in the future. Whenever I get to a point where I know I'm happy and contented, that's where I'd like to stop. So I can just keep on being happy forever."

"That's quite a proposition," the conductor mused. "I've got to admit I've never heard anything just like it before—and believe me, I've listened to some lulus in my day." He grinned at Martin. "You've really been thinking about this, haven't you?"

"For years," Martin admitted. Then he coughed. "Well, what do you say?"

"It's not impossible in terms of your own *subjective* time-sense," the conductor murmured. "Yes, I think it could be arranged."

"But I mean *really* to stop. Not for me just to *imagine* it."

"I understand. And it can be done."

"Then you'll agree?"

"Why not? I promised you, didn't I? Give me your hand."

Martin hesitated. "Will it hurt very much? I mean, I don't like the sight of blood, and—"

"Nonsense! You've been listening to a lot of poppycock. We already have made our bargain, my boy. No need for a lot of childish rigamarole. I merely intend to put something into your hand. The ways and means of fulfilling your wish. After all, there's no telling at just what moment you may decide to exercise the agreement, and I can't drop everything and come running. So it's better to regulate matters for yourself."

"You're going to give me a time-stopper?"

"That's the general idea. As soon as I can decide what would be practical." The conductor hesitated. "Ah, the very thing! Here, take my watch."

He pulled it out of his vest-pocket; a railroad watch in a silver case. He opened the back and made a delicate adjustment; Martin tried to see just exactly what he was doing, but the fingers moved in a blinding blur.

"There we are." The conductor smiled. "It's all set now. When you finally decide where you'd like to call a halt, merely turn the stem in reverse and unwind the watch until it stops. When it stops, Time stops, for you. Simple enough?"

"Sure thing."

"Then, here, take it." And the conductor dropped the watch into Martin's hand.

The young man closed his fingers tightly around the case. "That's all there is to it, eh?"

"Absolutely. But remember—you can stop the watch only once. So you'd better make sure that you're satisfied with the moment you choose to prolong. I caution you in all fairness; make very certain of your choice."

"I will." Martin grinned. "And since you've been so fair about it, I'll be fair, too. There's one thing you seem to have forgotten. It doesn't really matter *what* moment I choose. Because once I stop Time for myself, that means I stay where I am forever. I'll never have to get any older. And if I don't get any older, I'll never die. And if I never die, then I'll never have to take a ride on your train."

The conductor turned away. His shoulders shook convulsively, and he may have been crying. "And you said I was worse than a used-car salesman," he gasped in a strangled voice.

Then he wandered off into the fog, and the train-whistle gave an impatient shriek, and all at once it was moving swiftly down the track, rumbling out of sight in the darkness.

Martin stood there, blinking down at the silver watch in his hand. If it weren't that he could actually see it and feel it there, and if he couldn't smell that peculiar odor, he might have thought he'd imagined the whole thing from start to finish—train, conductor, bargain, and all.

But he had the watch, and he could recognize the scent left by the train as it departed, even though there aren't many locomotives around that use sulphur and brimstone as fuel.

And he had no doubts about his bargain. Better still, he had no doubts as to the advantages of the pact he'd made. That's what came of thinking things through to a logical conclusion. Some fools would have settled for wealth, or power, or Kim Novak. Daddy might have sold out for a fifth of whiskey.

Martin knew that he'd made a better deal. Better? It was foolproof. All he needed to do now was choose his moment. And when the right time came, it was his—forever.

He put the watch in his pocket and started back down the railroad track. He hadn't really had a destination in mind before, but he did now. He was going to find a moment of happiness . . .

Now young Martin wasn't altogether a ninny. He realized perfectly well that happiness is a relative thing; there are conditions and degrees of contentment, and they vary with one's lot in life. As a hobo, he was often satisfied with a warm handout, a double-length bench in the park, or a can of Sterno made in 1957 (a vintage year). Many a time he had reached a state of momentary bliss through such simple agencies, but he was aware that there were better things. Martin determined to seek them out.

Within two days he was in the great city of Chicago. Quite naturally, he drifted over to West Madison Street, and there he took steps to elevate his role in life. He became a city bum, a panhandler, a moocher. Within a week he had risen to the point where happiness was a meal in a regular one-arm luncheon joint, a two-bit flop on a real army cot in a real flophouse, and a full fifth of muscatel.

There was a night, after enjoying all three of these luxuries to the full, when Martin was tempted to unwind his watch at the pinnacle of intoxication. Then he remembered the faces of the honest johns he'd braced for a handout today. Sure, they were squares, but they were prosperous. They wore good clothes, held good jobs, drove nice cars. And for them, happiness was even more ecstatic; they ate dinner in fine hotels, they slept on innerspring mattresses, they drank blended whiskey.

Squares or no, they had something there. Martin fingered his watch, put aside the temptation to hock it for another bottle of muscatel, and went to sleep determining to get himself a job and improve his happiness-quotient.

When he awoke he had a hangover, but the determination was still with him. It stayed long after the hangover disappeared, and before the month was out Martin found himself working for a general contractor over on the South Side, at one of the big rehabilitation projects. He hated the grind, but the pay was good, and pretty soon he got himself a one-room apartment out on Blue Island Avenue. He was accustomed to eating in decent restaurants now, and he bought himself a comfortable bed, and every Saturday night he went down to the corner tavern. It was all very pleasant, but—

The foreman liked his work and promised him a raise in a month. If he waited around, the raise would mean that he could afford a second-hand car. With a car, he could even start picking up a girl for a date now and then. Lots of the other fellows on the job did, and they seemed pretty happy.

So Martin kept on working, and the raise came through and the car came through and pretty soon a couple of girls came through.

The first time it happened, he wanted to unwind his watch immediately. Until he got to thinking about what some of the older men always said. There was a guy named Charlie, for example, who worked alongside him on the hoist. "When you're young and don't know the score, maybe you get a kick out of running around with those pigs. But after a while, you want something better. A nice girl of your own. That's the ticket."

Well, he might have something there. At least, Martin owed it to himself to find out. If he didn't like it better, he could always go back to what he'd had.

It was worth a try. Of course, nice girls don't grow on trees (if they did, a lot more men would become forest rangers), and almost six months went by before Martin met Lillian Gillis. By that time he'd had another promotion and was working inside, in the office. They made him go to night school to learn how to do simple bookkeeping, but it meant another fifteen bucks extra a week, and it was nicer working indoors.

And Lillian *was* a lot of fun. When she told him she'd marry him, Martin was almost sure that the time was now. Except that she was sort of—well, she was a *nice* girl, and she said they'd have to wait until they were married. Of course, Martin couldn't expect to marry her until he had a little money saved up, and another raise would help, too.

That took a year. Martin was patient, because he knew it was going to be worth it. Every time he had any doubts, he took out his watch and looked at it. But he never showed it to Lillian, or anybody else. Most of the other men wore expensive wrist-watches, and the old silver railroad watch looked just a little cheap.

Martin smiled as he gazed at the stem. Just a few twists and he'd have something none of these other poor working slobs would ever have. Permanent satisfaction, with his blushing bride—

Only getting married turned out to be just the beginning. Sure, it was wonderful, but Lillian told him how much better things would be if they could move into a new place and fix it up. Martin wanted decent furniture, a TV set, a nice car.

So he started taking night courses and got a promotion to the front office. With the baby coming, he wanted to stick around and see his son arrive. And when it came, he realized he'd have to wait until it got a little older, started to walk and talk and develop a personality of its own.

About this time the company sent him out on the road as a troubleshooter on some of those other jobs, and now *he* was eating at those good hotels, living high on the hog and the expense-account. More than once he was tempted to unwind his watch. This was the good life. And he realized it could be even better if he just didn't have to *work*. Sooner or later, if he could cut in on one of the company deals, he could make a pile and retire. Then everything would be ideal.

It happened, but it took time. Martin's son was going to high school before he really got up there into the chips. Martin got the feeling that it was now or never, because he wasn't exactly a kid any more.

But right about then he met Sherry Westcott, and she didn't seem to think he was middle-aged at all, in spite of the way he was losing hair and adding stomach. She taught him that a toupée could cover the bald spot and a cummerbund could cover the potgut. In fact, she taught him quite a number of things, and he so enjoyed learning that he actually took out his watch and prepared to unwind it.

Unfortunately, he chose the very moment that the private detectives broke down the door of the hotel room, and then there was a long stretch of time when Martin was so busy fighting the divorce action that he couldn't honestly say he was enjoying any given moment.

When he made the final settlement with Lil he was broke again, and Sherry didn't seem to think he was so young, after all. So he squared his shoulders and went back to work.

He made his pile, eventually, but it took longer this time, and there wasn't much chance to have fun along the way. The fancy dames in the fancy cocktail lounges didn't seem to interest him any more, and neither did the liquor. Besides, the Doc had warned him about that.

But there were other pleasures for a rich man to investigate. Travel, for instance—and not riding the rods from one hick burg to another, either. Martin went around the world *via* plane and luxury liner. For a while it seemed as though he would find his moment after all. When he visited the Taj Mahal by moonlight, the moon's radiance was reflected from the back of the battered old watch-case, and Martin got ready to unwind it. Nobody else was there to watch him—

And that's why he hesitated. Sure, this was an enjoyable moment, but he was alone. Lil and the kid were gone, Sherry was gone, and somehow he'd never had time to make any friends. Maybe if he found a few congenial people, he'd have the ultimate happiness. That must be the answer—it wasn't just money or power or sex or seeing beautiful things. The real satisfaction lay in friendship.

So on the boat trip home, Martin tried to strike up a few acquaintances at the ship's bar. But all these people were so much younger, and Martin had nothing in common with them. Also, they wanted to dance and drink, and Martin wasn't in condition to appreciate such pastimes. Nevertheless, he tried.

Perhaps that's why he had the little accident the day before they docked in San Francisco. "Little accident" was the ship's doctor's way of describing it, but Martin noticed he looked very grave when he told him to stay in bed, and he'd called an ambulance to meet the liner at the dock and take the patient right to the hospital.

At the hospital, all the expensive treatment and expensive smiles and the expensive words didn't fool Martin any. He was an old man with a bad heart, and they thought he was going to die.

But he could fool them. He still had the watch. He found it in his coat when he put on his clothes and sneaked out of the hospital before dawn.

He didn't have to die. He could cheat death with a single gesture—and he intended to do it as a free man, out there under a free sky.

That was the real secret of happiness. He understood it now. Not even friendship means as much as freedom. This was the best thing of all—to be free of friends or family or the furies of the flesh.

Martin walked slowly beside the embankment under the night sky. Come to think of it, he was just about back where he'd started, so many years ago. But the moment was good, good enough to prolong forever. Once a bum, always a bum.

He smiled as he thought about it, and then the smile twisted sharply and suddenly, like the pain twisting sharply and suddenly in his chest. The world began to spin, and he fell down on the side of the embankment.

He couldn't see very well, but he was still conscious, and he knew what had happened. Another stroke, and a bad one. Maybe this was it. Except that he wouldn't be a fool any longer. He wouldn't wait to see what was still around the corner.

Right now was his chance to use his power and save his life. And he was going to do it. He could still move; nothing could stop him.

He groped in his pocket and pulled out the old silver watch, fumbling with the stem. A few twists and he'd cheat death; he'd never have to ride that Hell-Bound Train. He could go on forever.

Forever.

Martin had never really considered the word before. To go on forever—but *how*? Did he *want* to go on forever, like this; a sick old man, lying helplessly here in the grass?

No. He couldn't do it. He wouldn't do it. And suddenly he wanted very much to cry, because he knew that somewhere along the line he'd outsmarted himself. And now it was too late. His eyes dimmed; there was this roaring in his ears . . .

He recognized the roaring, of course, and he wasn't at all surprised to see the train come rushing out of the fog up there on the embankment. He wasn't surprised when it stopped, either, or when the conductor climbed off and walked slowly towards him.

The conductor hadn't changed a bit. Even his grin was still the same.

"Hello, Martin," he said. "All aboard."

"I know," Martin whispered. "But you'll have to carry me. I can't walk. I'm not even really talking any more, am I?"

"Yes, you are," the conductor said. "I can hear you fine.

And you can walk, too." He leaned down and placed his hand on Martin's chest. There was a moment of icy numbness, and then, sure enough, Martin could walk after all.

He got up and followed the conductor along the slope, moving to the side of the train.

"In here?" he asked.

"No, the next car," the conductor murmured. "I guess you're entitled to ride Pullman. After all, you're quite a successful man. You've tasted the joys of wealth and position and prestige. You've known the pleasures of marriage and fatherhood. You've sampled the delights of dining and drinking and debauchery, too, and you traveled high, wide and handsome. So let's not have any last-minute recriminations."

"All right," Martin sighed. "I guess I can't blame you for my mistakes. On the other hand, you can't take credit for what happened, either. I worked for everything I got. I did it all on my own. I didn't even need your watch."

"So you didn't," the conductor said, smiling. "But would you mind giving it back to me now?"

"Need it for the next sucker, eh?" Martin muttered.

"Perhaps."

Something about the way he said it made Martin look up. He tried to see the conductor's eyes, but the brim of his cap cast a shadow. So Martin looked down at the watch instead, as if seeking an answer there.

"Tell me something," he said softly. "If I give you the watch, what will you do with it?"

"Why, throw it into the ditch," the conductor told him. "That's all I'll do with it." And he held out his hand.

"What if somebody comes along and finds it? And twists the stem backwards, and stops Time?"

"Nobody would do that," the conductor murmured. "Even if they knew."

"You mean, it was all a trick? This is only an ordinary, cheap watch?"

"I didn't say that," whispered the conductor. "I only said that no one has ever twisted the stem backwards. They've all been like you, Martin—looking ahead to find that perfect happiness. Waiting for the moment that never comes."

The conductor held out his hand again.

Martin sighed and shook his head. "You cheated me after all."

"You cheated yourself, Martin. And now you're going to ride that Hell-Bound Train."

He pushed Martin up the steps and into the car ahead. As he entered, the train began to move and the whistle screamed. And Martin stood there in the swaying Pullman, gazing down the aisle at the other passengers. He could see them sitting there, and somehow it didn't seem strange at all.

Here they were: the drunks and the sinners, the gambling men and the grifters, the big-time spenders, the skirt-chasers, and all the jolly crew. They knew where they were going, of course, but they didn't seem to be particularly concerned at the moment. The blinds were drawn on the windows, yet it was light inside, and they were all sitting around and singing and passing the bottle and laughing it up, telling their jokes and bragging their brags, just the way Daddy used to sing about them in the old song.

"Mighty nice traveling companions," Martin said. "Why, I've never seen such a pleasant bunch of people. I mean, they seem to be really enjoying themselves!"

"Sorry," the conductor told him. "I'm afraid things may not be quite so enjoyable, once we pull into that Depot Way Down Yonder."

For the third time, he held out his hand. "Now, before you sit down, if you'll just give me that watch. I mean, a bargain's a bargain—"

Martin smiled. "A bargain's a bargain," he echoed. "I agreed to ride your train if I could stop Time when I found the right moment of happiness. So, if you don't mind, I think I'll just make certain adjustments."

Very slowly, Martin twisted the silver watch-stem.

"No!" gasped the conductor. "No!"

But the watch-stem turned.

"Do you realize what you've done?" the conductor panted. "Now we'll never reach the Depot. We'll just go on riding, all of us, forever and ever!"

Martin grinned. "I know," he said. "But the fun is in the trip, not the destination. You taught me that. And I'm looking forward to a wonderful trip."

The conductor groaned. "All right," he sighed at last. "You got the best of me, after all. But when I think of spending eternity trapped here riding this train—"

"Cheer up!" Martin told him. "It won't be that bad. Looks like we have plenty to eat and drink. And after all, these are *your* kind of folks."

"But I'm the conductor! Think of the endless work this means for me!"

"Don't let it worry you," Martin said. "Look, maybe I can even help. If you were to find me another one of these caps, now, and let me keep this watch—"

And that's the way it finally worked out. Wearing his cap and silver watch, there's no happier person in or out of this world— now and forever—than Martin. Martin, the new brakeman on That Hell-Bound Train.

Inspector Maigret Deduces

By Georges Simenon

*O*F ALL *the classic detectives created by writers of crime and suspense fiction, Georges Simenon's Inspector Maigret is perhaps the most human. While Maigret is of course brilliant in matters deductive, he is also prone to mistakes in judgment, fits of irascibility, impatience, and domestic worries—things with which we can all identify. As a result, the stories and novels about him contain a realism that enhances both the procedural story line and the psychological overtones that mark most of Simenon's fiction.*

"Inspector Maigret Deduces" is a prime example of the flesh-and-blood Maigret at work—on a complex train mystery in which a man is murdered on a European express that is traveling, via points in Belgium, from Berlin to Paris. Given the story's plot, most writers would have required a full-length novel to present it properly and to unravel it. Simenon, happily, is not "most

writers." Which is just one reason why he has achieved a world-wide reputation as a fictioneer par excellence.

Among his enormous output are a number of non-Maigret, in-depth behavioral crime studies; most critics agree that the best of these is The Man Who Watched the Trains Go By *(1946). A middle-period Maigret,* The Negro *(1959), also has a train background.*

Georges Simenon presently lives in Switzerland, where, at the age of seventy-four, he continues to produce first-rate novels at a prolific rate. The most recent, published last year and critically well received, is The Hatter's Phantoms.

Dimly through a deep sleep Maigret heard a ringing sound, but he was not aware that it was the telephone bell and that his wife was leaning over him to answer.

"It's Paulie," she said, shaking her husband. "He wants to speak to you."

"You, Paulie?" Maigret growled, half awake.

"Is that you, Nunk?" came from the other end of the wire.

It was three in the morning. The bed was warm, but the windowpanes were covered with frost flowers, for it was freezing outside. It was freezing even harder up at Jeumont, from where Paulie was telephoning.

"What's that you say? . . . Wait—I'll take the names . . . Otto . . . Yes, spell it; it's safer."

Madame Maigret, watching her husband, had only one question in her mind: whether he would have to get up or not. And of course he did, grumbling away. "Something very odd has happened," he explained, "over at Jeumont, and Paulie has taken it upon himself to detain an entire railway car."

Paulie was Maigret's nephew, Paul Vinchon, and he was a police inspector at the Belgian frontier.

"Where are you going?" Madame Maigret asked.

"First to Headquarters to get some information. Then I'll probably hop on the first train."

When anything happens it is always on the 106—a train that leaves Berlin at 11:00 A.M. with one or two cars from Warsaw, reaches Liége at 11:44 P.M.. when the station is empty—it closes as soon as the train leaves—and finally gets to Erquelinnes at 1:57 in the morning.

That evening the car steps had been white with frost, and slippery. At Erquelinnes the Belgian customs officials, who had virtually nothing to do as the train was on its way out, passed down the corridors, looking into a compartment here and there, before hurrying back to the warmth of the station stove.

By 2:14 the train got under way again to cross the frontier, and reached Jeumont at 2:17.

"Jeumont!" came the cry of a porter running along the platform with a lamp. "Fifty-one minutes' wait!"

In most of the compartments the passengers were still asleep, the lights were dimmed and the curtains drawn.

"Second- and third-class passengers off the train for customs," echoed down the train.

And Inspector Paul Vinchon stood frowning at the number of curtains that were drawn back and at the number of lights turned up. He went up to the conductor. "Why are there so many traveling first-class today?"

"Some international convention of dentists that starts in Paris tomorrow. We have at least twenty-five of them as well as the ordinary passengers."

Vinchon walked into the car at the head of the train, opened the doors one after the other, growling out mechanically, "Have your passports ready, please."

Wherever the passengers had not wakened and the light was still dimmed, he turned it up; faces rose out of the shadows, swollen with fatigue.

Five minutes later, on his way back up the corridor, he passed the customs men who were going through the first-class compartments, clearing the passengers into the corridor, while they examined the seats and searched every cranny.

"Passports, identity cards . . . "

He was in one of the red-upholstered German carriages. Usually these compartments held only four passengers, but because of the invasion of dentists this one had six.

Paulie threw an admiring glance at the pretty woman with the Austrian passport in the left corner seat by the corridor. The others he hardly looked at until he reached the far side of the compartment, where a man, covered with a thick rug, still had not moved.

"Passport," he said, touching him on the shoulder.

The other passengers were beginning to open their suitcases for the customs officials, who were now arriving. Vinchon shook his sleeping traveler harder; the man slid over on his side. A moment later Vinchon had ascertained he was dead.

The scene was chaotic. The compartment was too narrow for all the people who crowded in, and when a stretcher was brought in, there was some difficulty in placing the extremely heavy body on it.

"Take him to the first-aid post," Inspector Vinchon ordered. A little later he found a German doctor on the train.

At the same time he put a customs official on guard over the compartment. The young Austrian woman was the only one who wanted to leave the train to get some fresh air. When she was stopped, she gave a contemptuous shrug.

"Can you tell me what he died of?" Vinchon asked the doctor.

The doctor seemed puzzled; in the end, with Vinchon's help, he undressed the dead man. Even then there was no immediate sign of a wound; it took a full minute before the German pointed out, on the fleshy chest, a mark that could hardly be seen. "Someone stuck a needle into his heart," he said.

The train had still twelve or thirteen minutes before leaving again. The special Inspector was absent. Vinchon, feverish with excitement, had to make a snap decision: he ran to the station-master and gave orders for the murder car to be uncoupled.

The passengers were not sure what was happening. Those in the adjoining compartments protested when they were told that the car was staying at Jeumont and that they would have to find seats elsewhere. Those who had been traveling with the dead man protested even more when Vinchon told them he was obliged to keep them there till the next day.

However, there was nothing else for it, seeing that there was a murderer among them. All the same, once the train had left, one car and six passengers short, Vinchon began to feel weak at the knees, and rang up his uncle, the famous Inspector Maigret.

At a quarter to four in the morning Maigret was at the Quai des Orfèvres; only a few lights were burning and he asked a sergeant on duty to make him some coffee. By four o'clock, with his office already clouded with pipe smoke, he had Berlin on the line, and was dictating to a German colleague the names and addresses his nephew had given him.

Afterward he asked for Vienna, as one of the passengers in the compartment came from there, and then he wrote out a telegram for Warsaw, for there had also been a lady from Vilna by the name of Irvitch.

Meanwhile, in his office at the station at Jeumont, Paul Vinchon was taking a firm line with his five suspects, whose reactions varied according to their temperaments. At least there was a good fire on—one of those large station stoves that swallows up bucket after bucket of coal. Vinchon had chairs brought in from the neighboring offices, and good old administrative seats they were, too, with turned legs and shabby velvet upholstery.

"I assure you I am doing everything possible to speed things up, but in the circumstances I have no choice but to detain you here."

He had not a minute to lose if he wanted to draw up anything like a suitable report for the morning. The passports were on his desk. The body of Otto Braun—the victim's name, according to the passport found in his pocket—was still at the first-aid post.

"I can, if you like, get you something to drink. But you will have to make up your minds quickly—the buffet is about to close."

At ten past four Vinchon was disturbed by a ring on the telephone. "Hello? Aulnoye? What's that? Of course. There's probably some connection, yes. Well, send him over by the first train. And the packet, too, of course."

Vinchon went into an adjoining office to put through another call to Maigret unheard.

"Is that you, Nunk? Something else, this time. A few minutes ago, as the train was drawing into the station at Aulnoye, a man was seen getting out from under a car. There was a bit of a chase, but they managed to get him in the end. He was carrying a waxed-paper packet of bearer bonds, mostly oil securities, for quite an amount. The man gave his name as Jef Bebelmans, native of Antwerp, and his profession as an acrobat . . . Yes . . . They're bringing him over on the first train. You'll be on that one, too? . . . No? . . . At 10:20? Thanks, Nunk."

And he returned to his flock of sheep and goats, which is the way he thought of them . . .

When day broke, the frosty light made it seem even colder than the night before. Passengers for a local train started to arrive, and Vinchon worked on, deaf to the protests of the detained passengers, who eventually subsided, overwhelmed with fatigue.

No time was lost. This was essential, for it was the kind of business that could bring diplomatic complications. One could not go on indefinitely holding five travelers of different nationalities, all with their papers in order, just because a man had been killed in their railway compartment.

Maigret arrived at 10:20, as he said he would. At 11:00, on a siding where the death car had been shunted, the reconstruction of the crime took place.

It was a little ghostly, with the gray light, the cold, and the general weariness. Twice a nervous laugh rang out, indicating that one of the lady passengers had helped herself too freely to the drinks to warm herself.

"First of all, put the dead man back in his seat," Maigret ordered. "I suppose the curtains on the outside window were drawn?"

"Nothing's been touched," said his nephew.

Of course, it would have been better to wait until night, until the exact time of the affair. But as that was impossible—

Otto Braun, according to his passport, was 58, born at Bremen, and formerly a banker at Stuttgart. He certainly looked the part, neatly dressed, with his comfortable, heavy build and close-cropped hair.

The information that had just arrived from Berlin stated: *Had to stop his financial activities after the National Socialist revolution, but gave an undertaking of loyalty to the Government, and has never been disturbed. Said to be very rich. Contributed one million marks to party funds.*

In one of his pockets Maigret found a hotel bill from the Kaiserhof, in Berlin, where Otto Braun had stayed three days on his way from Stuttgart.

Meanwhile, the five passengers were standing in the corridor, watching, some dismally and others angrily, the comings and goings of Inspector Maigret. Pointing to the luggage rack above Braun, Maigret asked, "Are those his suitcases?"

"They're mine," came the sharp voice of Lena Leinbach, the Austrian.

"Will you please take the seat you had last night?"

She did so reluctantly, and her unsteady movements betrayed the effects of the drinks. She was beautifully dressed, and wore a mink coat, and a ring on every finger.

The report on her that was telegraphed from Vienna said: *Courtesan of the luxury class, who has had numerous affairs in the capitals of Central Europe, but has never come to the attention of the police. Was for a long time the mistress of a German prince.*

"Which of you got on at Berlin?" Maigret asked, turning to the others.

"If you will allow me," someone said in excellent French. And, in fact, it turned out to be a Frenchman, Adolphe Bonvoisin, from Lille.

"I can perhaps be of some help to you as I was on the train from Warsaw. There were two of us. I myself came from Lvov,

where my firm—a textile concern—has a Polish subsidiary.
Madame boarded the train at Warsaw at the same time as I
did." He indicated a middle-aged woman in an astrakhan coat,
dark and heavily built, with swollen legs.

"Madame Irvitch of Vilna?"

As she spoke no French, the interview was conducted in
German. Madame Irvitch, the wife of a wholesale furrier, was
coming to Paris to consult a specialist, and she wished to lodge a
protest—

"Sit down in the place you were occupying last night."

Two passengers remained—two men.

"Name?" Maigret asked the first, a tall, thin, distinguished-
looking man with an officer's bearing.

"Thomas Hauke, of Hamburg."

On Hauke, Berlin had had plenty to say: *Sentenced in 1924 to
two years' imprisonment for dealing in stolen jewelry . . . closely
watched since . . . frequents the pleasure spots of various European
capitals . . . suspected of engaging in cocaine and morphine
smuggling.*

Finally, the last one, a man of 35, bespectacled, shaven-
headed, severe. "Dr. Gellhorn," he said, "from Brussels."

A silly misunderstanding then arose. Maigret asked him why,
when his fellow passenger was discovered unconscious, he had
done nothing about it.

"Because I'm not a doctor of medicine. I'm an archeologist."

By now the compartment was occupied as it had been the
previous night:

| Otto Braun | Adolphe Bonvoisin | Madame Irvitch |
| Thomas Hauke | Dr. Gellhorn | Lena Leinbach |

Naturally, except for Otto Braun, henceforth incapable of
giving evidence one way or another, each one protested entire
innocence. And each one claimed to know nothing.

Maigret had already spent a quarter of an hour in another room
with Jef Bebelmans, the acrobat from Antwerp who had appeared
from under a car at Aulnoye carrying more than two million
in bearer bonds. At first, when confronted with the corpse,

Bebelmans had betrayed no emotion, merely asking, "Who is it?"

Then he had been found to be in possession of a third-class ticket from Berlin to Paris, although that had not prevented him from spending part of the journey hiding under a car, no doubt to avoid declaring his bonds at the frontier.

Bebelmans, however, was not a talkative fellow. His one observation revealed a touch of humor: "It's your business to ask questions. Unfortunately, I have absolutely nothing to tell you."

The information on him was not too helpful, either: *Formerly an acrobat, he has since been a night-club waiter in Heidelberg, and later in Berlin.*

"Well, now," Maigret began, puffing away at his pipe, "you, Bonvoisin, and Madame Irvitch were already in the train at Warsaw. Who got in at Berlin?"

"Madame was first," Bonvoisin said, indicating Lena Leinbach.

"And your suitcases, madame?"

She pointed to the rack above the dead man, where there were three luxurious crocodile bags, each in a fawn cover.

"So you put your luggage over this seat and sat down in the other corner, diagonally opposite."

"The dead man—I mean, that gentleman—came in next." Bonvoisin asked nothing better than to go on talking.

"All he had with him was a traveling rug."

This was the cue for a consultation between Maigret and his nephew. Quickly they made another inventory of the dead man's wallet, in which a luggage slip was found. As the heavy baggage had by then reached Paris, Maigret sent telephone instructions that these pieces should be opened at once.

"Good! Now, this gentleman—" He motioned toward Hauke.

"He got in at Cologne."

"Is that right, Monsieur Hauke?"

"To be precise, I changed compartments at Cologne. I was in a non-smoker."

Dr. Gellhorn, too, had got on at Cologne. While Maigret, hands in pockets, was putting his questions, muttering away to himself, watching each of them in turn, Paul Vinchon, like a good secretary, was taking notes at a rapid rate.

These notes read:

Bonvoisin: Until the German frontier, no one seemed to know anyone else, except for Madame Irvitch and myself. After the customs we all settled down to sleep as best we could, and the light was dimmed. At Liége I saw the lady opposite (Lena Leinbach) try to go out into the corridor. Immediately the gentleman in the other corner (Otto Braun) got up and asked her in German what she was doing. "I want a breath of air," she said. And I'm sure I heard him say, "Stay where you are."

Later in his statement Bonvoisin returned to this point:

At Namur she tried once more to get out of the train, but Otto Braun, who seemed to be asleep, suddenly moved, and she stayed where she was. At Charleroi they spoke to each other again, but I was falling asleep and have only a hazy recollection.

So, somewhere between Charleroi and Jeumont, in that hour and a half or so, one of the passengers must have made the fatal move, must have approached Otto Braun and plunged a needle into his heart.

Only Bonvoisin would not have needed to get up. He had only to move slightly to the right to reach the German. Hauke's position, directly opposite the victim, was the next best, then Dr. Gellhorn's and finally the two women's.

Despite the cold, Maigret's forehead was bathed with sweat. Lena Leinbach watched him furiously, while Madame Irvitch complained of rheumatism and consoled herself by talking Polish to Bonvoisin.

Thomas Hauke was the most dignified of them all, and the most aloof, while Gellhorn claimed that he was missing an important appointment at the Louvre.

To return to Vinchon's notes, the following dialogue appears:

Maigret, to Lena: Where were you living in Berlin?

Lena: I was only there for a week. I was staying as usual at the Kaiserhof.

M: Did you know Otto Braun?

L: No. I may have run across him in the hall or the lift.

M: *Why, then, after the German frontier did he start talking to you as if he knew you?*

L: *(dryly) Perhaps because he grew bolder away from home.*

M: *Was that why he forbade you to get off the train at Liége and Namur?*

L: *He merely said I'd catch cold.*

The questioning was still going on when there was a telephone call from Paris. Otto Braun's luggage—there were eight pieces—contained a great amount of clothing, and so much linen and personal stuff that one might have assumed the banker was going off on a long trip, if not forever. But no money—only four hundred marks in a wallet.

As for the other passengers: Lena Leinbach was carrying 500 French francs, 50 marks, 30 crowns; Dr. Gellhorn, 700 marks; Thomas Hauke, 40 marks and 20 French francs; Madame Irvitch, 30 marks, 100 francs, and letters of credit on a Polish bank in Paris; Bonvoisin, 12 zloty, 10 marks, 5000 francs.

They still had to search the hand luggage that was in the compartment. Hauke's bag held only one change of clothes, a dinner jacket, and some underwear. In Bonvoisin's there were two marked decks of cards.

But the real find came in Lena Leinbach's suitcases in which, under the crystal-and-gold bottles, the fragile lingerie, and the gowns, there were beautifully contrived false bottoms.

But the false bottoms were empty. When questioned, all Lena Leinbach said was, "I bought these from a lady who went in for smuggling. They were a great bargain. *I've* never used them for anything like that."

Who had killed Otto Braun in the bluish half light of the compartment between Charleroi and Jeumont?

Paris was beginning to get worried. Maigret was summoned to the telephone. This business was going to cause a stir, and there would be complications. The numbers of the bonds found on Jef Bebelmans had been transmitted to the leading banks, and everything was in order—there was no record of any large theft of bonds.

It was eleven o'clock when they had started this laborious

reconstruction in the railway car. It was two o'clock before they got out, and then only because Madame Irvitch fainted after declaring in Polish she could no longer bear the smell of the corpse.

Vinchon was pale, for it seemed to him that his uncle was not showing his usual composure—that he was, in fact, dithering.

"It's not going well, Nunk?" he said in a low voice as they were crossing the tracks.

Maigret's only response was to sigh, "I wish I could find the needle. Hold them all another hour."

"But Madame Irvitch is ill!"

"What's that to do with me?"

"Dr. Gellhorn claims—"

"Let him," Maigret cut him short.

And he went off to lunch on his own at the station bar.

"Be quiet, I tell you!" Maigret snapped, an hour later. His nephew lowered his head. "All you do is bring me trouble. I'm going to tell you my conclusions. After that, I warn you, you can get yourself out of this mess, and if you don't, you needn't bother to ring up your nunk. Nunk's had enough."

Then, changing his tone, he went on, "Now! I've been looking for the one logical explanation of all the facts. It's up to you to prove it, or to obtain a confession. Try to follow me.

"First, Otto Braun, with all his wealth, would not have come to France with eight suitcases and goodness knows how many suits—and, on the other hand, with precisely four hundred marks.

"Second, there must have been some reason for him to pretend during the German part of the journey not to know Lena Leinbach, and then as soon as they were over the Belgian border for them to be on familiar terms.

"Third, he refused to let her get out of the train at Liége, at Namur, and at Charleroi.

"Fourth, in spite of that she made several desperate attempts to get out.

"Fifth, a certain Jef Bebelmans, a passenger from Berlin who had never seen Braun—or he would have shown some sign on seeing the corpse—was found carrying more than two million in bonds."

And, still in a very bad temper, Maigret rumbled on, "Now I'll explain. Otto Braun, for reasons of his own, wanted to smuggle his fortune, or part of it, out of Germany. Knowing that his luggage would be minutely searched, he came to an agreement with a demimondaine in Berlin, and had double-bottomed suitcases made for her, knowing that they would stand less chance of being closely examined, being full of feminine articles.

"But Lena Leinbach, like all self-respecting members of her calling, has one real love: Thomas Hauke. Hauke, who is a specialist in this line, arranged with Lena in Berlin—perhaps even in the Kaiserhof—to make off with the bonds hidden in her suitcases.

"She gets on the train first, and puts the cases where Braun, still suspicious, has told her to put them. She sits down in the opposite corner, for they are not supposed to know each other.

"At Cologne, Hauke, to keep an eye on things, comes to take his place in the compartment. Meanwhile, another accomplice, Jef Bebelmans, probably a professional burglar, is traveling third-class with the bonds, and at each frontier he has orders to hide for a while underneath the car.

"Once the Belgian frontier is crossed, Otto Braun obviously runs no further risk. He could at any moment take it into his head to open his companion's suitcases and remove his bonds. That is why, first at Liége, then at Namur, and again at Charleroi, Lena Leinbach tries to get off the train.

"Is Braun mistrustful? Does he suspect something? Or is he just in love with her? Whichever it is, he watches Lena closely, and she begins to panic, for in Paris he will inevitably discover the theft, the empty false bottoms.

"He may even notice it at the French frontier, where, having no further reason to hide the bonds, he may want to open the suitcases. Thomas Hauke, too, must be aware of the danger of discovery—"

"And it's he who kills Braun?" Vinchon asked.

"I'm certain it is not. If Hauke had got up to do that, one or another of his traveling companions would have noticed. In my opinion Braun was killed when you went past the first time, calling, 'Have your passports ready, please.'

"At that moment everyone got up, in the dark, still half asleep. Only Lena Leinbach had a reason to go over to Braun, press close to him to take down her suitcases, and I am convinced that it was at that moment—"

"But the needle?"

"Look for it!" Maigret grunted. "A long brooch pin will do. If this woman had not happened on someone like you, who insisted on undressing the corpse, for a long time it would have seemed to be a death from natural causes.

"Now draw your plan. Make Lena think Bebelmans has talked, make Bebelmans think Hauke has been broken—all the old dodges, eh?"

And he went off to have a beer while Vinchon did what his uncle had told him. Old dodges are good dodges because they work. In this case they worked because Lena Leinbach was wearing a long arrow-shaped pin of brilliants in her hat, and because Paulie, as Madame Maigret called him, pointing at it, said to her, "You can't deny it. There's blood on the pin!"

It wasn't true. But, for all that, she had a fit of hysterics and made a full confession.

Sweet Fever

By Bill Pronzini

*F*OR *a professional writer most fiction, alas, is the product of
hard work and a lot of head-scratching and brain-cudgeling; but
on rare occasions a story suddenly and rather startlingly comes
to him full-born (nonwriters like to call this simple if unusual
act of the subconscious "inspiration" or "a visit from the Muse").
Everything is there: plot, characters, title, whole sentences and
paragraphs. All the writer has to do is transfer it to paper, the
easiest and most pleasant part of the creative process.*

*This blessed event has only happened to me four times in ten
years, and all four of those stories are among my personal
favorites. The most recent is "Sweet Fever," which deals with a
man who has railroading in his blood, and with obsession and
its effects on mind and soul.*

I won't say any more about it. After all, I'm biased. . . .

Quarter before midnight, like on every evening except the Sabbath or when it's storming or when my rheumatism gets to paining too bad, me and Billy Bob went down to the Chigger Mountain railroad tunnel to wait for the night freight from St. Louis. This here was a fine summer evening, with a big old fat yellow moon hung above the pines on Hankers Ridge and mocking-birds and cicadas and toads making a soft ruckus. Nights like this, I have me a good feeling, hopeful, and I know Billy Bob does too.

They's a bog hollow on the near side of the tunnel opening, and beside it a woody slope, not too steep. Halfway down the slope is a big catalpa tree, and that was where we always set, side by side with our backs up against the trunk.

So we come on down to there, me hobbling some with my cane and Billy Bob holding onto my arm. That moon was so bright you could see the melons lying in Ferdie Johnson's patch over on the left, and the rail tracks had a sleek oiled look coming out of the tunnel mouth and leading off toward the Sabreville yards a mile up the line. On the far side of the tracks, the woods and the rundown shacks that used to be a hobo jungle before the county sheriff closed it off thirty years back had them a silvery cast, like they was all coated in winter frost.

We set down under the catalpa tree and I leaned my head back to catch my wind. Billy Bob said, "Granpa, you feeling right?"

"Fine, boy."

"Rheumatism ain't started paining you?"

"Not a bit."

He gave me a grin. "Got a little surprise for you."

"The hell you do."

"Fresh plug of blackstrap," he said. He come out of his pocket with it. "Mr. Cotter got him in a shipment just today down at his store."

I was some pleased. But I said, "Now you hadn't ought to go spending your money on me, Billy Bob."

"Got nobody else I'd rather spend it on."

I took the plug and unwrapped it and had me a chew. Old

man like me ain't got many pleasures left, but fresh blackstrap's one; good corn's another. Billy Bob gets us all the corn we need from Ben Logan's boys. They got a pretty good sized still up on Hankers Ridge, and their corn is the best in this part of the hills. Not that either of us is a drinking man, now. A little touch after supper and on special days is all. I never did hold with drinking too much, or doing anything too much, and I taught Billy Bob the same.

He's a good boy. Man couldn't ask for a better grandson. But I raised him that way—in my own image, you might say—after both my own son Rufus and Billy Bob's ma got taken from us in 1947. I reckon I done a right job of it, and I couldn't be less proud of him than I was of his pa, or love him no less, either.

Well, we set there and I worked on the chew of blackstrap and had a spit every now and then, and neither of us said much. Pretty soon the first whistle come, way off on the other side of Chigger Mountain. Billy Bob cocked his head and said, "She's right on schedule."

"Mostly is," I said, "this time of year."

That sad lonesome hungry ache started up in me again—what my daddy used to call the "sweet fever." He was a railroad man, and I grew up around trains and spent a goodly part of my early years at the roundhouse in the Sabreville yards. Once, when I was ten, he let me take the throttle of the big 2-8-0 Mogul steam locomotive on his highballing run to Eulalia, and I can't recollect no more finer experience in my whole life. Later on I worked as a callboy, and then as a fireman on a 2-10-4, and put in some time as a yard tender engineer, and I expect I'd have gone on in railroading if it hadn't been for the Depression and getting myself married and having Rufus. My daddy's short-line company folded up in 1931, and half a dozen others too, and wasn't no work for either of us in Sabreville or Eulalia or any-wheres else on the iron. That squeezed the will right out of him, and he took to ailing, and I had to accept a job on Mr. John Barnett's truck farm to support him and the rest of my family. Was my intention to go back into railroading, but the

Depression dragged on, and my daddy died, and a year later my wife Amanda took sick and passed on, and by the time the war come it was just too late.

But Rufus got him the sweet fever too, and took a switchman's job in the Sabreville yards, and worked there right up until the night he died. Billy Bob was only three then; his own sweet fever comes most purely from me and what I taught him. Ain't no doubt trains been a major part of all our lives, good and bad, and ain't no doubt neither they get into a man's blood and maybe change him, too, in one way and another. I reckon they do.

The whistle come again, closer now, and I judged the St. Louis freight was just about to enter the tunnel on the other side of the mountain. You could hear the big wheels singing on the track, and if you listened close you could just about hear the banging of couplings and the hiss of air brakes as the engineer throttled down for the curve. The tunnel don't run straight through Chigger Mountain; she comes in from the north and angles to the east, so that a big freight like the St. Louis got to cut back to quarter speed coming through.

When she entered the tunnel, the tracks down below seemed to shimmy, and you could feel the vibration clear up where we was sitting under the catalpa tree. Billy Bob stood himself up and peered down toward the black tunnel mouth like a bird dog on a point. The whistle come again, and once more, from inside the tunnel, sounding hollow and miseried now. Every time I heard it like that, I thought of a body trapped and hurting and crying out for help that wouldn't come in the empty hours of the night. I swallowed and shifted the cud of blackstrap and worked up a spit to keep my mouth from drying. The sweet fever feeling was strong in my stomach.

The blackness around the tunnel opening commenced to lighten, and got brighter and brighter until the long white glow from the locomotive's headlamp spilled out onto the tracks beyond. Then she come through into my sight, her light shining like a giant's eye, and the engineer give another tug on the whistle, and the sound of her was a clattering rumble as loud to my ears as a mountain rock-slide. But she wasn't moving fast, just kind of easing along, pulling herself out of that tunnel like a night crawler out of a mound of earth.

The locomotive clacked on past, and me and Billy Bob watched her string slide along in front of us. Flats, boxcars, three tankers in a row, more flats loaded down with pine logs big around as a privy, a refrigerator car, five coal gondolas, another link of boxcars. Fifty in the string already, I thought. She won't be dragging more than sixty, sixty-five. . . .

Billy Bob said suddenly, "Granpa, look yonder!"

He had his arm up, pointing. My eyes ain't so good no more, and it took me a couple of seconds to follow his point, over on our left and down at the door of the third boxcar in the last link. It was sliding open, and clear in the moonlight I saw a man's head come out, then his shoulders.

"It's a floater, Granpa," Billy Bob said, excited. "He's gonna jump. Look at him holding there—he's gonna jump."

I spit into the grass. "Help me up, boy."

He got a hand under my arm and lifted me up and held me until I was steady on my cane. Down there at the door of the boxcar, the floater was looking both ways along the string of cars and down at the ground beside the tracks. That ground was soft loam, and the train was going slow enough that there wasn't much chance he would hurt himself jumping off. He come to that same idea, and as soon as he did he flung himself off the car with his arms spread out and his hair and coattails flying in the slipstream. I saw him land solid and go down and roll over once. Then he knelt there, shaking his head a little, looking around.

Well, he was the first floater we'd seen in seven months. The yard crews seal up the cars nowadays, and they ain't many ride the rails anyhow, even down in our part of the country. But every now and then a floater wants to ride bad enough to break a seal, or hides himself in a gondola or on a loaded flat. Kids, oldtime hoboes, wanted men. They's still a few.

And some of 'em get off right down where this one had, because they know the St. Louis freight stops in Sabreville and they's yardmen there that check the string, or because they see the rundown shacks of the old hobo jungle or Ferdie Johnson's melon patch. Man rides a freight long enough, no provisions, he gets mighty hungry; the sight of a melon patch like Ferdie's is plenty enough to make him jump off.

"Billy Bob," I said.

"Yes, Granpa. You wait easy now."

He went off along the slope, running. I watched the floater, and he come up on his feet and got himself into a clump of bushes alongside the tracks to wait for the caboose to pass so's he wouldn't be seen. Pretty soon the last of the cars left the tunnel, and then the caboose with a signalman holding a red-eye lantern out on the platform. When she was down the tracks and just about beyond my sight, the floater showed himself again and had him another look around. Then, sure enough, he made straight for the melon patch.

Once he got into it I couldn't see him, because he was in close to the woods at the edge of the slope. I couldn't see Billy Bob neither. The whistle sounded one final time, mournful, as the lights of the caboose disappeared, and a chill come to my neck and set there like a cold dead hand. I closed my eyes and listened to the last singing of the wheels fade away.

It weren't long before I heard footfalls on the slope coming near, then the angry sound of a stranger's voice, but I kept my eyes shut until they walked up close and Billy Bob said, "Granpa." When I opened 'em the floater was standing three feet in front of me, white face shining in the moonlight—scared face, angry face, evil face.

"What the hell is this?" he said. "What you want with me?"

"Give me your gun, Billy Bob," I said.

He did it, and I held her tight and lifted the barrel. The ache in my stomach was so strong my knees felt weak and I could scarcely breathe. But my hand was steady.

The floater's eyes come wide open and he backed off a step. "Hey," he said, "hey, you can't—"

I shot him twice.

He fell over and rolled some and come up on his back. They wasn't no doubt he was dead, so I give the gun back to Billy Bob and he put it away in his belt. "All right, boy," I said.

Billy Bob nodded and went over and hoisted the dead floater onto his shoulder. I watched him trudge off toward the bog hollow, and in my mind I could hear the train whistle as she'd sounded from inside the tunnel. I thought again, as I had so many times, that it was the way my boy Rufus and Billy Bob's ma must have sounded that night in 1947, when the two floaters from the hobo jungle broke into their home and raped her and shot Rufus to death. She lived just long enough to tell us about the floaters, but they was never caught. So it was up to me, and then up to me and Billy Bob when he come of age.

Well, it ain't like it once was, and that saddens me. But they's still a few that ride the rails, still a few take it into their heads to jump off down there when the St. Louis freight slows coming through the Chigger Mountain tunnel.

Oh my yes, they'll *always* be a few for me and Billy Bob and the sweet fever inside us both.

The Man
Who Loved
the Midnight Lady

By Barry N. Malzberg

*A*ND WHAT *of trains in the future—the far future? As most everyone reluctantly and unhappily concedes, the days of the transcontinental, intrastate and interstate railroads appear numbered; with the ever-increasing emphasis on speed, there seems to be no place for the iron horse in the highly technologized world of the twenty-first century. If indeed there comes a time when freight trains, passenger trains, even subway trains are reduced to total obsolescence, how will they be remembered? Nostalgically? Or, when enough time has passed to dissipate legend and desensitize fact, as nothing more than historical curiosities?*

There is no way we can know today, of course; but the question fascinated me enough to want, as the final story in this anthology, a possible and extrapolative answer. A writer who has specialized in science-fiction seemed the best source of such an explanation, and since I could not find a published s-f story on the theme, I asked my close friend and sometimes-collaborator, Barry Malzberg, to do an original for me. "The Man Who Loved the Midnight Lady" is the result, and quite a result it is—a haunting look at the year 2112, and a sad, glad celebration of trains (and something equally relevant to this book) unlike any other in fiction.

Barry Malzberg is a writer of major talent whose experimental work in science-fiction has brought him a controversial reputation; he has been called, variously, "a genius," "a degenerate," "a writer of stunning power," "a merchant of gloom and depression." Among his novels are Beyond Apollo, *for which he received the John W. Campbell Memorial Award for the best science-fiction novel of 1972;* Herovit's World; Screen; Oracle of the Thousand Hands; *and, in collaboration with your editor,* The Running of Beasts. *He has written at least a dozen brilliant short stories; to my mind, "The Man Who Loved the Midnight Lady" is among the best five of these—and proves once and for all that "writer of stunning power" is the only valid appelation.*

Here it is 2112. And so I report for the next sequence arranged by the Bureau of Historical Reconstruction and am diverted to the IRT uptown Seventh Avenue Express from New Lots Avenue to 242nd Street–Van Cortlandt Park. On the midnight run there are only six of us in the second car, two of whom are sleeping drunks. The other three are two old men with dreaming expressions and a woman with several shopping bags at her feet.

The train lurches its way out of 72nd Street and then stalls in the tunnel approaching 79th. The fans shut down along with the bulbs; small emergency lights go on. We sit there for ten to fifteen minutes before the first gentle wisps of smoke begin to fill the car.

"My God," says the woman with the shopping bags, "there's a fire in the tunnel. We'll all be incinerated."

"Not to worry, madam," I say. "It's probably only smoke from debris which has touched the third rail." Historicity has its uses; a fixed past, when relived, can at least quell panic. "We'll be on our way in just a little while, I'm sure."

"We'll never be on our way," she says. She reaches down, clutches two of her bags. "We'd better make a run for it while there's still time."

The two old men stare at her quizzically. The sleeping drunks say nothing; subway drunks are notably quiescent.

"My jewels, my life," the woman says. "Also my helpless grandchildren. My chest is tight. I can't breathe. Oh my God, let's get out of here.'

"Everything will be well, madam," I say with superb calm, and at that moment the train lurches forward, upsetting the bags still on the floor. Little rags and pieces of paper spill from one of them. The woman stares at it fixedly. The train gathers speed. "As you see," I say, "you had nothing to worry about at all."

The train is moving furiously past 86th Street now, the stanchions like pinwheels through the dirty windows. The old men are looking at me intensely and the drunks are twitching in their places, but the Procedural Technicians are notorious for this kind of thing anyway—out of some perversity they squeeze in extraneous matter to taunt subjects—and it is not worth worrying about. We stagger into 96th Street. The woman begins to sing, atonally.

So I come through that unscathed and report for the next Reconstruction and go under the receptors and find myself in the Orient Express for a midnight border crossing. The car is packed with sinister people of all types, to say nothing of children who cling to uninterested mothers. Almost everybody looks like a smuggler or a spy. I try to look inconspicuous, but it is very difficult, considering the simplicity of my costume and manner in a situation where everyone looks exotic.

A man with large mustaches across the aisle motions to me, then leans forward and says, "Who are you?"

"I am just a traveler," I say.

"You do not look like a traveler," he says with overtones of menace; "you look like the police."

I look around the car, seeking some sympathy or assistance, but instead find that in the sudden quiet many people are staring at me with dangerous expressions. "That is ridiculous," I say. "I am not the police."

"And if you were, would you admit this? We know how to deal with police on the Orient Express," the man says. He reaches inside his turban and extracts a large knife. "We have our own justice here—crude justice, but it suits all of our purposes."

He puts the knife against my forehead and I feel the thin sensation of skin parting. "All of our purposes," he repeats.

It occurs to me that I am being threatened with death. There are rumors that this has happened in the Reconstructive Process; there are even hints that on occasion death has ensued, "hysteric overload" being the phrase, but I attempt to hold onto my superb calm. I am being closely observed at all times, and it is all part of the examination procedure.

"Don't be ridiculous," I repeat. "There are a hundred witnesses here, and I am innocent."

"All of them are my friends," the man with the mustaches says, "and your manner is that of the distinctly guilty. Rude interpositions make for extravagant deals." He brings the knife slowly down my forehead. Something falls into my eyes that is not sweat. The car is silent, and everyone, particularly the children, leans forward with an interested expression.

I move away from the knife and try to parry it with certain movements I learned in the Orientation Center, but the edges of my calm have already become ragged, and I feel I am on the verge of committing a dangerous *faux pas* which will abort my training or recycle me to a much earlier stage; but it is at that instant that the train comes to a screaming halt, and with shouts and cries several dozen uniformed men push their way into the already overcrowded car, waving dangerous armaments.

"We are the Kiev police," one of them cries, "and we have information that there is a smuggler on this train. Everybody will present themselves at once and divest themselves of all of their outer garments."

My assailant moves quickly from me and disappears behind a seat: no small accomplishment, considering the degree to which the car is now occupied. I feel an arm around my shoulders and look up into kindly gray features underneath a helmet.

"I am the Chief Inspector," the features say, "and I want to thank you for all of your help in preparing for our surprise entrance. Thanks to your courageous efforts, we have already deduced the identity of the smuggler."

I am unable to do anything but nod, although pleasure must show clearly on my own features.

"If it were not for the efforts of those such as you," the Chief Inspector says, "this dangerous passage would be unchecked, and within less than a generation all of the world would be in the snare of that terrible drug opium."

I nod in acceptance of his praise. My assailant, surrounded by police, is taken off struggling. The Chief Inspector reaches into his pockets and hands me a special award of merit suitable for framing and a badge granting me honorary status with the Kiev police. Nonetheless, even after his presentation and exit, the train does not move, and I come to understand that the sudden halt has led to a locking of the brake mechanism, which is very common among locomotives of such ancient vintage as exist on the Orient Express.

So I am brought before the Bureau and am told that I am doing fairly well, nothing extraordinary, *comme ci comme ça*, as the old expression goes, but that my command of the lexicon of trains is still somewhat shaky.

"What is a Pullman?" they ask. "What is a siding? What is a first-class compartment, a caboose, a trip-signal, a firebox?"

Some of their questions I answer correctly, others I answer incorrectly, a few I cannot answer at all. They remind me that the practicum is necessarily eighty percent of the examinations and that I am right to concentrate upon a good performance; but they remind me also that a good performance on the verbal section can often be the difference between failure and passing and I would be well advised to pay some attention to the texts during interim periods. All in all, though, they are not condemnatory and cite my performance under pressure on the Orient Express as being a distinguished example which they will keep as part of their training classes.

"It is an exotic and arcane area of study which you have selected," they conclude, "and certainly singles you out as unusual, but you must understand that the rarity of your goal is not sufficient basis for a passing mark. We certainly do need a new scholar on passenger trains in this Section, but he must conform to the same rigorous standards as anyone aspiring to be a flotation pilot."

"I understand that," I say. "I'm genuinely interested in the subject or I never would have applied for the training. I have no objection to conforming to a high standard of knowledge; I wish to know it for my own sake."

"Of course," they say, "and by the way, there is no such thing as hysteric, suggestion-induced death during training; this is an institutional rumor which we have never been able to quash and is worthless," and then they send me away, although hardly reassured because it is the material that they take the trouble to deny that more often than not turns out to be the truth.

So I am on the Yankee Clipper, coach car, heading toward Boston, and after a while, soothed but bored by the gliding of forest shapes outside, I decide to go to the club car for a drink. A porter tells me that all of the tables are occupied, but if I desire I may join a young lady in the rear where there is an empty chair. I say that I will do this and find that she is blonde, very young and very beautiful, with pained eyes; she is having a soft drink and staring through the windows wistfully.

We fall into conversation, as usually happens in club cars at night, and in the space of less than half an hour we fall deeply and truly in love in the manner of men and women who meet on trains. I ask her if she will join me at our mutual destination, but her eyes become filmed and she says that she has a dark and terrible secret which forever precludes consummation of our relationship. I do not press her for further details, but merely sit there and hold her hand, feeling the warm pressure of her spirit pass into mine.

After a time she suggests that we stand on the observation car, which we do. We stand there embracing and kissing for a long time as the train bears us due east from Albany to the closed spaces of old Boston.

"If only it could be," she says, "if only it could be," and leans against me. I feel her body shaking, and then at last the secret comes out: she is not alive; she is merely a ghost, the ghost of a beautiful young woman who threw herself to death from a train one hundred and fifty years ago because of an unhappy romance, and who is now doomed through eternity to ride the Yankee Clipper and fall into hopeless relationships with young men like myself, whose presence can only hurt her over and again. This is her purgatory for the crime of suicide. She is the midnight lady, the specter of passage.

Hearing her story quite unmans me, which is to be expected under the circumstances, and I find her suddenly cold within my grasp, then insubstantial, and soon she has faded away. I am alone on the observation car. Slowly I return to the club car, which is now almost empty, find a deserted table, and slowly, bleakly, drink myself toward unconsciousness, thinking of the midnight lady as, all unaware of its terrible legacy, the steel coffin of my hopes carries me toward Henry James's Boston.

So I am now a public official in Promontory, Utah, and hold between my hands the golden spike which will splice one section of rail to another section of rail, meaning that trains will now run across all of the wild and beautiful continent. A laborer hands me a hammer; I take it clumsily, the spike almost falling from the grasp of my other hand. I steady it, hit it off-center once to the sound of cheering. The workman takes both spike and hammer from me, and I mount a podium and make a short speech.

"Now the continent is joined," I say. "We have the rail link that makes all of us one people, one commerce. The trains will run through the heart of the wilderness and through the canyons of the cities, the passage that will keep us vital and make this country last as long as the trains last; only when the last train has gone to the last siding will this country perish." Well, you know political rhetoric of that period.

There is more cheering, although I can barely hear it; it must be the sound of the hammer blow still filling my ears. "The trains are our lives," I conclude and step down. The workman assists me, wavering, from the podium, and in the distance I can hear a whistle. The great train: the great train is coming. I lean forward, trying to catch the first vision of its gaunt bulk at the far edge of the tablelands.

So the Bureau says that I have done satisfactorily on the practicum; nothing remarkable, but a good command of all the materials; if a slight lack of originality, an ease with the material which shows the results of study and application. They are mildly congratulatory. They proceed with the verbal, and I tell them what a "diesel" is, and a "gondola" and a "steel-driving man," and at the end of that they ask me to leave the room. When I return they tell me I have been commissioned, and then they rise, one by one, to solemnly shake my hand and welcome me to the ranks of the Bureau.

Trained for this by my experience as a politician, to say nothing of the dangers of the Orient Express, I accept their congratulations with humility, with the mildest and least self-important of demeanors. At length they confer upon me a certificate and an oath; then I am escorted from the room and taken to my larger quarters, which will be my residence as long as I remain part of the Bureau.

These quarters are six-by-eleven and contain a bed, a wooden table, a mirror and a basin. I am overwhelmed with such

amenities and understand for the first time how truly worthwhile
all of my endeavors have been and what it will mean to me to be
part of the Bureau.

So I report to the Bureau the next day and am given my first
assignment. It is very much like the practicum, of course,
because there is no difference between practicum and assignment,
except that in assignment they trust you and leave you alone.
Also, there is no difference between the imagined and the real,
as my own difficulties on the Orient Express made so clear. History
is dream; dreams are history. At least in 2112.

In due course I find myself on the Calais Coach, sipping
from a small carafe of wine while thinking about the problems
of cabbage cultivation which await me in the south of Belgium,
that home to which in retirement I am now returning. "We have
a great problem, Monsieur," someone says to me, and I look
up to see an excited conductor. "We have deduced your identity
and need the assistance of the great and famous Monsieur. One
of the passengers in the next car has been murdered in his
sleep; there are twelve fellow passengers, and it can only be one
of them, but all of them deny it. We must solve this mystery
before we reach the south of Belgium or it will become a serious
police matter of much disgrace to the company."

"Yes, yes," I say and move my round little bulk from the
seat, hands behind me for purchase, then twirl my mustaches
with a flourish and slowly follow the conductor into the next
car, catching for just a moment between cars the enormous sense
of speed, heat, light, power and distance from which the trains
have so briefly shielded me before I go into the insulated spaces
within to face, not for the first time in my long and illustrious
career, the problem of murder in the night.

But I am comforted in the knowledge that the train will go on;
that precisely because of me and those like me the great trains
will go on forever and ever. And ever.

Hallelujah.

Bibliography

*W*HILE the following lists are extensive, they are not intended as an all-inclusive bibliography; the sheer volume of published material in magazines alone would have made such an undertaking lamentably prohibitive. Starred (*) items are personal favorites—those works which seem to me to contain the most suspense as well as to deal most extensively with trains, train travel and travelers, and train personnel.

SHORT STORIES: In Anthologies and Collections

Barr, Robert. "The Great Pegram Mystery." In *The Misadventures of Sherlock Holmes*, edited by Ellery Queen. Little, Brown (Boston), 1944.

Bond, Nelson. "On Schedule." In *Murder for the Millions*, edited by Frank Owen. Frederick Fell, 1946.

Bradbury, Ray. "The Town Where No One Got Off." In *Twice Twenty-Two*. Doubleday, 1966.

262   [Bibliography]

Bramah, Ernest. "The Knight's Cross Signal Problem." In *Max Carrados*. Methuen (London), 1914.

Bruce, Leo. "Murder in Miniature." In *Evening Standard Detective Book, Second Series*. Gollancz (London), 1951.

Carter, Nick, pseud. "Nick Carter's Enemy." In *Nick Carter, Detective*, edited and with an introduction by Robert Clurman. Macmillan, 1963.

Charteris, Leslie. "The Rhine Maiden." In *The Saint in Europe*. Hodder & Stoughton (London), 1954.

*Christie, Agatha. "The Girl in the Train." In *The Listerdale Mystery and Other Stories*. Dodd, Mead, 1934.

_____. "The Plymouth Express." In *The Under Dog and Other Stories*. Dodd, Mead, 1926.

Clouston, J. Storer. "The Envelope." In *World's Great Spy Stories*, edited by Vincent Starrett. Forum Books (Cleveland, Ohio), 1944.

Cohen, Octavus Roy. "Common Stock." In *Jim Hanvey, Detective*. Dodd, Mead, 1923.

*Crispin, Edmund. "Beware of the Trains." In *Beware of the Trains*. Gollancz (London), 1953.

*Crofts, Freeman Wills. "Crime on the Footplate." In *Many a Slip*. Hodder & Stoughton (London), 1955.

_____. "East Wind." In *The Mystery of the Sleeping Car Express and Other Stories*. Hodder & Stoughton (London), 1956.

*_____. "The 8:12 from Waterloo." In *Many a Slip*.

_____. "The Landing Ticket." In *The Mystery of the Sleeping Car Express and Other Stories*.

_____. "The Level Crossing." In *The Mystery of the Sleeping Car Express and Other Stories*.

*_____. "The Mystery of the Sleeping Car Express." In *The Mystery of the Sleeping Car Express and Other Stories*.

_____. "The Raincoat." In *The Mystery of the Sleeping Car Express and Other Stories*.

_____. "The Relief Signalman." In *Murderers Make Mistakes*. Hodder & Stoughton (London), 1947.

_____. "The Suitcase." In *Many a Slip*.

Davies, Rhys. "Fear." In *Collected Stories*. William Heineman (London), 1955.

*Derleth, August. "The Adventure of the Lost Locomotive." In *The Memoirs of Solar Pons*. Mycroft & Moran (Sauk City, Wisconsin), 1951.

*_____. *The Adventure of the Orient Express*. Candlelight Press, 1955. (A novella published in booklet form.)

_____. "The Battle over the Teacups." In *World's Best Spy Stories*, edited by Vincent Starrett. Forum Books (Cleveland, Ohio), 1944.

_____. "The Extra Passenger." In *Mr. George and Other Odd Persons*. Arkham House (Sauk City, Wisconsin), 1963.

_____. "The Night Train to Lost Valley." In *Mr. George and Other Odd Persons*.

Donovan, Dick, pseud. "The Robbery of the London Mail." In *Caught at Last! Leaves from the Note-Book of a Detective*. Chatto & Windus (London), 1899.

_____. "A Railway Mystery." In *Riddles Read*. Chatto & Windus (London), 1896.

*Donovan, Frank P., and Henry, Robert Selph. *Headlights and Markers*. Creative Age Press, 1946. (All stories.)

*Doyle, Sir Arthur Conan. "The Adventure of the Bruce-Partington Plans." In *His Last Bow*. Doran, 1917.

_____. "The Lost Special." In *Round the Fire Stories*. Doubleday, 1909.

Ellin, Stanley. "Broker's Special." In *Mystery Stories*. Simon & Schuster, 1956.

Elston, Allan Vaughan. "Drawing Room B." In *The Best American Mystery Stories*, edited by Carolyn Wells. John Day, 1931.

Fitzgerald, F. Scott. "The Night Before Chancellorsville." In *The Bedside Esquire*, edited by Arnold Gingrich. Tudor Publishing Co., 1940.

Freeman, R. Austin. "The Blue Sequin." In *Dr. Thorndyke's Cases*. Dodd, Mead, 1931.

_____. "The Case of Oscar Brodski." In *The Singing Bone*. W. W. Norton, 1965.

*Gardner, Erle Stanley. "Death Rides a Boxcar." In *The Case of the Murderer's Bride and Other Stories*, edited by Ellery Queen. Davis Publications, 1969.

_____. "Flight to Disaster." In *The Case of the Murderer's Bride and Other Stories*.

Hemingway, Ernest. "The Battler." In *In Our Time*. Charles Scribner's Sons, 1925.

Henry, O. "The Roads We Take." In *Whirligigs*. Doubleday, Page, 1910.

Isla, L. A. "The Case of the Southern Arrow." In *Latin Blood*, edited by Donald A. Yates. Herder & Herder, 1972.

Jakes, John. "Cloak and Digger." In *Award Espionage Reader*, edited by Hans Stefan Santesson. Award Books, 1965.

*Jameson, Malcolm. "Train for Flushing." In *The Pulps*, edited by Tony Goodstone. Chelsea House, 1970.

*Kantor, MacKinlay. "The Second Challenge." In *The Fantastic Pulps*, edited by Peter Haining. St. Martin's Press, 1975.

Leblanc, Maurice. "The Mysterious Railway Passenger." In *Fifty Famous Detectives of Fiction*. Odhams Press (London), 1938.

*Lynde, Francis. *Scientific Sprague*. Charles Scribner's Sons, 1912. (All stories.)

McCulley, Johnston. "Thubway Tham, Thivilian." In *Ellery Queen's Rogue's Gallery*, edited by Ellery Queen. Little, Brown (Boston), 1945.

Merwin, Sam, Jr. "Death Meets the Ski Train." In *Master Mystery Stories*, edited by Leo Margulies. Hampton Publishing Co., 1945.

*Morgan, Bryan (editor). *Crime on the Lines*. Routledge and Kegan Paul (London), 1975. (All stories.)

Neidig, William J. "Alibi." In *The Best American Mystery Stories*, edited by Carolyn Wells. John Day, 1931.

Orczy, Baroness. "The Mysterious Death on the Underground Railway." In *The Man in the Corner*. Dodd, Mead, 1909.

*Packard, Frank L. *The Night Operator*. Doran, 1919. (All stories.)

*_____. *Running Special*. Doran, 1925. (All stories.)

Palmer, Stuart, and Rice, Craig. "Once Upon a Train." In *People Vs. Withers and Malone*. Simon & Schuster, 1963.

*Post, Melville Davisson. "The Spread Rails." In *The Sleuth of St. James Square*. D. Appleton, 1920.

Queen, Ellery. "The Black Ledger." In *Queen's Bureau of Investigation*. Little, Brown (Boston), 1954.

Reeve, Arthur B. "The Treasure Train." In *The Treasure Train*. Harper, 1917.

Russell, John. "Boston Limited." In *Cops 'n Robbers*. W. W. Norton, 1930.

Sale, Richard. "Figure a Dame." In *Fireside Mystery Book*, edited by Frank Owen. Lantern Press, 1947.

Savage, David. "Killer in the Club Car." In *This Week's Stories of Mystery and Suspense*, edited by Stewart Beach, Random House, 1957.

Scott, R. T. M. "The Killer." In *Secret Service Smith*. E. P. Dutton, 1923.

_____. "The Trap." In *Secret Service Smith*.

Train, Arthur. "The Escape of Wilkins." In *McAllister and His Double*. Charles Scribner's Sons, 1905.

_____. "Extradition." In *McAllister and His Double*.

Twain, Mark. "Cannibalism in the Cars." In *The Complete Short Stories of Mark Twain*, edited by Charles Neider. Doubleday, 1957.

*Walsh, Thomas. "Journey by Night." In *As Tough as They Come*, edited by Will Oursler. Doubleday, 1951.

*Whitechurch, Victor L. *Thrilling Stories of the Railway*. Pearson (London), 1912. (All stories.)

Williams, Ben Ames. "Man Afraid." In *The Best American Mystery Stories*, edited by Carolyn Wells. John Day, 1931.

*Woolrich, Cornell. "Death in the Air." In *Nightwebs*, edited by Francis M. Nevins, Jr. Harper & Row, 1971.

SHORT STORIES: In Magazines

Anderton, Seven. "Railroaded." *Railroad Man's Magazine*, June 1930.

Baldwin, William. "The Last Man Aboard." *Ellery Queen's Mystery Magazine*, February 1964.

*Barnard, Leslie Gordon. "The Talkative Stranger." *Alfred Hitchcock's Mystery Magazine*, February 1957.

Bloch, Robert. "Hobo." *Ed McBain's Mystery Book*, #2, 1960.

*Blochman, Lawrence G. "Madnight Train." *Argosy*, March 8, 1941. (Also appears as "Midnight Train to Death." *The Saint Mystery Magazine*, January 1959.)

Boucher, Anthony. "The Last Hand." *Ellery Queen's Mystery Magazine*, August 1958.

Davis, Dorothy Marie. "And Never Come Back." *Suspense Magazine*, Winter 1952.

*Davis, Norbert. "A Vote for Murder." *Detective Fiction Weekly*, July 15, 1939.

_____. "Blue Bullets." *Argosy*, March 13, 1937.

*Deutsch, A. J. "A Subway Named Mobius." *Astounding Science-Fiction*, December 1950.

Dresner, Hal. "I'll Go With You." *Alfred Hitchcock's Mystery Magazine*, November 1962.

*Flynn, T. T. "The Snow Train." *Short Stories*, February 1931. (Also appears in *Short Stories Digest*, December 1958.)

_____. "Tried by Fire." *Complete Story Magazine*, July 10, 1926.

Frazee, Steve. "The Thin Edge." *Detective Story Magazine*, November 1952.

*Gordons, The. "Case File—FBI: Faceless Killer." *American Magazine*, June 1953. (Also appears as "The Terror Racket." *Ellery Queen's Mystery Magazine*, August 1967.)

*Hayes, William Edward. "Banjo Boy." *Short Stories Digest*, September 1958.

*_____. "Death Watch at Dexter." *Railroad Man's Magazine*, December 1931.

*_____. "Red Rails." *Dime Detective*, December 1, 1934.

January, Jason. "Express Stop." *Manhunt*, April 1957.

*Packard, Frank L. "The Spotter." *Railroad Stories*, September 1935.

Patrick, Q. "Who Killed the Mermaid?" *Ellery Queen's Mystery Magazine*, February 1951.

Perowne, Barry. "The Raffles Special." *Ellery Queen's Mystery Magazine*, July 1974.

Pronzini, Bill. "Night Freight." *Mike Shayne's Mystery Magazine*, March 1967.

Rohde, William L. "Thunder from the Grave." *Short Stories*, September 1949.

*Schisgall, Oscar. "Murder Aisle." *Dime Detective*, February 1, 1934.

Selig, Frank. "Yard Bull." *Manhunt*, August 1954.

Watson, Frank. "Tar and Feathers." *Trapped Detective Story Magazine*, June 1956.

West, John. "The Vanishing Passenger." *The Mysterious Traveler Magazine*, June 1952.

NOVELS

*Ambler, Eric. *Background to Danger*. Knopf, 1937.

Audemars, Pierre. *Confessions of Hercule*. Sampson Low, Marston & Co. (London), 1947.

_____. *Hercule and the Gods*. Rinehart, 1946.

_____. *The Obligations of Hercule*. Sampson Low, Marston & Co. (London), 1947.

_____. *The Temptations of Hercule*. The Pilot Press, Ltd. (London), 1945.

Avallone, Michael. *The Case of the Violent Virgin*. Ace Books, 1957.

*Bedwell, Harry. *The Boomer*. Farrar & Rinehart, 1943.

Bellairs, George. *Death on the Last Train*. Macmillan, 1949.

Blochman, Lawrence G. *Bombay Mail*. Little, Brown (Boston), 1934.

*Brock, Lynn. *The Slip-Carriage Mystery*. Harper, 1928.

Browne, Douglas. *The Stolen Boat Train*. Methuen (London), 1934.

Burton, Miles. *Dark Is the Tunnel* (British title: *Death in the Tunnel*). Doubleday, Doran, 1936.

*Cain, James M. *Double Indemnity*. Knopf, 1943.

Chalmers, Stephen. *The Crime in Car 13*. Doubleday, Doran, 1930.

*Christie, Agatha. *Murder on the Calais Coach* (British title: *Murder on the Orient Express*). Dodd, Mead, 1934.

_____. *The Mystery of the Blue Train*. Dodd, Mead, 1928.

_____. *What Mrs. McGillicuddy Saw!* (British title: *The 4:50 from Paddington*). Dodd, Mead, 1957.

*Creasy, John. *Murder on the Line*. Charles Scribner's Sons, 1963.

*Crichton, Michael. *The Great Train Robbery*. Knopf, 1975.

Crofts, Freeman Wills. *The Cask*. Collins (London), 1920.

_____. *Dark Journey*. Dodd, Mead, 1951.

*_____. *Death of a Train*. Dodd, Mead, 1947.

*_____. *Double Death* (British title: *Death on the Way*). Harper, 1932.

_____. *Sir John Magill's Last Journey*. Harper, 1930.

_____. *Young Robin Brand, Detective*. University of London Press (London), 1947.

Dekobra, Maurice. *The Madonna of the Sleeping Cars*. T. Werner Laurie (London), 1927.

Farjeon, J. J. *The 5:18 Mystery*. Dial Press, 1929.

_____. *Holiday Express*. Collins (London), 1935.

Fleming, Ian. *From Russia with Love*. Macmillan, 1957.

*Fox, James M. *Free Ride*. Popular Library, 1957.

Garnett, Bill. *Down Bound Train*. Doubleday, 1973.

Garve, Andrew. *The Cuckoo-Line Affair*. Harper, 1953.

*Godey, John. *The Taking of Pelham One Two Three*. G. P. Putnam's Sons, 1973.

*Gordons, The. *Campaign Train*. Doubleday, 1952.

*Greene, Graham. *Orient Express* (British title: *Stamboul Train*). Doubleday, Doran, 1933.

Harvester, Simon. *Obols for Charon*. Jerrolds (London), 1951.

Highsmith, Patricia. *Strangers on a Train*. Harper, 1949.

*Hitchens, Bert & Dolores. *End of the Line*. Doubleday, 1957.

*_____. *F.O.B. Murder*. Doubleday, 1955.

_____. *The Grudge*. Doubleday, 1963.

*_____. *The Man Who Followed Women*. Doubleday, 1959.

_____. *One-Way Ticket*. Doubleday, 1956.

Holt, Henry. *The Midnight Mail*. Doubleday, Doran, 1931.

Jack, Jeremiah. *Train Wreck!* Manor Books, 1975.

Japrisot, Sebastien. *The 10:30 from Marseilles*. Doubleday, 1963.

Kendrick, Baynard. *The Last Express*. Doubleday, Doran, 1937.

*Laurenson, R. M. *The Railroad Murder Case*. Phoenix Press, 1948.

Lenehan, J. C. *The Tunnel Mystery*. Mystery League, 1931.

MacVeigh, Sue. *Grand Central Murder*. Houghton Mifflin (Boston), 1939.

*_____. *Murder Under Construction*. Houghton Mifflin (Boston), 1939.

_____. *Streamlined Murder*. Houghton Mifflin (Boston), 1940.

McCary, Reed. *Kiss and Kill*. Avon Books, 1958.

*Masterson, Whit. *The Gravy Train*. Dodd, Mead, 1971.

Meyer, Nicholas. *The Seven-Per-Cent Solution*. E. P. Dutton, 1974.

*Millar, Kenneth. *Trouble Follows Me*. Dodd, Mead, 1946.

*Nebel, Frederick. *Sleepers East*. Little, Brown (Boston), 1933.

*Noble, Hollister. *One Way to Eldorado*. Doubleday, 1954.

Norman, James. *Murder, Chop Chop*. William Morrow, 1942.

*O'Rourke, Frank. *Concannon*. Ballantine Books, 1952.

*Packard, Frank L. *The Wire Devils*. Doran, 1918.

*Parker, Robert. *Passport to Peril*. Rinehart, 1951.

_____. *Ticket to Oblivion*. Rinehart, 1950.

Phillips, Austin. *The Man on the Night Mail*. Hutchinson (London), 1927.

Reilly, Helen. *Compartment K*. Random House, 1955.

Rhode, John. *Death on the Boat Train*. Dodd, Mead, 1940.

Rinehart, Mary Roberts. *The Man in Lower Ten*. Bobbs-Merrill (Indianapolis, Indiana), 1909.

Rohde, William L. *High Red for Dead*. Gold Medal, 1951.

Ross, Barnaby (Ellery Queen). *The Tragedy of X*. Viking, 1932.

Later editions published as by Ellery Queen.

Sayers, Dorothy. *Suspicious Characters* (British title: *Five Red Herrings*). Brewer Warren, 1931.

Simenon, Georges. *The Man Who Watched the Trains Go By*. Reynal & Hitchcock, 1946.

*_____. *The Negro*. Hamish Hamilton (London), 1959.

Timins, Douglas. *The Extra Passenger*. Hutchinson (London), 1928.

*_____. *The Phantom Train*. Hutchinson (London), 1926.

Tucker, Wilson. *Last Stop*. Doubleday, 1964.

*Westheimer, David. *Von Ryan's Express*. Doubleday, 1964.

White, Ethyl Lina. *The Wheel Spins*. Harper, 1936.

Williams, Valentine. *The Three of Clubs*. Houghton Mifflin (Boston), 1924.

NONFICTION

*Block, Eugene B. *Great Train Robberies of the West*. Coward-McCann, 1959.

Botkin, E. A., and Harlow, Alvin F. *A Treasury of Railroad Folklore*. E. P. Dutton, 1953.

*Bromley, Joseph. *Clear the Tracks!* Whittlesey House (McGraw-Hill), 1943.

*Gosling, John, and Craig, Dennis. *The Great Train Robbery*. Bobbs-Merrill (Indianapolis, Indiana), 1965.

Griswold, Wesley S. *Train Wreck!* S. Greene Press (Brattleboro, Vermont), 1969.

*Hogg, Garry. *Orient Express*. Walker & Co., 1968.

Horan, James D. *The Pinkertons*. Crown, 1967.

Hubbard, Freeman H. *Railroad Avenue: Great Stories and Legends of American Railroading*. Whittlesey House (McGraw-Hill), 1945.

King, Ernest L., and Mahaffey, Robert E. *Main Line*. Doubleday, 1948.

*London, Jack. *The Road*. Macmillan, 1907.

Reinhardt, Richard (editor). *Workin' on the Railroad*. American West Publishing Co. (Palo Alto, California), 1970.

*Siringo, Charles A. *A Cowboy Detective*. W. B. Conkey Co. (Chicago), 1912.

*Theroux, Paul. *The Great Railway Bazaar*. Houghton Mifflin (Boston), 1975.

PLAYS

Hecht, Ben, and MacArthur, Charles. *Twentieth Century*. First produced in New York, 1932. Script published by Samuel French, Inc.
Rose, Edward E. *The Rear Car*. A 1920s stage melodrama.

FILMS

Alcatraz Express (1962). Robert Stack, Neville Brand.
*Background to Danger (1943). George Raft, Sydney Greenstreet, Peter Lorre. Directed by Raoul Walsh. Based on the novel by Eric Ambler.
Berlin Express (1948). Merle Oberon, Robert Ryan.
Bombay Mail (1934). Edmund Lowe, Onslow Stevens. Based on the novel by Lawrence G. Blochman.
Boxcar Bertha (1972). David Carradine, John Carradine, Barbara Hershey.
Bulldog Drummond's Revenge (1937). John Howard, John Barrymore.
Crack-Up (1946). Pat O'Brien, Claire Trevor, Herbert Marshall. Based on the novel *Madman's Holiday* by Fredric Brown.
Dark of the Sun (1968). Rod Taylor, Jim Brown.
*Destination Unknown (1942). William Gargan, Irene Hervey, Turhan Bey.
*Double Indemnity (1944). Fred MacMurray, Edward G. Robinson, Barbara Stanwyck. Directed by Billy Wilder; screenplay by Raymond Chandler and Billy Wilder. Based on the novel by James M. Cain.
*Emperor of the North (1973). Lee Marvin, Ernest Borgnine. Directed by Robert Aldrich.
Enemy Agents Meet Ellery Queen (1942). William Gargan, Margaret Lindsay, Gilbert Roland, Gale Sondergaard.
French Connection, The (1971). Gene Hackman, Roy Scheider.
*From Russia, With Love (1964). Sean Connery (as James Bond), Lotte Lenya, Robert Shaw. Based on the novel by Ian Fleming.
General, The (1927). Buster Keaton.
Ghost Train, The (British, 1941). Wilfred Lawson, Carola Lynn.
Grand Central Murder (1942). Van Heflin, Cecilia Parker. Based on the novel by Sue MacVeigh.

*Great Train Robbery, The (1903). Directed by Edwin S. Porter.

Horror Express (1972). Telly Savalas, Peter Cushing.

Human Desire (1954). Glenn Ford, Broderick Crawford, Gloria Grahame.

Iron Horse, The (1924). George O'Brien, Madge Bellamy. Directed by John Ford.

Istanbul Express (1968). Gene Barry, Senta Berger, John Saxon.

Lady on a Train (1945). Deanna Durbin, Ralph Bellamy.

*Lady Vanishes, The (British, 1938). Michael Redgrave, Margaret Lockwood, Paul Lukas, Dame May Whitty. Directed by Alfred Hitchcock. Based on the novel The Wheel Spins by Ethyl Lina White.

*Murder on the Orient Express (1974). Albert Finney (as Hercule Poirot), Sean Connery, Ingrid Bergman, Anthony Perkins, Lauren Bacall, Martin Balsam, John Gielgud, Vanessa Redgrave, Richard Widmark, Michael York. Directed by Sidney Lumet. Based on the novel Murder on the Calais Coach by Agatha Christie.

*Murder in the Private Car (1934). Charles Ruggles, Una Merkel.

Murder, She Said (British, 1962). Margaret Rutherford (as Jane Marple), Arthur Kennedy, James Robertson Justice. Based on the novel What Mrs. McGillicuddy Saw! by Agatha Christie.

*Narrow Margin, The (1952). Charles McGraw, Marie Windsor.

*Night Train, The (British, 1940). Rex Harrison, Margaret Lockwood, Paul Henried. Directed by Carol Reed.

Powder Keg (1970). Rod Taylor, Dennis Cole.

Railway Children, The (British, 1972). Dinah Sheridan, William Mervyn. Directed by Lionel Jeffries.

Red Lights (1923). Directed by Clarence Badger. A Samuel Goldwyn film. Based on The Rear Car by Edward S. Rose.

*Seven-Per-Cent Solution, The (1976). Nicol Williamson (as Sherlock Holmes), Robert Duval (as Dr. Watson), Sir Laurence Olivier, Joel Grey, Alan Arkin. Based on the novel by Nicholas Meyer.

*Silver Streak (1976). Gene Wilder, Jill Clayburgh, Richard Pryor.

*Sleepers West (1941). Lloyd Nolan, Lynn Bari, Mary Beth Hughes. Based on the novel Sleepers East by Frederick Nebel.

Sleeping Car Murders, The (French, 1967). Yves Montand, Simone Signoret. Based on the novel The 10:30 from Marseilles by Sebastien Japrisot.

Stop Train 349 (1964). Sean Flynn, Jose Ferrer, Nicole Courcel.

272 [Bibliography]

Strangers on a Train (1951). Robert Walker, Ruth Roman, Farley Granger. Directed by Alfred Hitchcock. Based on the novel by Patricia Highsmith.

*Taking of Pelham One Two Three, The (1974). Walter Matthau, Robert Shaw, Martin Balsam. Based on the novel by John Godey.

Terror by Night (1946). Basil Rathbone (as Sherlock Holmes), Nigel Bruce (as Dr. Watson), Alan Mowbray.

Titfield Thunderbolt, The (British, 1953). Stanley Holloway, George Relph.

*Train, The (1965). Burt Lancaster, Jean Moreau. Directed by John Frankenheimer.

Train to Alcatraz (1948). Donald Barry, Janet Martin.

*Von Ryan's Express (1965). Frank Sinatra, Trevor Howard. Based on the novel by David Westheimer.